A/MORAL ECONOMICS

A/MORAL ECONOMICS

*Classical Political Economy and
Cultural Authority in Nineteenth-Century
England*

Claudia C. Klaver

The Ohio State University Press
Columbus

Copyright © 2003 by The Ohio State University Press
All rights reserved.

Library of Congress Cataloging-in-Publication Data

Klaver, Claudia C.
  A/moral economics : classical political economy and cultural authority in nineteenth-century England / Claudia C. Klaver.
      p. cm.
  Includes bibliographical references and index.
  ISBN 0-8142-0944-0 (hardcover : alk. paper) — ISBN 0-8142-9021-3 (CD-ROM)
  1. English prose literature—19th century—History and criticism. 2. Economics in literature. 3. Economics and literature—England—History—19th century. 4. Economics—England—History—19th century. 5. England—Economic conditions—19th century. I. Title.

PR868.E37 K56 2003
824'.809433—dc21
                              2003008551

"Revaluing Money: *Dombey and Son*'s Moral Critique," which appeared in *Literature and Money* (Rodopi Perspectives on Modern Literature 13), edited by Anthony Purdy (1993) was used with permission from Rodopi Press.

Paper (ISBN: 978-0-8142-5657-2)

Cover design by Dan O'Dair.
Type set in Adobe Garamond.

*In loving memory of my mother,
Joan Celeste Klaver, 1930–1989*

contents

ACKNOWLEDGMENTS	VIII
INTRODUCTION: Economic Authority and Discursive Form in Nineteenth-Century England	XI
1. Ricardian Economics: Rhetoric and the Form of Science in Early-Nineteenth-Century Political Economy	1
2. Providential Economics: J. R. McCulloch's Nationalist Narratives	31
3. Sentimental Science: Harriet Martineau's *Illustrations of Political Economy*	53
4. Revaluing Money: *Dombey and Son*'s Moral Critique	78
5. The Economics of Working-Class Masculinity in Mayhew's Letters to the *Morning Chronicle*	109
6. Rewriting Ricardo/Renewing Smith: The New, Expanded Political Economy of J. S. Mill	134
7. Morals and Mathematics: Critical Revisions of Scientific Economic Theory in the 1860s and 1870s	161
NOTES	189
BIBLIOGRAPHY	211
INDEX	221

acknowledgments

Because this book and I have lived together for so long, many, many people and institutions have contributed to and participated in its conceptualization, writing, rethinking, and revision. At opposite ends of the process, however, two people stand out to whom I owe particular thanks. The first of these is Mary Poovey, my dissertation advisor, mentor, and intellectual inspiration. Without the stimulus of working closely with her, this book would probably never have been imagined, much less written. The second person who has been crucial to the creation of this book—as a book—is my high school friend and copyeditor, Connie Oehring. She not only helped me make the cuts necessary to bring this unwieldy manuscript into line with OSU Press's word limit, but also signed on with the Press as a freelance copyeditor just so she could copyedit the manuscript for me. Her moral support and professional assistance were invaluable in the process of turning "manuscript" into "book."

I also want to thank a several other professors and mentors with whom I worked while attending graduate school in English at Rutgers University and John Hopkins University. George Levine, Jerome Christensen, and Frances Ferguson all helped to develop my understanding of literary historical methodologies and of late-eighteenth- and nineteenth-century British culture in ways that were invaluable for this project. In revising and expanding this project, I have continued to benefit from the intellectual stimulus, historical knowledge, and professional guidance of many of my colleagues at Syracuse University, especially my senior colleagues Linda Shires and Susan Edmunds, both of whom read and commented upon many drafts of large portions—if not all—of the manuscript.

I would also like to thank the members of three different faculty writing groups whose comments on earlier versions of many chapters not only helped to improve those chapters, but also helped me focus and refine the book as a whole. Most recently, the English Department Faculty Writing

Group helped me refine my final chapter on Ruskin and Jevons, for which I sincerely thank Crystal Bartolovich, Michael Echeruo, Susan Edmunds, Bob Gates, Christian Thorne, and Monika Wadman. In my first years at Syracuse, I was given guidance and immense support through a process of substantial reconceptualization and rewriting from "Critical Mass," an interdisciplinary women's junior faculty writing group that included Monisha Das Gupta, Gail Hamner, Dana Harrington, Jackie Orr, and Eileen Schell. Finally, I would like to thank the first "non-professorial" readers of and advisors on my manuscript, the members of another interdisciplinary junior women's writing group (at the Claremont Colleges), which included Audrey Bilger, Lora Wildenthal, Stacey Freeman, and Cynthia Humes.

I would also like to thank my friends Catherine Jurca and Margaret Russet whose support has moved with me as I myself have moved from Baltimore to southern California and then to Syracuse.

I have received crucial financial support for this project from the Woodrow Wilson Foundation (for a Charlotte M. Newcombe dissertation fellowship), the W. M. Keck Foundation (for a Huntington Library junior scholars fellowship), and Syracuse University. This financial support has provided me the time to undertake and complete this project. I also want to thank the interlibrary loan offices at John Hopkins University, the Claremont Colleges, and Syracuse University for their assistance in helping me access the important and at times quite obscure primary texts that were unavailable in the libraries themselves.

I have benefited greatly, too, from the thoughtful comments of two anonymous readers at The Ohio State University Press who helped me further conceptualize and refocus my manuscript.

I save my final thanks to my partner, Penny Lee Dean, whose support of me and of this project, combined with her determination for me to finish it and to make it the best book it could be, have been "invaluable"—at least in any "value" terms other than those idealist formulations articulated in the face of nineteenth-century political economy by Charles Dickens and John Ruskin.

introduction

Economic Authority and Discursive Form in Nineteenth-Century England

This is the history of the uneven development of economic discourse in nineteenth-century England. More accurately, this is one chapter in a discontinuous history, one part of a complex and contradictory narrative. This history at once plays off and contests the traditional histories that trace the "progress" of economic thought, the increasing rationalization, mathematization, and specialization of economic theory from Adam Smith and David Ricardo through W. Stanley Jevons and Alfred Marshall.[1] This is also a history that both depends upon and seeks to complicate histories of social scientific thought that identify "economics" as the first aspirant to and model for "social science" because of its successful methodological construction and disaggregation of its object—the economic—from the earlier discursive domains of moral philosophy and theories of civil society.[2] My narrative depends upon these histories because they construct a plot of disciplinary and institutional development whose basic outline I find descriptively persuasive and politically important. At the same time, my narrative complicates these histories by demonstrating the unevenness and internal contradictions of a process that becomes linear and teleological only in retrospect and through the suppression of the texts and contexts of early-nineteenth-century culture. I argue that in that culture, theories about the social—including the production, distribution, and consumption of material wealth—found little support when they were not embedded in the very discourses of morality, providentialism, and nationalism from which, according to such histories, economic theory had already been disaggregated. Furthermore, this cultural context for economic theory enabled and authorized a series of self-conscious critiques of the very process such histories claim to describe. Finally, this is a history of a moment during which the very terms that we bring to the categorization and organization of history—"economic," "social," "political," and "cultural"—were being contested as well as formed.

Three threads in particular constitute the significance of this complex moment in the history of economic discourse. The first is the emergence and convergence of scientific and economic modes of thought in such a way that scientific forms of knowledge about the economy began to attain a new kind of cultural authority. The second involves the material discursive forms through which this convergence was effected, enabled, and contested. The third thread interwoven into this critical historical moment is the discourse of morality, ethics, and virtue.[3] This final thread plays a particularly complex and shifting role throughout nineteenth-century economic discourse. Whether as discarded remainder, as supplemental effect, as disturbing factor, or as ground for a radical reenvisioning of economic knowledge, the discourse of morality, ethics, and virtue plays a key and troubling role in the discursive and institutional foundation of economic authority in nineteenth-century Britain.

In 1817, with encouragement, editing, and coaching from his friend, disciple, and sometime mentor James Mill, David Ricardo completed and published *Principles of Political Economy and Taxation*. In part through his development and synthesis of what was, in effect, a new discursive form for economic theory, Ricardo's text isolated a discrete set of concerns that he defined as "economic" and then created a self-enclosed discursive model of the interaction of those terms. While the disaggregation of the "economic" from its earlier discursive contexts in studies of domestic economy and moral philosophy had already begun in Adam Smith's *The Wealth of Nations* (1776), Ricardo took this discursive process much further.[4]

Ricardo's separation of "economic" concerns from those we now term "social," "political," "psychological," "moral," and "cultural" was a result of his own and James Mill's desire to establish a "scientific" model of political economy that borrowed from the methods and authority of the natural sciences. While Ricardo's text built on the content of his contemporary Thomas Malthus's infamous and influential *Essay on the Principle of Population* (1798; 1803), he distanced his model of political economy from the concerns of Christian morality and providence that were fundamental to Malthus's conception of "economic" law. Ricardo considered only such "economic laws" to be the appropriate object of a "scientific" political economy. Furthermore, through the discursive and rhetorical forms he deployed in the *Principles*, Ricardo was able to construct a treatise in which such laws were represented and constituted as autonomous and self-acting. I argue that Ricardo's apparently successful disaggregation of economic from moral, social, religious, and political concerns depended upon his institution of a different set of discursive technologies than those utilized by his predecessors and contemporaries.

At the same time that these new rhetorical strategies helped to constitute an autonomous domain of "the economy" and of "economic law," they also rendered Ricardo's text alienating and difficult for much of its potential readership among the educated gentry and middle classes. The very rhetorical strategies that enabled Ricardo to represent and constitute political economy as a scientific rather than a political or moral discourse also effectually excluded the reading public on which much of the science's authority was forced to depend. Because political economy was largely excluded from the curriculum of the universities, or was taught primarily as an extension of history and moral philosophy, early-nineteenth-century writers on economic issues aspired instead to the cultural authority that could be won from an elite, but relatively large, general public. There were some institutional and discursive forms in which political economy could be constituted as a coherent and discrete body of knowledge. For example, thinkers and writers on economic issues were able to speak among themselves in the Political Economy Club, through personal correspondence, and through such events as the Ricardo Memorial Lectures. Until the 1870s, however, they lacked the institutional power and support that would enable them to constitute their own audience for each other's theoretical writings; provide authority to legislate the validity of these writings; and determine their appropriate deployment into the public discursive spaces of moral, social, and political controversy. Thus, in the early-nineteenth-century institutional and discursive contexts into which Ricardo's scientific approach to political economy was introduced, his text's alien and alienating format proved a significant disadvantage so that he was unable to fulfill his desire—or that of James Mill and John Ramsey McCulloch—to establish the "scientific" approach to political economy as the legitimate and authoritative form of economic discourse.

One of the "solutions" to this dilemma developed by James Mill, J. R. McCulloch, and, later, Harriet Martineau was to "popularize" scientific economic discourse, to retain the content of Ricardo's economic theories while recontextualizing them in rhetorical and generic forms that were more accessible and appealing to the educated reading public of the 1820s and 1830s. Mill's *Elements of Political Economy* was the first of these projects, but it was so dry and abstract that it did not gain significantly more readers than Ricardo's *Principles*. Ricardo's "scientific" economic theories first reached a wide general audience through J. R. McCulloch's writings in the 1820s and 1830s. McCulloch's review of Ricardo's *Principles* in the *Edinburgh Review* was for the most part a summary, explanation, and defensive celebration of Ricardo's difficult text. In his other regular contributions to the *Edinburgh Review,* McCulloch used Ricardian models of production, distribution, and consumption to advocate specific political, economic, and social policies in addressing contemporary problems. In his *Encyclopedia Britannica* article on political economy, he not only rehearsed Ricardo's theories but also constructed a developmental narrative in which those theories were seen as the teleological fulfillment of one hundred years of "progress" in the scientific study of the economy. Finally, from 1832 to 1834, Harriet Martineau published her series of twenty-five novellas entitled *Illustrations of Political Economy*. This extremely popular didactic project systematically explained and promulgated economic theory by developing individual fictional narratives around clusters of economic "laws" or "principles."

Just as Ricardo's prose style at once enabled and limited the emergence of a "scientific" discourse on the economy, the popularizing projects of McCulloch and Martineau had contradictory effects on the process of establishing social and cultural authority for the discourse of political economy. On the one hand, they succeeded in creating a broader audience for Ricardo's economic theories: there were many more readers of their texts than of Ricardo's, and the discursive construction of political economy *as* science became a widely recognized element of the educated reading public's vocabulary. On the other hand, the generic and rhetorical forms that enabled McCulloch and Martineau to reach and influence this wider public also decontextualized Ricardo's "ideas" from the discursive forms that had helped to constitute them, thus inevitably altering the structures that, in Ricardo's text, functioned to create the economic domain as an autonomous set of concerns and laws that could be authoritatively analyzed, understood, and predicted only through a "scientific" methodology. In other words, the popularizers of Ricardo's economic theories undermined the discursive foundations of the "scientific" authority Ricardo—and they—claimed for his *Principles*.

The undermining of Ricardo's discursive authority in McCulloch's and Martineau's texts had, I argue, two important sets of effects on the emergence of an authoritative cultural discourse in early and mid-Victorian England that have been elided in most histories of economic thought. The first set involves the way the popularizers' discursive recontextualization of Ricardian tenets repeatedly exposed the incomplete disaggregation of an autonomous "economic" domain from discourses and concerns that Ricardo's textual project had seemed to leave behind—concerns of religion and morality, politics and policy, and social or civic virtue. While Ricardo argued in a letter to Malthus that political economy had more affinity to mathematics than to ethics or national policy, the essays and narratives of McCulloch and Martineau exposed the way political economy in the early and mid-nineteenth century—even in its "scientific" forms—was inextricably linked to the discourses from which it had sought to separate itself. If there was no autonomous domain of the economic that political economy could study and theorize, then the very claims that Ricardians made for their theories were threatened: if the economic was connected to a dense tissue of other discourses, practices, and concerns, then perhaps the narrowly "scientific" approach to its study was not the only—or even the most effective—way to understand it.

The other way in which Ricardo's popularizers undermined, even as they sought to establish, the authority of his economic discourse was closely related to the first. Attendant on Ricardo's attempt to "identify" and represent an autonomous domain of economic law was the assumption that only a "scientific" analysis of this domain could generate reliable knowledge about issues of material productivity, distribution, exchange, and consumption. By extension, only someone trained in the scientific methodology deployed by theorists such as Ricardo, James Mill, and, to a lesser extent, Thomas Malthus and J. R. McCulloch could make authoritative claims about the structure and working of these "economic" activities. The claims and criticisms of those not scientifically trained (whether formally or informally) were irrelevant to the creation of economic knowledge; these nonspecialists were, in effect, defined as outside the emergent discipline or domain of "economics." However, precisely because that domain was only beginning to emerge within the discursive and institutional structures of early-nineteenth-century England, Ricardo's popularizers had to step beyond its nascent boundaries in order to win cultural authority for the new methodology and practice. Their transgression of these boundaries inadvertently marked the gap between discursive and institutional practice that was instantly noted by critics of the emergent model of scientific economic discourse. Perhaps even more importantly, nonspecialist critics of political economy could claim authority to speak on these issues because Ricardo's popularizers, despite their retention of the vocabulary of "science," did not maintain the fundamental discursive structures that had enabled him to constitute the "economy" *as* a naturally occurring, autonomous, and law-bound domain of human activity that could only be understood "scientifically."

Thus, such Victorian nonspecialist critics of the discourse of political economy as Thomas Carlyle, Charles Dickens, and Henry Mayhew should be accorded a more central role in the development and transformations of this discourse than they have been assigned in most disciplinary, intellectual, or even cultural histories of economic thought. Their criticisms not only attacked specific tenets of the emergent discourse but also—and more importantly—undermined the authority of that form of discourse in defining and understanding what political economy constructed as "economic concerns." In particular, writers such as Dickens and Mayhew argued for the fundamental connection between issues defined by Ricardian economics as solely "economic" and those defined as noneconomic—issues of morality, religion, and social stability. If questions of morality were *not* essentially different and distinct from those political economy labeled "economic," then writers who isolated and privileged the "economic" questions of material production and distribution in their analysis of contemporary social problems were producing distorted diagnoses of and prescriptions for those social ills. Rather than establishing the authority of economic discourse in addressing these objects, the disaggregation of "economic" issues from broader moral and social concerns was precisely what popular critics of political economy identified as the central weakness—as well as hubris—of the emergent public discourse.

Dickens and Mayhew, for example, argued that by constructing social dynamics as competition in solely "economic" terms, political economists mistakenly had been led to embrace and celebrate such competition as an inevitable, necessary, and reliable (if not always benevolent) "economic" mechanism. Ricardian economic theorists viewed any "extra-economic" interventions as an unnatural and dangerous disruption of the self-regulating functions of the market mechanism (i.e., the "market" as mechanism). In contrast to this discursive construction of competition, Dickens and Mayhew invoked and constructed alternative discursive models that represented competition as a complex dynamic with social, moral, and psychological as well as "economic" elements. Furthermore, they represented competition as an extremely dangerous and destructive social dynamic if unmoored from mediating discourses, practices, and institutions. Yet it was just such an unmooring that scientific economics sought to effect and naturalize, not only discursively but also through the practices and institutions that the discourse sought to influence and construct. I argue that the attacks of such writers as Charles Dickens and Henry Mayhew on the discourse of political economy, and the alternative solutions they offered to the problems they saw around them, should be read as part of a significant discursive contest waged in early- and mid-nineteenth-century England over what counted as "economic," how "economic" concerns were to be understood and addressed, and what practices and institutions should address the instabilities of Victorian culture and society.

While such a reading of popularizations and popular critiques of political economy is by no means completely new, my analysis revises and makes significant contributions to existing accounts. The most important contribution concerns my assumption that the materiality of language results in uneven developments within historically specific discourses that have come to be viewed as reified "thought," "theory," and even "truth."[5] In particular, my reading shows that the emergence of even the most abstracted and reified theories of "scientific" or classical political economy in early- and mid-nineteenth-century England was caught up in such uneven development. Hence, traditional histories of economic thought that chart the emergence of economic truth in and through the writings of such "theoretical predecessors" as Adam Smith, David Ricardo, John Stuart Mill, and W. Stanley Jevons need to be rewritten to explain the ways in which such "truth" always took specific material forms and the way those forms created the truths they purported to simply communicate. By rehistoricizing and denaturalizing such discourses, we can avoid the danger of simply reinscribing and reinforcing their truth effects as we attempt to understand the development of what has come to be seen as the largely autonomous domain of "the economic" and of the apparent inevitability and inescapability of its laws.

Likewise, we can and must simultaneously rehistoricize and denaturalize the other discourses that were disaggregated from the economic in the eighteenth and nineteenth centuries and that were, in turn, reified into the semi-autonomous domains of religion, morality, politics, culture, and the social. However, because of the privileged place that "economic truth" continues to occupy in contemporary scholarly and political discourse, and because the discourses of literature, culture, and the social have already begun to be compellingly historicized in the work of other scholars, my narrative centers on the nineteenth-century discourse of "the economic."[6]

In arguing for and examining the historicity of scientific political economy, I recognize that my project overlaps with Karl Marx's in his *Critique of Political Economy, Capital,* and *Theories of Surplus Value*. My analysis of the texts of Ricardo, McCulloch, Martineau, Dickens, Mayhew, and J. S. Mill, however, does not lead up to or feed into a totalizing narrative and critique of industrial capitalism as a mode of production; nor, ultimately, does it identify any such mode of production as the final determinant of the unevenness it exposes. Indeed, my argument seeks to problematize the very construction of "the economic" as the law-bound object of scientific inquiry on which Marx's historical materialism depends. My analysis is more a Foucauldian reading of this quintessentially Marxist moment of theoretical reification and mystification. In other words, while recognizing the development of industrial-imperialist capitalism as probably the most powerful historical force in nineteenth-century England, my analysis of the scientific and popular discourses that explained, justified, and contested that force also remains committed to exposing the ways in which other forms of materiality—other discourses, conventions, and practices—continued to exist and exert pressures within, underneath, and alongside the material forces that Marx and other analysts have linked to the development of historical capitalism.

In invoking Michel Foucault as model for my historical and analytical project, I recognize that Foucault's own work does not yield a completely coherent and noncontradictory historiographical methodology.[7] Nor do I embrace all aspects and implications of Foucault's archaeological and genealogical analyses. Rather, I draw upon Foucault as the contemporary cultural and institutional historian whose theoretical premises and practices most fully explain the discursive contestations I explore and the implications of those contestations for the emergence of an autonomous discipline and domain of "the economic." In my analysis of Victorian attempts to popularize and popularly contest scientific political economy, I draw on three aspects of Foucault's work in particular: his commitment to the constitutive power of discourse, his examination of the relationship between discursive and nondiscursive practices and institutions, and his positing of a nontotalizing model of historical development.

In *The Archaeology of Knowledge,* where Foucault theorizes his earlier historical projects *Madness and Civilization, The Birth of the Clinic,* and the *Order of Things,* he emphatically distinguishes his discursive histories from more traditional histories of science and thought. The problem with histories of science, Foucault argues, is that they tend to accept without question the identities formed by our own contemporary disciplinary demarcations without interrogating the specificities of the discursive field in which various statements or discursive events took place. In so doing, such histories presume that it is the object of the discipline under examination—the referent—that gives rise to its continuities and regularities rather than recognizing that the discursive formation itself participates in the constitution of any such object. The aim of Foucault's work, in contrast, is "not to neutralize discourse . . . but on the contrary to maintain it in its consistency, to make it emerge in its own complexity. . . . To substitute for the enigmatic treasure of 'things' anterior to discourse, the regular formation of objects that emerge only in discourse. To define these *objects* without reference to the *ground,* the *foundation of things,* but by relating them to the body of rules that enable them to form as objects of a discourse and thus constitute the conditions of their historical appearance."[8] Foucault, then, is not interested in how the social sciences "capture" nondiscursive truths but in how the discourses of the sciences themselves bring such truths into being. This approach shifts the emphasis of the historiographical enterprise away from the relationship of texts to "truth" toward the relationships within and among texts themselves, what Foucault calls the "consistency" and "complexity" of discourse.

While Foucault criticizes disciplinary histories of science for reading through the specificities of discursive practices and events in order to recover a prediscursive referent, he criticizes traditional histories of thought for reading through those same specificities in order to recover a prediscursive subject—they attempt to "rediscover beyond the statements themselves the intention of the speaking subject" (*AK* 27). By trying to unearth the intentions of the speaking subject, such analyses implicitly grant to the subject the constitutive possibilities that Foucault locates within the discursive field itself. It is within this discursive field, Foucault argues, that "we must grasp the statement in the exact specificity of its occurrence; determine its conditions of existence, fix at least its limits, establish its correlations with other statements that may be connected with it, and show what other forms of statement it excludes" (*AK* 28).

In examining what seems, in retrospect, to be the unevenness with which a discourse of the economic emerged in the early years of the nineteenth century, I find compelling Foucault's conception of discourse as subject and force of history. Certainly the intentions of the writers that I examine—whether they sought to popularize or excoriate "scientific" economic discourse—cannot explain the complex and contradictory discursive formations that emerge in their individual writing projects. So, while their explicitly stated and implied intentions form an aspect of my analysis, they cannot be its primary object. Instead, I will examine their texts as discursive sites that are themselves a form of historical event or object. Similarly, in my examinations of more popular articulations of Ricardian economic theory in early-nineteenth-century England, I am concerned with the specific discursive forms in which definitions and discussion of "the economic" took shape rather than in how accurately or inaccurately those articulations might "capture" a nondiscursive economic truth. This focus enables me to show the ways in which the objects of such discursive practices were themselves in the process of being formed.

By examining discursive formations as a constitutive historical force, Foucault is not asserting that the forms and structures of language are themselves ahistorical givens that univocally predetermine their objects. On the contrary, as Foucault demonstrates throughout his work, these forms and structures are themselves historical formations and events. I argue that it is precisely the textual specificity—the discursive regularities—of Ricardo's theoretical project that enables his *Principles of Political Economy and Taxation* to constitute the "economy" as an autonomous object of scientific analysis. The same discursive regularities that produce this effect, however, produce other discursive effects for many of Ricardo's would-be readers—alienation and illegibility.[9] Both of these sets of effects are crucial to understanding the ways in which economic discourse constituted its object and authority in the early nineteenth century. They are historically specific effects that, in "Politics and the Study of Discourse," Foucault describes as *"intradiscursive"* and *"interdiscursive"* dependencies."[10] In addition to analyzing the historical specificity of discursive formations themselves, Foucault recognizes that such discursive formations carry out functions within "a field of nondiscursive practices," which he names "*extradiscursive* dependencies" (PSD 58). In the early nineteenth century, the nondiscursive practices and institutions involved in the emergence of economic discourse were not only those of industrial capitalism but also those of the institutional structures of the university and the press. Thus, while my emphasis will be on economic discourse itself, I will also discuss the intersection of this discourse with some of the specific nondiscursive institutions and practices through which it functioned and in relation to which it wielded its constitutive force.

Foucault is, of course, by no means the only cultural historian who articulates a fundamental and mutually constitutive relationship between discursive and nondiscursive materialities. But he is the most prominent of such historians to theorize this relationship within a nontotalizing model of history. After defining his criteria for the individualization of discourses, whether historical or contemporary, Foucault explains in "Politics and the Study of Discourse" that "these criteria make it possible to substitute differentiated analyses for the theme of totalizing history ('the progress of reason,' 'the spirit of a century')" (PSD 54–55). Such "differentiated analyses" seek to understand the "episteme" of a period not as a "grand underlying theory" but rather as "the divergence, the distances, the oppositions, the differences, the relations of its various scientific discourses" (PSD 55). Later in the same essay, when he introduces the "interdiscursive" and "extradiscursive" dependencies mentioned earlier, Foucault further explains his model of a nontotalizing history: "I would like to substitute the study of this whole play of dependencies for the uniform, simple activity of allocating causality; and by suspending the indefinitely renewed privileges of cause, to render apparent the polymorphous interweaving of correlations" (PSD 58). In rejecting what he calls "the uniform, simple activity of allocating causality," Foucault distances his historiographical project not only from idealist histories of "mind" and "thought" but also from liberal and Marxist histories that identify political or economic realities as the engine and organizing force of history. While Marxist cultural theory and history since Antonio Gramsci and Louis Althusser has not been a "uniform, simple activity," it retains a commitment to totality that ultimately does "allocate causality" to modes of production. Foucault's genealogies attempt to move away from just this assumption of a determinate causality.[11] Thus, instead of a general causality, Foucault's explorations of discursive and nondiscursive materialities demarcate "correlations" and assign what might be called "local causalities"—conjunctions so close, but often also so contingent, that questions of determination cannot move beyond the specific and limited historical field under examination.

I undertake the same kind of nontotalizing historical project in exploring the uneven development of economic discourse in nineteenth-century England. While Marxist cultural theories and histories constitute invaluable resources for my analysis, I am ultimately unwilling to bring the discursive events I examine into a narrative that identifies the capitalist mode of production as its final determining factor. Perhaps more accurately, I am unwilling to adopt any of the available theoretical-historiographical narratives of that mode of production as a satisfactory organizing lens for this history. This unwillingness does not mean that I reject the insights into and tools for cultural analysis provided by such Marxist theorists as Louis Althusser, Fredric Jameson, and Raymond Williams. The Althusserian formulation of the relative autonomy of cultural domains in relation to each other and to a society's productive materialities has provided me, and many other cultural historians, with a way of thinking of cultural and "economic" practices as developing at once according to their own logics and in a constitutive relationship with each other, as has Jameson's revisionary model of mediation.[12] Thus, I use the term "capitalist ideology" to acknowledge the ways in which certain discursive structures and logics were fundamentally, even deterministically, linked to the operation of industrial-imperial capitalism in nineteenth-century England. Likewise, Raymond Williams's formulation of residual, dominant, and emergent social formations has enabled me to theorize the uneven development of social and cultural practices through the coexistence and interaction of conceptually discrete but experientially nontotalized social and economic forms.[13] Indeed, this model is perhaps the most useful for understanding the relationship between Ricardo's discursive project and the work of his popularizers: the abstract, "scientific" formulations that Ricardo used in his *Principles* were part of an emergent discursive form, while the narrative formulations of McCulloch and Martineau used dominant and residual discursive forms to try to articulate the "content" of the emergent mode. My project would have been impossible without the theoretical models provided and utilized by these and other Marxist scholars; my work departs from theirs primarily at the crucial question of ultimate historical determination or causality.

In simultaneously drawing upon and coming to terms with the contradictory theoretical legacies of Foucault and structuralist and poststructuralist Marxism, the model of historical work toward which my own project aspires is that of Mary Poovey in what she has called, following Lorraine Daston, "historical epistemology." In her recent book, *A History of the Modern Fact*, Poovey argues that the very categories through which knowledge is organized, such as facts and disciplines, "inform *what* can be known at any given time, as well as *how* this knowledge can be used."[14] Historical epistemology studies these categories and how they change over time, but, unlike more traditional histories of scientific thought and method, "it is less a study of the inexorable march of 'science' toward a fully adequate description of nature than an investigation of those developments that have increasingly made Westerners believe this march is underway" (*HMF* 7). Poovey's version of this methodology focuses specifically on historical discourses and their relationship to the particular material practices, technologies, and institutions through which those discourses were articulated. She makes this methodological orientation clear as she distinguishes her work from that of other intellectual historians:

> Unlike most intellectual historians . . . I am not primarily interested in the influence one individual's ideas had on the ideas of others, nor am I primarily concerned with the development of particular abstractions (liberalism, for example), which intellectual historians typically detach from their original formulations for analysis. As I have already noted, these abstractions were a characteristic product of the kind of writing I examine here, and instead of simply taking them as given, I want to see how they acquired sufficient vitality to produce material effects. As I have also noted, one can identify epistemological effects like these abstractions only by looking at *the way an argument was conducted* and how the mode of argumentation delimited *what could and could not be said*. . . . I assume that *how an argument is conducted constitutes the argument itself*: there are no ideas apart from their articulation. (*HMF* 16–17).

Poovey's methodology, then, like Foucault's, reads the history of "ideas" through the specific rhetorics through which those ideas were articulated.

While distancing herself from traditional intellectual histories by emphasizing the materiality of language and "ideas," Poovey also refuses to identify her work as "Foucauldian." Foucauldian methodology, she argues, "privileges ruptures or focuses only on discourses," liabilities her work self-consciously strives to avoid (*HMF* 17). While I agree with Poovey that these are tendencies to which the work of some Foucauldians and, at times, Foucault himself are prone, I choose to adopt a broader, less literalist, and perhaps more generous reading of the Foucauldian project. As I argued before, I have adopted a Foucauldian methodology in part because of its attempts to analyze the intersection or embeddedness of "discourses" with nondiscursive institutions and practices rather than limiting itself to a purely linguistic analysis. Likewise, I see no reason to define a "discourse" solely along the highly specified lines that Foucault articulates in such examples as "Politics and the Study of Discourse"[15] but rather adopt a broader application of the term that allows for more heterogeneity within a "discursive formation" and thus, also, more sense of continuity among unevenly developing discursive practices. My conception of the Foucauldian project is more in line with the vision of the editors Ellen Messer-Davidow, David Shumway, and David Sylvan in their interdisciplinary collection of essays, *Knowledges: Historical and Critical Studies in Disciplinarity,* than with what Poovey sees as a more limited project.[16]

My analysis of the uneven development of economic discourse should also be read as part of the intellectual work that Immanuel Wallerstein calls for in his essay "Should We Unthink the Nineteenth Century?" a critique and critical rethinking of "the basic assumption that [the contemporary Western world's] collective activity occurred in three different arenas, or at three different levels—the economy (or the market), the state (or the polity), and the society (or the culture)."[17] While working through a Marxist tradition of social science, Wallerstein argues that both liberal *and* Marxist social scientific traditions have mistakenly written into their analyses of human activity these artificial distinctions inherited from the nineteenth century. Many historians, particularly in recent years, have been more critical of the naturalized categories inherited from the nineteenth century and institutionalized in the disciplinary divisions of twentieth-century Western universities than their colleagues in the "harder" social sciences of economics, sociology, political science, and even anthropology. Intellectual historians, historians of science and the social sciences, and cultural historians have written narratives that chart the construction of these naturalized domains in the thought and writings of such enlightenment figures as Rene Descartes, Thomas Hobbes, David Hume, and Adam Smith and such nineteenth-century thinkers as David Ricardo, Thomas Malthus, William Whewell, and John Stuart Mill.[18] Furthermore, the traditional history of economic thought that implicitly reinscribes positivistic assumptions about a knowable, autonomous realm of "the economic" and about the "progress" of economic theory toward more accurate knowledge of that realm has been supplemented in recent years with persuasive accounts of the ways in which the scientific study of economics emerged alongside and through the "nonscientific" discourses of theology, Anglicanism, Evangelicism, Tractarianism, romanticism, and moral and political anti–Corn Law polemics.[19] My own understanding of the uneven development and contradictions of economic discourse in the early and mid-nineteenth century is deeply indebted to both sets of historians, and I see this book as a contribution to the revisionary history of economic thought undertaken by the latter group, including A. C. Waterman, Boyd Hilton, Donald Winch, and Alon Kadish.

Where my work departs from and thus makes a unique contribution to this revisionary history is my emphasis on the materiality of thought and theory, an emphasis that draws attention to the formal specificities of the texts that I examine and serves as the foundation of my argument that these specificities are themselves a part of the development of "scientific" economic thought in the nineteenth century. It is precisely this materiality, I argue, that makes necessary what might otherwise seem to be an irrelevant detour—or even dead end—into the popular economic texts of John Ramsey McCulloch and Harriet Martineau in the early nineteenth century and, through them, the popular critiques of scientific economic theory written by Charles Dickens and Henry Mayhew in the mid-nineteenth century. In my final chapters, I use the methodology of formal discourse analysis to examine John Stuart Mill's more canonical project in scientific economic discourse, *Principles of Political Economy* (1848–62); the alternative economics of John Ruskin's *Unto This Last* (1862); and the marginalist revisions of Jevons's *Theory of Political Economy* (1871).

In addition to charting a new, supplementary course for the development of scientific economic thought in the nineteenth century, my study also contributes an analysis of rhetorical form and genre as technologies that, like the technologies of nondiscursive practices and institutions, have a relative autonomy and thus develop unevenly in relation to one another and other forms of human activity. Finally, my epistemological assumptions about and methodological interrogation of the historical constructedness of such domains as the "economic," the "literary," the "social," the "moral," and the "political" enable me to contribute to the projects of cultural and epistemological historians to resituate "literary" and other nonspecialist critiques of economic theories within a shared discursive domain.[20]

In my first chapter, I lay out the some of the basic history and historiography of classical or scientific political economy. I explain why I have begun my discussion of scientific political economy with Ricardo, as opposed to Adam Smith, and show how Ricardo, more than any of the political economists who preceded him, attempted to disaggregate economic concerns from their broader moral, social, and political contexts.

In chapter 2, I show how John Ramsey McCulloch's adaptation of Ricardian theory to more familiar genres and a more readable prose style also importantly altered the content of "Ricardian" economics. While Ricardo strove to be aggressively amoral, McCulloch's writing relied on large narrative structures that explicitly remoralized the stakes of profit and loss and of scientific knowledge itself. By joining economic issues to political, social, and psychological concerns, McCulloch created for economic theory a moral urgency that appealed directly to his readers' beliefs and fears. The familiarity of the narratives that McCulloch adopted constituted a bridge between

Ricardo's striking claims and the expectations of an educated and politically engaged, but not specialized or radical, general public. However, while McCulloch's recontextualization of Ricardo's theories made them more urgent, relevant, and familiar to the public, that recontextualization also led McCulloch to transgress Ricardo's most fundamental economic laws.

Harriet Martineau's project for educating her Victorian contemporaries in the fundamental principles of political economy was even more ambitious than McCulloch's. Through twenty-five original novellas, Martineau "illustrated" the whole science of political economy, beginning with its basic definitions and principles in the earlier novellas and continuing through the more complex permutations of economic law in the final volumes. Whereas Martineau's novellas could appeal to an even wider range of readers than McCulloch's popular treatises and journalism, their reliance on the conventions of popular narrative fiction further complicated the theoretical core of her didactic message. Because the generic conventions of such fiction were so far removed from the scientific tradition in which Ricardo's ideas were developed, Martineau's stories were riddled with tensions between the formal demands and expectations of the divergent traditions. As in McCulloch's journalism, Martineau's formal recontextualization of classical economic theory powerfully altered the abstract content of scientific political economy as well as its abstract form.

In addition to the local textual effects of McCulloch's and Martineau's popularizing projects, their economic writings also had the more general effect of placing economic theory back within the moral, social, and political discourses from which Ricardo had so painstakingly isolated it. By interjecting economic theory into these nonspecialist discourses, Ricardo's popularizers made that theory vulnerable to attacks from within these same discourses. These attacks were launched not only from the extreme positions of Tory paternalism, which we see in the writings of Thomas Carlyle, or working-class radicalism, which we see in the writings of Thomas Hodgskin, John Francis Bray, John Gray, and William Thompson. They were also launched from more moderate positions that were potential sources of support for aspects of classical economic theory—liberal middle-class writers concerned with the moral and social well-being of the nation who were looking for solutions to the problems that they saw destroying English culture and society. What these writers perceived and disparaged in the popular writings of political economists was the privileging of economics as the center of and key to all of England's concerns and the refusal of economic writers to accept any ground other than economic law as a basis for moral authority. In the remaining chapters of my book, I explore four representative examples of projects critical of classical political economists' hubristic claims and reductive worldview. The first two projects I examine, those of Charles Dickens (in the novel *Dombey and Son*) and Henry Mayhew (in his letters to the *Morning Chronicle*), totally reject the claims of classical economics. The third, John Stuart Mill's *Principles of Political Economy,* attempts to retain the fundamental claims of Ricardian economics while at the same time broadening the scope of those "economics" to include explicitly moral, psychological, social, and political concerns. In my final chapter, I contrast John Ruskin's and W. Stanley Jevons's revisionary critiques of the entire tradition of classical political economy, including both Ricardo and J. S. Mill, from their differing positions within and outside the increasingly institutionalized discourse of economic science.

chapter one

Ricardian Economics: Rhetoric and the Form of Science in Early-Nineteenth-Century Political Economy

> It is, indeed, a peculiarity of our times, that we must instruct so many people. On politics, on religion, on all less important topics still more, everyone thinks himself competent to think,—in some casual manner does think,—to the best of our means must be taught to think rightly. Even if we had a profound and far-seeing statesman, his deep ideas and long-reaching vision would be useless to us, unless we could import a confidence in them to the mass of influential persons, to the unelected Commons, the unchosen Council, who assist at the deliberations of the nation. . . . And this appeal to the many necessarily brings with it a consequence. We must speak to the many so that they will listen, that they will like to listen, that they will understand. It is of no use addressing them with the forms of science, or the rigour of accuracy, or the tedium of exhaustive discussion. The multitude are impatient of system, desirous of brevity, puzzled by formality.
>
> —WALTER BAGEHOT, 1855

In his 1855 essay on the first Edinburgh Reviewers, Walter Bagehot identifies the democratization of the British reading public as a determining factor in the forms of knowledge made available to that public. Bagehot's multitude is "impatient of system, desirous of brevity, and puzzled by formality" even while it demands to be instructed in how to think about the issues that confront the nation.[1] Paradoxically, at the same time that this multitude was demanding accessible and palatable forms of authoritative knowledge, knowledge production was beginning to be reorganized into disciplines and increasingly claimed as the special province of various experts or professionals. In other words, knowledge production was being reformed in ways that increasingly demanded system, science, and accuracy—the very qualities that Bagehot's public rejects.

Early-nineteenth-century political economy, in particular, was caught up in this paradox of cultural and discursive history. In the writings of David Ricardo, James Mill, and, to a lesser extent, Thomas Malthus, knowledge about "the economy" was self-consciously systematized and modeled on the natural sciences. This process of attempting to render economic theory "scientific" in turn became the basis of many political economists' claims to have produced authoritative knowledge. At the same time, the institutional structures of the universities did not yet support these claims or the secular, systematic knowledges produced by these writers.[2] Instead, early-nineteenth-century political economists appealed to the "unelected Commons" of Bagehot's public, not only to instruct the public but also to authorize this new form of knowledge about the production, distribution, and consumption of material wealth.

"Scientific" knowledge and claims about the economy did not originate suddenly with the writings of the early-nineteenth-century classical economists. In fact, many historians of economic thought identify Adam Smith's *The Wealth of Nations* as the founder of "scientific" economics, while Ricardo is seen merely as continuing and extending, if not corrupting, Smith's theories.[3] The question of who is the "true" founder of classical or scientific economic thought is, indeed, a key point of contention among historians of economic ideas. While one school of economic and intellectual historians identifies Smith as the key originator of modern economic theory, the other dominant school sees a radical break between Smith and Ricardo and emphasizes the differences between them rather than the continuities. Historians of economic thought as diverse as Donald Winch, Marc Blaug, S. G. Checkland, Frank Fetter, Karl Polanyi, and Gertrude Himmelfarb see Ricardo as breaking with the eighteenth-century traditions of moral, political, and economic philosophy epitomized by Smith's authorship of both *The Theory of Moral Sentiments* and *The Wealth of Nations*.[4] Instead of being Smith's heir, Ricardo is seen as the originator of a new strain of secular and "scientific" economic thought that explicitly rejects the Smithian legacy of a politically and socially contextualized economic theory. Both sets of historians see the development of classical or "scientific" political economy as a crucial moment in the emergence of modern economic theory and of the contemporary discipline of "economics." The notion of a "scientific" political economy is fundamentally linked to the current self-definition of economics as an authoritative discipline. Even historians who are skeptical about the category and claims of science recognize its centrality to the historiography of economic theory and disciplinarity.

In this chapter, I argue with the second group of historians that Ricardo's methodological reconstruction of political economy was a crucial stage in the development of what is now defined as modern, "scientific" economic theory, and in doing so, I complicate existing histories in several crucial ways. First, I broaden the analysis of Ricardo's break with Smithian political economy by reinserting Smith's explicitly economic writings into the eighteenth-century tradition of moral philosophy of which they were a part. On the one hand, this analysis shows how the normative, moral, and psychological concerns articulated in Smith's *The Theory of Moral Sentiments* are integral to his economic theory; on the other hand, it shows how the same project of moral philosophy also helps to construct a key feature of the discursive space in which Ricardo writes. Second, by contending that Ricardo's secular, scientific version of economic theory sought to appeal to a specialized audience and institutional context that did not exist in early-nineteenth-century Britain, I complicate this narrative of economic *thought* with questions of discursive legibility. A close examination of the rhetoric and structure of Ricardo's prose reveals the way in which his development of his new economic ideas, methodology, and approach depended upon certain formal generic and rhetorical innovations that would have been alien to Bagehot's reading public. Third and finally, by reading against the grain of Ricardo's self-consciously amoral formulations, I expose the providential logic embedded in Ricardo's "scientific" theories.[5] This "moral logic" seemingly contradicts Ricardo's discourse of a secular and scientific economics, but it is in large part facilitated by the form of that discourse. The very reductive gestures through which Ricardo's *Principles of Political Economy and Taxation* works to constitute a narrow, reified domain of "the economy" also enable the text to create the effect of a totalizing, law-bound system that mediates and legislates human affairs as profoundly, if not as comprehensively, as divine providence. Thus Ricardo's economic theory provides the basis not only for the emergent "scientific" study of the economy but also for a secular alternative to divine law and a bourgeois version of "virtue" that places capitalist economic organization at the center of a reassuring narrative of human development and progress. This formulation of "natural economic law" as a kind of "secular providence" remains largely implicit in Ricardo's canonical economic text, subordinated to complex explanations, hypothetical scenarios, and quantified "illustrations" of the "laws" themselves. Such rhetorical formulations predominate and create the discursive texture of Ricardo's prose; only in the work of Ricardo's popularizers is this economic logic displayed in its fully providential guise.

Before examining the distinctiveness of Ricardian economic discourse, I want to briefly contextualize the term "science" as it was used in nineteenth-century England and to place Ricardo's project within this context. "Science" was an intensely contested term and practice in early- and mid-nineteenth-century Britain. Issues involving method, scope, epistemology, and forms of knowledge complicated questions of scientific authority and imbricated "science" with discourses of nationalism and religion. Most of the definitions and uses of "science" in early- and mid-nineteenth-century England were organized around four major sets of oppositions. The first and most obvious of these was the distinction between scientific inquiry focused on the natural world and such inquiry focused on aspects of individual or collective human experience. As the definitions provided by the *Oxford English Dictionary* make clear, the term "science" in the eighteenth and nineteenth centuries could be used to apply to virtually any body of knowledge. During the course of these two centuries, however, methods and standards developed in the physical sciences became increasingly authoritative. At the same time, and certainly by the nineteenth century, the differences between the *objects* of scientific study were being specified in distinctions between the "natural" and the "moral" sciences. Thus, nineteenth-century references to political economy as a "scientific" field of study can mean many different things and are not necessarily appeals or references to the models of the emergent natural sciences. In the case of Ricardo, the term "scientific" was self-consciously associated with the methods and standards of the natural sciences and just as self-consciously distinguished from what were seen as other, less rigorous and less authoritative forms of knowledge. In *Principles of Political Economy,* Ricardo repeatedly refers to the "laws" of political economy as "the laws of nature."[6] Ricardo considers these natural laws of political economy to be as real, immutable, and ascertainable as the laws of physics or astronomy. In criticizing the English Poor Laws that guaranteed each person subsistence, for example, Ricardo emphasizes his point through an analogy of the laws of political economy with the laws of Newtonian physics: "The principle of gravitation is not more certain than the tendency of such laws to change wealth and power into misery and weakness" (*PPE* 63).

The second key distinction within nineteenth-century science is between the use of inductive and deductive methodologies. These methods were nationalized through the association of induction with Bacon and Newton, and thus with English forms of science, whereas deduction was disparagingly associated with Descartes and French "theory." In the hands of William Whewell and his followers at Cambridge, English inductivism was also linked to the theistic assumptions of natural theology.[7] Thus, for many in the early nineteenth century, deductive reasoning was seen, a priori, as subversive of both religion and the nation in addition to being discredited as untestable or otherwise "unscientific." At the same time, despite the dominance of the empiricist tradition in the rhetoric of Victorian intellectuals, their scientific practice was in reality a mixture of inductive and deductive methodologies.[8] A small but influential number of nineteenth-century scientists and philosophers, including notably David Ricardo, continued to make arguments for the necessity, if not inevitability, of a priori forms of thought. Even Sir Isaac Newton was frequently quoted in support of the necessity for hypotheses, analogies, and other aspects of deductive reasoning in the scientific enterprise.

Many of the writers advocating the continued cultivation of deductive methodologies traced these methodologies not to Descartes and France but rather to the tradition of eighteenth-century Scottish philosophy represented by David Hume, Adam Smith, and Dugald Stewart. The legacy of this tradition was particularly powerful within political economy and the other emergent social sciences that followed in its wake.[9] Ricardo deployed this discursive strain of deductive reasoning, especially through his deep indebtedness to Adam Smith's *The Wealth of Nations*. In particular, Ricardo drew upon Smith's idea of "natural" social progress via commercial expansion and economic growth. Indeed, a version of this "natural law" constitutes the implicit providential logic that structures Ricardo's *Principles*. Significantly, however, unlike other inheritors of the Scottish tradition such as J. R. McCulloch and the Mills, Ricardo's interest in "the progress of society"—at least in his canonical *Principles*—is subordinated to his model of economic functioning, a model that is in turn rigorously derived from a specific and fundamental set of *economic* principles. Ricardo, that is, unlike his allies and supporters, developed a model of the economic domain that formally resembled the Cartesian deductive or "derivational" model in which, as Stephen Gudeman explains, "one or another premise serves as the core from which the remaining elements of the model may be derived."[10] Gudeman identifies Ricardo's use of such a model for economic theory as constituting an "epistemological break" at the beginning of the nineteenth century. The problem with Gudeman's reading is that this form, rather than "allow[ing] for effective communication between Ricardo and his audience," as Gudeman claims, actually constituted a significant barrier between Ricardo and many of his English contemporaries.[11] Such elaborate theoretical constructions, as the cultural historian David Simpson has shown, triggered the Francophobic hostilities of the English public.[12] Furthermore, the very prose necessary to construct such rigorous and complex derivational models was acknowledged by Ricardo's supporters to be alien to the majority of the reading public.

The final two significant distinctions within nineteenth-century science are those through which scientists increasingly defined their endeavors against the "unscientific" discourses of art, governance, and legislation or, alternatively, morality and ethics. Thus, in the third major distinction, "science" became increasingly associated with the discovery and description of "truths" rather than with issues of how those truths might be "applied." Ricardo, despite his experience as a stockbroker and member of Parliament, constructs his project as one of scientific *knowledge* rather than one of *praxis*. In the Preface to his *Principles,* Ricardo states: "If the principles which he [Ricardo] deems correct should be found to be so, it will be for *others,* more able than himself, *to trace them to their important consequences*" (emphasis mine, *PPE* 3). John Stuart Mill and Nassau Senior later formalized this type of distinction by defining political economy as a *science* versus an *art.* As a science, according to these constructions, political economy theorized and produced knowledges that were distinct from their practice, either in commerce or in government legislation. In the fourth and final distinction, during the nineteenth century the "science" of political economy also began to be differentiated from its moral and ethical implications: the knowledge or truth that Ricardo attempts to "discover" is imagined as positive and predictive rather than normative and prescriptive. Such distinctions became crucial discursive devices in the separation of economic science not only from the nonscientific others of politics and business practices but also from the whole question of morality. Furthermore, these distinctions point to the more fundamental discursive distinction that emerged in the nineteenth century: the opposition between the rationally governed realities formulated and theorized by scientific forms of knowledge and the irrational—or at least nonrationalizable—realities and knowledges relegated to the domain of the nonscientific.

This final differentiation between positive and normative knowledges is the one that most strikingly distinguishes Ricardo's version of political economy from that of his predecessor Adam Smith. For Smith, political economy is part of the "science" of jurisprudence, which is itself part of a larger system of morality and virtue. In other words, for Smith, economic theory is fully imbricated with questions of morality and virtue. At the same time, Smith, unlike later social scientists, does not see morality and virtue as outside the domain of the rational and scientific. The imbrication of his economic theory with moral concerns becomes clear when Smith's *The Wealth of Nations,* instead of being read through the retrospective and anachronistic lens of nineteenth- and twentieth-century economic theory, is read in conjunction with Smith's earlier published work, *The Theory of Moral Sentiments.* The notion of an "Adam Smith Problem" that presumes and attempts to reconcile the apparent disjunctions between these two works is in fact a production of the "two cultures" divide that emerged in the nineteenth century—a divide that reifies the distinction between positive, supposedly objective science and the normative subjectivity of nonscientific judgments, knowledges, and activities. Recent Smith scholars, by resituating both works within the discursive and intellectual contexts of late-eighteenth-century England and Scotland, have been able to demonstrate the continuities and shared commitments of these two texts.[13]

Perhaps the most important of these contexts for understanding the normative aspects of Smith's economic science is the debate on civic virtue in which both *The Theory of Moral Sentiments* and *The Wealth of Nations* intervened. As J. G. A. Pocock and others have shown, the growth of commerce and mobile forms of property in the seventeenth and eighteenth centuries was seen as a threat to the classical model of civic humanism that associated virtue with the "independence" of the landed aristocracy.[14] Adam Smith was among a number of eighteenth-century moral philosophers (including Francis Hutcheson, his teacher, and his radically skeptical contemporary, David Hume) who responded to conservative Tory concerns about the commercial erosion of civic virtue by reimagining virtue in such a way that it was not only compatible with the growth of commercial society but actually supported and fostered by that growth. This new model, called "bourgeois virtue" by some historians, linked individual virtue to political and economic liberalism, particularly free trade. For these writers, the liberal economic policy of free trade was valued not only because it promoted economic growth but also because of its capacity to produce virtuous, albeit largely private, citizens.[15]

This concern with the positive moral possibilities of commercial society, while present in *The Wealth of Nations* (1776), is explored much more fully in *The Theory of Moral Sentiments* (1759). Thus, in order to fully appreciate Ricardo's break with the Smithian tradition of political economy, Ricardo's economic writings must be contrasted not only with the more narrowly economic treatise but also with Smith's text of moral philosophy. In addition to demonstrating the discursive effects of Ricardo's decontextualization of political economy from earlier traditions of moral and political philosophy, such a contrast also makes visible some of the crucial erasures and suppressions on which modern "scientific" economic theory depends.

Adam Smith's economic theory was embedded in normative forms of knowledge at a number of levels, two of which are particularly important for understanding the alternative history of economic discourse that I am tracing. The first and broadest level is systemic. In his university lectures and published writings, Smith outlined a complex but unified system of the interdependent functioning of the political, economic, social, moral, and psychological domains. Most contemporary Smith scholars agree that his theory of jurisprudence is the linchpin of this system.[16] Smith's economic theory, in turn, is seen as a branch of his moralized science of jurisprudence.[17] In particular, Smith's theorization and advocacy of economic liberalism are linked to a moral-political vision that identifies human labor as the moral foundation of property and, through the "natural" human desire to better one's condition, as the basis for individual moral development.[18] The individual moral development fostered by human labor and the desire for bettering one's condition includes the virtues of prudence, justice, and self-command. The virtue of prudence stimulates the individual's self-command and reasoning capacities in order to enable the individual to restrain his or her immediate selfish appetites in the anticipation of more distant but noble—or at least more long-lasting—rewards. The desire to reap the rewards of one's own labor and self-restraint, in turn, fosters the virtue of justice and, again, of self-command. Because the individual sympathetically imagines himself in the situations of others, he will demand for them the justice that he desires for himself, even when that justice is to his own immediate disadvantage. The development of all of these virtues in individual social agents, or "citizens," guarantees further economic growth *and* collective social development—processes that are themselves interdependent within Smith's stage-based theory of human social development.[19]

Justice is the only enforceable virtue in Smith's *The Theory of Moral Sentiments*—and, along with self-command, it is also the highest.[20] While the self-interested virtue of prudence fuels the cycle of economic and social development sketched in the preceding paragraphs, the nonselfish virtue of justice is what Smith calls the "main pillar" of the human social building.[21] Justice constructs the framework through which individuals can pursue their own economic advancement (within legitimate boundaries) *and* can make their own individual moral decisions in relation to the other virtues of prudence, benevolence, and self-command.[22] Since these virtues are unenforceable, only a liberal judicial and legislative system can foster their growth. On the other hand, only a liberal economic policy of free trade can provide the economic rewards and growth that propel and sustain this moral social economy.

For Smith, then, scientific economic theory is logically subordinated to the larger positive *and* normative project of describing how human economic behavior interacts with human moral, social, and political behavior and prescribing a course of governmental, legislative, and commercial policy that could best foster what he considered the natural, beneficial development of human civilization. In contract, Ricardo's scientific economic theory describes narrowly economic processes that are natural laws unto themselves. Ricardo does not attempt to explain how such laws might be linked to any individual or collective good beyond that of "economic growth." Some vestiges of Smith's "providential" liberalism remain embedded in the structure of Ricardo's prose and paradigm, as do implicit commendations of the "bourgeois virtues" of prudence and self-denial. But in Ricardo's economic writings, even these vestiges of Smith's broader moral and social vision are articulated as a positive, objective description of a narrowly defined and rationalized economic system rather than advocated as the best route to individual virtue and the beneficent development of the social body.

Smith's concern with individual virtue, as well as collective social development, is related to a second level at which his system of social or moral "science" encompasses both positive and normative forms of knowledge. While *The Wealth of Nations* focuses on the individual as an economic agent largely pursing his or her own self-interest, *The Theory of Moral Sentiments* establishes the broader psychological and moral context in which self-interest or prudence functions. This broader context is crucial to Smith's intervention in the debate on commerce and civic virtue, for it is through his unique conception of human psychology that Smith develops the foundation for his entire social and moral system.[23] Like other "liberal" eighteenth-century theorists, Smith attempts to reconcile capitalist commerce and civic virtue by relocating the source of civic virtue from the public domain of martial, judicial, and legislative action to the private domain of the individual subject.[24] Despite this liberalizing theoretical move, Smith's model of the individual is still intricately tied to a moral social vision and thus significantly different from the model of the individual presumed within the theoretical paradigms of nineteenth-century scientific economics.[25]

This difference between the two models of individual subjectivity constructed or assumed in their theories is a second crucial distinction between Smithian and Ricardian political economy. At the simplest level, this distinction involves the difference between an individual agent motivated solely by the rational pursuit of self-interest, in the Ricardian model, and an agent motivated by multiple and competing passions, only partially reined in and guided by the dictates of reason, in the Smithian model.[26] This is already a striking distinction, but it is related to an even more complex and significant distinction between the two theorists' psychological models. For Ricardo, the individual is fully autonomous as well as rational and singly motivated. "Self"-interest straightforwardly refers to this singular and autonomous economic agent. For Smith, in contrast, the "self" is not only animated by a more complex set of psychological motivations but also enfolds *others within* "itself" through the fundamental psychological process of sympathy.[27] Thus, while Smith's psychological paradigm does help to construct that liberal subject—the individual—it also complicates this subject by making it fully dependent upon its intersubjective relations. Smith identifies this mutual dependence of individuals, in turn, as enabling a commercial system to produce virtue as well as wealth.[28]

Smith's model of individual psychology involves three distinct theoretical movements, all of which are crucial for his model of individual subjectivity: first, the internalization of morality and virtue within the individual; second, the external projection of the self through sympathy; and third, the internalization of others' moral sentiments and perceptions in the form of the "impartial spectator" or "inhabitant of the breast" (*TMS* 215, 137) The first of these movements seems straightforward: the internalization here is a movement away from the classical and republican models of what we might, in retrospect, consider a more "public" or social model of virtue. The second movement, however, complicates the first significantly because it immediately refers the internal sentiments of the individual outward toward others. The very first sentence of *The Theory of Moral Sentiments* announces this orientation, foregrounding the complexity of Smith's model of individual psychology: "How selfish soever man may be supposed, there are evidently some principles in his nature, which interest him in the fortune of others, and render their happiness necessary to him, though he derives nothing from it except the pleasure of seeing it" (*TMS* 9). Smith elaborates upon this sympathetic process several paragraphs later: "Whatever is the passion which arises from any object in the person principally concerned, an analogous emotion springs up, at the thought of his situation, in the breast of every attentive spectator" (*TMS* 10). For Smith, sympathy is not only pity and compassion for others but "our fellow-feeling with any passion whatever" (*TMS* 10).

Another distinctive aspect of Smith's notion of sympathy is that it arises not from the view of the other person's passion but rather from the situation that excited the passion. Because of this indirection, Smith argues, "the compassion of the spectator must arise altogether from the consideration of what he himself would feel if he was reduced to the same unhappy situation, and what perhaps is impossible, was at the same time able to regard it with his present reason and judgment" (*TMS* 12). Sympathy, that is, involves the spectator's imaginative projection of him- or herself into the situation of the other while *at the same time* retaining the critical distance granted by the spectatorial position. This process of sympathy and the self-division involved is, in fact, the crux of an individual's capacity for moral sentiment in Smith's psychological model. We approve of another's passions only when we imagine that we would feel the same passion if we were placed in the same situation; we disapprove of them if we imagine that we would feel otherwise in the situation (*TMS* 16).

The interplay between sympathy and self-division is crucial not only for moral judgment of others but also for the development of the individual's own virtues, particularly what Smith calls the "great, the awful and respectable virtues" associated with self-command (*TMS* 23). Smith argues that just as "nature," via sympathy, teaches the individual, as spectator, to place himself in the situation of the sufferer or person primarily concerned, "so he [the sufferer] is constantly placing himself in theirs, and *thence conceiving some degree of that coolness about his own fortune*, with which he is sensible that *they will view it*" (emphasis mine, *TMS* 22). In other words, just as the individual judges another's emotions according to what she would feel in the same situation, so she judges—and attempts to moderate—her own emotions according to her perception of the feelings of less immediately involved others.

For Smith, the desire for mutual sympathy—for concurrence between one's own emotions and the emotions of those around one—is the most fundamental feature of human psychology, the basis of all the virtues, and the primary motivator of human feeling and action. Thus, even though humans are by nature selfish, their psychological makeup demands that they constantly move beyond their own self-interested passions in order to obtain the sympathetic correspondences that they, also by nature, desire. Significantly, within Smith's moral-psychological model, even the virtue most closely associated with selfishness—prudence—is motivated and sustained by the individual's desire for such sympathetic correspondences. The individual's desire to "better one's condition" that motivates prudent behavior is actually a desire to have those around him sympathetically enter into his situation, and the course of prudent action necessary for bettering his condition is supported more by others' sympathetic approval of his behavior than by the calculation and anticipation of long-term gains.

The role of others' sympathy and approval in the fostering of one's own virtues points to the third movement in Smith's moral-psychological model. This final feature of Smith's model of the individual involves a movement back inward, the folding of others' perceptions permanently back into the self in the form of the "impartial spectator" or the "man within." The impartial spectator is, in effect, the desire for others' approval or "mutual sympathy" internalized as conscience. It is particularly crucial in mediating conflicts between one's own immediate self-interest and others' needs and desires. Thus, Smith writes:

> When our passive feelings are almost always so sordid and so selfish, how comes it that our active principles should often be so generous and so noble? . . . It is a stronger power, a more forcible motive, which exerts itself upon such occasions. It is reason, principle, conscience, the inhabitant of the breast, the man within, the great judge and arbiter of our conduct. It is he who, whenever we are about to act so as to affect the happiness of others, calls to us, with a voice capable of astonishing the most presumptuous of our passions, that we are but one of the multitude . . . and that when we prefer ourselves so shamefully and so blindly to others, we become the proper objects of resentment, abhorrence, and execration. (*TMS* 137)

Because of the presence of conscience, or "the inhabitant of the breast," within all persons, "self-interest" is not necessarily selfish. The "man within" reminds the individual that if he hopes to retain the sympathy and approval of others, he must moderate his emotions and actions according to *their* interests.

For Smith, then, the individual is a highly complex entity. Even his or her interest cannot be understood without reference to others because those others are crucial to his or her happiness, whether or not they are necessary for his or her material well-being. The individual's very "self" is multiple because it involves an entity with "its own" usually selfish passions *and* a second and often more powerful entity that speaks for others and for the self's passion for harmony with those others. At the same time that this Smithian psychological model is oriented outward toward others, it also, ultimately, does locate morality and virtue within the individual rather than in a social structure (as did civic humanism). The perceptions and interests of others make their claims on the self most powerfully and authoritatively through the figure of an *internalized* other—the man *within* or the *inhabitant of the breast*. It is this figure, rather than specific others with whom the individual comes in contact, that bears the authority of impartiality. Likewise, it is this entity with whom the virtuous man comes most fully to identify himself, whose approval he seeks more than that of the actual others he encounters in his day-to-day life.

The fact that Smith reinternalizes the sympathetic, outward-looking orientation of his psychological model has significant consequences for the development of political, economic, and moral discourse in the late eighteenth and the nineteenth centuries. Once moral and economic agency have been located within the individual, that individual can be divided between public and private, with the "public" aspects of the individual theorized in terms of rationality while the "private" aspects are implicitly coded as irrational and relegated to the domain of the untheorizable and unsystematic, the subjective and idiosyncratic. This is precisely the opposition on which Ricardo's economic project depends. Ricardo's version of scientific economic theory deals only with the rational, public aspects of the individual's narrowly defined economic behavior, and much of its authority depends upon this exclusive focus. For Ricardo, the sympathy that is fundamental to Smith's psychological model of the individual—and that results in its complexity—can be dismissed as irrelevant to the operation of natural economic law because it is outside the psychological model of rational, self-interested economic man that Ricardo's theory at once assumes *and* constructs. While Smith attempts to synthesize and explain all aspects of collective and individual human behavior into a moral "science," Ricardo depends upon the opposition between public and private to carve out a discrete domain of human activity that can be fully rationalized, leaving behind the domain of the "private" as the untheorized, untheorizable space of individual moral agency.

The feminist intellectual historian Kathryn Sutherland, in looking only at Smith's *The Wealth of Nations,* reads Smith as the inaugurator of this public/private opposition within economic theory—and of the consequent narrowing specialization of political economy—through his erasure of female productive labor from the public space of the market.[29] When we contextualize Smith's economic project within his larger moral science, however, his role in this process becomes more complex and conflicted than Sutherland suggests. While Smith's writings do function to gender certain spaces, activities, and personal attributes as male and female, they do not follow the nineteenth-century model of assigning individual morality and subjective judgment to the private aspects of the nonrational and nonrationalizable aspects of individual character or to the equally nonrational spaces of female domesticity. At the same time, Smith's internalization of the processes of virtue does set the stage for the kind of move that Ricardo makes several decades later, as does Smith's decision to write *The Wealth of Nations* as an independent book.[30] While it now seems relatively easy to trace out the underlying theoretical and systematic connections between Smith's "moral" and his "economic" text, the very disaggregation effected by nineteenth-century political economists made it appear just as self-evident, for over one hundred years, that there was a sharp, radical break between the text of moral philosophy and the text of political economy. In the remainder of this chapter, I will examine more closely exactly how Ricardo attempted, with only partial success, to effect this disaggregation of the economic from the moral as well as from the nonrational, the nonsystematic, the private, and the subjective.

Ricardo structures his writing in the *Principles of Political Economy* in ways that facilitate the discursive construction of "the economy" and of political economy as the "science" that can explain the law and logic of that entity. For the most part, the effect of Ricardo's "scientific" methodology and rhetorical form is an image of the economy as an autonomous, law-bound, and amoral entity. At the same time, however, due in large part to Ricardo's commitment to systemic totality structured according to deductive logic, his text also creates a more marginal, often unremarked-upon effect: a narrative of coherent social development that is reassuring in its very coherence and an attendant set of behavioral assumptions that *structurally* mimic the prescriptions of divine providential law.

Ricardo's *Principles* begins with a brief Preface in which he defines what he sees as "the principal problem in Political Economy," the problem that becomes the center of his theoretical project. The opening statement of the Preface is a universalizing principle differentiating humankind according to three economic categories, or "classes"—landlords, capitalists, and laborers—among whom "the produce of the earth" is divided. Ricardo's second statement introduces into the universal principle the variable of "history": "But in different stages of society, the proportions of the whole produce of the earth which will be allotted to each of these classes, under the names of rent, profit, and wages, will be essentially different; depending mainly on the actual fertility of the soil, on the accumulation of capital and population, and on the skill, ingenuity, and instruments employed in agriculture" (*PPE* 3). The "laws which regulate this distribution," which can accurately calculate and predict the effect of these historical variables, are for Ricardo precisely the problem of political economy that his text is constructed to address. Although acknowledging the "improvements" made to the science of political economy by his predecessors and peers Anne-Robert-Jacques Turgot, Sir James Steuart, Smith, Jean-Baptiste Say, and J.-C.-L. Simonde de Sismondi, Ricardo argues that these writers "afford very little satisfactory information respecting the natural course of rent, profit, and wages."[31] This "natural course" is the subject of Ricardo's *Principles* (*PPE* 3).

The uniqueness of Ricardo's approach to this issue lies in his labor theory of value and his methodology. Ricardo derives much of the labor theory of value from Smith's discussion in *The Wealth of Nations*. Always more systematic than Smith, however, Ricardo clearly distinguishes between labor as productive of value and the amount of goods that can be exchanged for a certain amount of labor. The significance of this distinction was crucial for classical political economy on multiple levels. First, Ricardo's value theory provided the coherent theoretical core from which the remainder of the system could be derived. Second, Ricardo's definition of value solely in terms of labor linked economic value to the process of material production rather than the process of exchange. Third, by defining value solely in terms of labor, Ricardo's theory excluded rent and profits as productive of value and made the issue of the distributive share of labor value one of the central problematics of classical economic theory. Classical political economy's focus on distribution is linked to the fourth and final level on which the labor theory of value functions. That is, Ricardo's labor theory of value, along with his focus on the distribution of that value, provided the theoretical basis for the contestatory socialist economic theories of the Ricardian socialists in the early decades of the nineteenth century and, later, for the more systematic and influential socialist writings of Marx and Engels. After the marginalist revolution in orthodox economic theory rejected the labor theory of value in the final decades of the nineteenth century, it was primarily Marxist economic theorists who retained this theoretical claim and kept alive the macroeconomic analysis and discourse of *political* economy. This powerful legacy of classical economic theory has been ably traced by historians of nineteenth-century socialist thought, including G. D. H. Cole, Max Beer, Noel Thompson, and Gregory Claeys.[32] For the purposes of my project, Ricardo's labor theory of value is important primarily for its structural role within Ricardo's *Principles* and for the formal effects of its construction of an economic system based on material productivity and the notion of a "natural," subsistence wage.

After Ricardo sets up his labor theory of value in the opening chapter, this economic principle becomes the "core" of his quasi-Euclidean model, the initial premise of his Cartesian system. His second chapter on rent reintroduces history in the form of population growth and pressures on the "means of subsistence" but does so less in terms of narrative progression than in terms of another set of universal principles: the theory of rent and Malthus's population principle, along with its attendant assumptions about human reproduction. In fact, throughout Ricardo's text, "history" is reified into abstract principles of "natural" and inevitable development, the most common being the "progress of society" involving capital accumulation, population growth, and a concomitant bringing into cultivation of inferior lands.[33] This principle of "progress" is invoked particularly in Ricardo's discussion of wages, profits, and foreign trade in his fifth through seventh chapters. The remaining chapters of *Principles* use the economic principles already established to explain the economic operations of taxation, colonial trade, currency and banking, and other issues of concern to Ricardo and his contemporaries. Even when he examines such "contemporary" issues, however, Ricardo retains the deductive methodology and discursive form introduced in his first chapter. Within Ricardo's primary text of economic theory, then, both history and current political and economic issues are structurally subordinated to a few narrowly specified and carefully defined economic principles.

In addition to the overall structure of his text, Ricardo bases his scientific version of political economy on three interlocking rhetorical and methodological features—disaggregation, abstraction, and systematization. Ricardian theory shares all of these features to some extent with the theories of Ricardo's predecessor Adam Smith and his contemporary Thomas Malthus, but Ricardo's *Principles* depends on each of these features to a much greater extent than *The Wealth of Nations, Essay on the Principle of Population,* or Malthus's *Principles of Political Economy.* Intellectual and economic historians who locate the origin of modern economics in *The Wealth of Nations* identify precisely Smith's ability to disaggregate or separate economic issues from moral and political issues as his revolutionary accomplishment.[34] Ricardo, however, is even more radical than Smith in his disaggregation of the "economic." In addition to their differing intellectual commitments and methodologies, one of the reasons that Ricardo was able to effect disaggregation so much more radically than Smith was that, unlike Smith, he rigorously subordinated his expository style to his theoretical methodology. In other words, while both Smith and Ricardo worked to specify a distinct domain of human activity as "economic," Ricardo used the structure, as well as the content, of his economic prose as a way to effect this discursive separation. Thus, part of the difference between the economic visions of Smith and Ricardo is a difference in "style" as well as a difference in "substance" or principle.

A brief look at one of the most famous passages from Smith's *The Wealth of Nations*, his analysis of the division of labor through a pin factory, will set up some of the stylistic differences between the two writers as well as suggesting the way in which Smith's style is linked to the methodology and shape of his project. In the first sentence of the first chapter of *Wealth*, Smith states that it is through the division of labor that "the greatest improvement in the productive powers of labour" has resulted.[35] Smith immediately moves from this general and rather abstract claim to an example, explaining that a particular illustration will assist the reader in understanding the general principle. To further facilitate the reader's imaginative grasp of this process, Smith says that he will examine the division of labor as it works on a smaller scale, where all of the workmen are collected into the same workhouse "and placed at once under the view of the spectator" (*WN* 8). In other words, Smith implicitly acknowledges that a coherent visual image of this economic process is important to the reader's analytical understanding and thus constructs a scene in which the reader can position him- or herself as a spectator. Furthermore, Smith notes that the example of the pin factory is "one in which the division of labour has been very often taken notice of"; in other words, it may already be familiar to the reader.

The passage begins by Smith explaining that without the division of labor, a single unskilled workman, on his own, could at best produce one to twenty pins in the course of a day's labor. In contrast, he continues,

> the way in which this business is now carried on . . . it is divided into a number of branches, of which the greater part are likewise peculiar trades. One man draws out the wire, another straights it, a third cuts it, a fourth points it, a fifth grinds it at the top for receiving the head; to make the head requires two or three distinct operations; to put it on, is a peculiar business, to whiten the pins is another; it is even a trade by itself to put them into the paper; and the important business of making a pin is, in this manner, divided into about eighteen distinct operations, which, in some manufactories, are all performed by distinct hands, though in others the same man will sometimes perform two or three of them. I have seen a small manufactury of this kind where ten men

only were employed. . . . But though they were very poor, and therefore but indifferently accommodated with the necessary machinery, they could, when they exerted themselves, make among them about twelve pounds of pins in a day. (8–9)

Smith continues on to calculate how many pins per day each laborer would be making under this regimen, estimating the figure at 4,800 pins per day and comparing that with the one to twenty pins of the single laborer. There are several features of this passage that distinguish it stylistically from the kind of prose developed by Ricardo. First, as already mentioned, it is self-consciously and highly visual. Second, the main portion of the passage is constructed around the narrative progression provided by the movement of the "pin" through its various stages of making. In short, it tells a story. Third, while Smith inserts numerous phrases specifying and qualifying aspects of the process illustrated, such qualifications do not interrupt the rhetorical flow. They do slow down some of the sentences, but they never seem to halt the forward movement of the sentences themselves. Finally, toward the end of the passage, Smith gestures beyond the imaginary scenario he has constructed and refers to a specific pin factory within his own experience: "I have seen a small manufactury of this kind." In other words, Smith not only creates a visual image and a miniature narrative to illustrate an abstract and general claim, he then also refers his illustration to the specific historical reality of his own experience.

This is only one brief passage from a book that is over nine hundred pages long, but it gives a sense of Smith's commitment to communicating with his reader and his concern with linking economic theory to specific historical applications and variations rather than simply elaborating the theory itself. Even the title of Smith's book demonstrates his sense that the "economic" is historically and politically embedded. Rather than the common title adopted by nineteenth-century writers, *The Principles of Political Economy* (to which Ricardo adds "and Taxation"), Smith's *Inquiry into the Nature and Causes of the Wealth of Nations* suggests the subordination of "wealth," that is, "economics," to the larger discursive entities of the polis and society, the "nation." In fact, book 3 of volume 1 and virtually the entirety of volume 2 of *The Wealth* deal specifically with the interpenetration of economics with the social and political domains of national well-being.

In contrast, in order to develop a "science" of the economy, Ricardo first delineated a distinct domain of "the economic" that by definition excluded many of the concerns associated with the earlier term "oeconomy."[36] This specifically economic domain went hand in hand with a new narrowing of the definition of political economy. Ricardo does not explicitly define political economy in the *Principles*, but the theoretical specificity of both the science and its object are implicit throughout. The definition with which McCulloch prefaces his encyclopedia article is an accurate articulation of these implicit definitions and in fact constitutes the very first sentence of McCulloch's article: "Political economy is the science of the laws which regulate the production, distribution, and consumption of those material products which have exchangeable value, and which are either necessary, useful, or agreeable to man."[37] McCulloch makes clear the exclusive specificity of this definition a few paragraphs later when he focuses on the term "wealth," which he has intentionally excluded from his definition because for many, the word "is synonymous with '*all that man desires as useful and agreeable to him*'" (emphasis in original, *Outlines* 9–10). In contrast to this broader term, McCulloch insists that it is only objects that have "exchange value"—a term that he defines in opposition to "use value"—that can be categorized as wealth. Scientific political economy, then, defines as its object of analysis only those kinds of wealth and value that are produced in or can be registered by the market.

McCulloch's definition of the science of political economy demonstrates this disaggregation of a distinctly economic domain from other spheres of activity and knowledge, but it does not fully capture the extent to which Ricardian scientific political economy refused to engage with moral and ethical problems. Ricardo himself announces this exclusion as a fundamental aspect of his theory during an argumentative correspondence with Malthus when he writes that the duty of the political economist "is to tell you how you may become rich, but he is not to advise you to prefer riches to indolence, or indolence to riches."[38] The apparent facetiousness of this statement does not lessen the significance of its claim. Richard Olson writes that "nothing is more important to the emergence of political economy as a science . . . than the initial isolation of economic issues from broader issues relating to religion and social concerns."[39]

The disaggregation of Ricardo's economic project is accomplished through methodological and stylistic abstraction. Indeed, abstraction is one of the primary mechanisms through which the exclusion of moral, theological, political, and social concerns from Ricardian economic theory was effected. The abstraction of Ricardo's prose is particularly important for his representation of human agency and psychology. One of the central features of the deductive, Cartesian methodology Ricardo adopted was the theoretical gesture through which all human agents were rendered identical for the purposes of analysis. This process was effected by the science's reduction of all human considerations to the one set of components—in this case, the economic—defined as the scientific object of analysis. This radical process of abstraction was most strongly and explicitly articulated in the nineteenth century by J. S.

Mill in his early essay on the definition of political economy: "[Political economy] does not treat of the whole of man's nature . . . nor the whole conduct of man in society. It is concerned with him solely as a being who desires to possess wealth, and who is capable of judging the comparative efficacy of means for obtaining that end. . . . It makes entire abstraction of every other human passion or motive; except those which may be regarded as perpetually antagonizing principles to the desire for wealth. . . . Political Economy considers mankind as occupied solely in acquiring and consuming wealth."[40] Although Mill's essay was written years after Ricardo's *Principles,* it explains the reductionary definition of human agency inherent in Ricardo's examination of the economy. This definition of human nature allows the economist to identify human actors solely as functions of the economic system—as, for example, landlords, capitalists, and laborers. Through this process of double abstraction, Ricardo's mathematical reasoning effectually erases any ground for broader moral or social considerations. And while Ricardo was by no means alone in his analytical reliance on abstraction in nineteenth-century social and economic theory, he, more than his predecessors or contemporaries, created a prose style that approached the ideal of mathematical abstraction.

One of the most striking stylistic abstractions of Ricardo's *Principles* is its complete lack of illustrative anecdote. This feature is noted repeatedly even by Ricardo's most loyal supporter, J. R. McCulloch. In his *Discourse on Political Economy,* McCulloch ends his laudatory discussion of Ricardo's contribution to the development of political economy with an entire paragraph discussing the difficulty of Ricardo's prose. He lists three sources of that difficulty, all of which can be linked to the abstraction of his master's project: "the brevity with which [he] has stated some of his most important propositions, the fewness of his illustrations, and the mathematical cast he has given to his reasoning."[41] All of these features, especially Ricardo's lack of illustrating anecdotes, make the medium of the *Principles* alien to what McCulloch at another point calls "the generality of readers."[42] Instead of anecdotes, Ricardo relies heavily on the use of hypothetical scenarios. These scenarios allow Ricardo to recreate the abstraction of his theories in the prose through which he explains them. They enable him to strip his human representations of all features except those directly related to his economic point. There are no complicating circumstances unwittingly imported by an actual, or even realistic, anecdote. Collaterally, there are no grounds for the complicating emotions of sympathetic identification in the reader. In fact, because Ricardo reifies the actors in these scenarios into one-dimensional economic figures, he produces a narrative version of rational economic man without the capacity for mutual sympathy—or any other moral or affective capacities. The reader can relate to this figure only through his or her rational capacities, rather than through the nonrational and subjective sensibilities that stimulate sympathetic investment in other narrative forms and agents.

Just as Ricardo's disaggregation of the economic from the domains of the moral, political, and social depends on the abstraction of his representation, so the third important rhetorical feature of his economic discourse—its systematization—depends and builds upon the disaggregation and abstraction of his theory. S. G. Checkland writes, "the primary objective of Ricardo was to establish a universal theory, yielding absolute conclusions."[43] Such an absolutist, universal theory requires an extremely high degree of systematization involving careful definition and tight internal coordination. When the system is the product of a priori reasoning, most of the validity of the universal depends precisely on the rigors of its internal logic and the details of its systematization. Rather than being responsible for explaining any actual event, action, or incident, the system is responsible only for accounting for the logical arrangement of abstract, highly reductive representations of such events or behaviors. Thus, Ricardo responds to Malthus's declaration that "the science of political economy bears a nearer resemblance to the science of morals and politics than to that of mathematics" by shifting the terms of the debate slightly to argue, "If I am too theoretical, which I really believe is the case— you I think are too practical. There are so many combinations—so many operating causes in Political Economy, that there is a great danger in appealing to experience in favour of a particular doctrine, unless we are sure that all the causes of variation are seen and their effects duly estimated."[44] Of course, Ricardo believes that such estimation in relation to actual events is impossible. By criticizing the grounds of Malthus's empiricism, Ricardo is arguing for a different standard of evidence. That standard is derived from Euclidean geometry and other forms of a priori reasoning and amounts, in effect, to the internal coherence of the system. Such a systematization of economic theory, in turn, relies heavily on the processes of disaggregation and abstraction. It is these features that enable Ricardo to control the variables within the scenarios that constitute much of the "evidence" offered within his text. By tightly controlling what gets put into the system through these variables, Ricardo creates his absolute, "universal" theory; although this theory is, in effect, completely self-referential and self-enclosed, it gains from that containment precisely the rhetorical control needed to construct his compelling logic.[45]

The extent to which such control is rhetorical as well as theoretical becomes clear when one examines Ricardo's *Principles* at the basic linguistic levels of the phrase, the sentence, and the paragraph. The connection between Ricardo's writing style and his theoretical project is crucial because it demonstrates the necessity of the linguistic difficulty that both of his popularizers, McCulloch and Martineau, felt it necessary to justify, explain, and, ultimately, supplement with their own textual projects. At the same time, an examination of the rhetorical aspects of Ricardo's theoretical project also points to some of the unacknowledged slippages between his narrowly scientific aspirations and the broader ideological and imaginative appeals of his economic text.

Perhaps the most obvious and immediately "difficult" aspect of Ricardo's prose, as mentioned before, is the absence of illustrative anecdote. Like many eighteenth- and nineteenth-century writers, he begins most chapters with what looks like a summary of the main points to be made in those chapters. In this case, those "points" are the various economic principles that are to be elaborated in the paragraphs that follow. Here the similarity to the more standard expository prose of the period ends. The paragraphs that follow these opening headings develop the initial statements through a process of what might be called elaboration, as distinct from illustration. For example, in his opening chapter on value, Ricardo writes: "In the same country double the quantity of labour may be required to produce a given quantity of food and necessaries at one time than may be necessary at another and a distant time; yet the labourer's reward may possibly be very little diminished" (*PPE* 8). In this sentence, Ricardo invokes a place, two different times, and an actor—what would seem to be the very stuff of narrative. But in Ricardo's prose, all of these elements remain abstractions, never individualized or located in history—even a fictional history—by description. Instead, place and time are the nowhere and everywhere of scientific abstraction, and the actor—the laborer—remains a personification rather than becoming a person. This level of abstraction allows Ricardo to use the scenario to make predictions that escape the limitations of historical place and time. Only the abstraction of the scenario insulates it from those unaccounted-for "causes of variation" that Ricardo decries in Malthus's appeal to "experience."

Into this completely abstract scenario Ricardo goes on to insert a particular—"if the shoes and clothing of the labourer could, by improvements in machinery, be produced by one-fourth of the labour now necessary to their production. . . ." This highly specified alteration of the original scenario is followed by a prediction and an explanation of the mechanics that lead to the predicted result. The particulars complicate Ricardo's original scenario but do not render it more narrative. Rather, they are like the insertion of a variable into a highly simplified mathematical equation: the variable makes the equation more complex and allows the equation to account for another kind of experience, but it is not itself any closer to "experience" than the simple equation. The variable, despite its specificity, is itself an abstraction. Ricardo's paragraphs and chapters, like a mathematical equation or the diagram of an increasingly complex sentence, unfold *spatially* rather than *temporally.*

Much of the difficulty of Ricardo's prose stems from the fact it is so spatially complex at the level of the sentence. After Ricardo has articulated a few of the most basic principles of his political economy in his opening chapters, the remainder of his discussion is in large part the working out of these principles in terms of different sets of variables. Because he is trying to control so rigorously the equation into which the variable is being inserted and the definition of the variable itself, his direct assertions or statements are hedged in by layer upon layer of qualifying phrases and clauses. In his chapter distinguishing value from riches, for example, Ricardo begins with a fairly simple statement: "Value, then, differs essentially from riches, for value depends not on abundance, but on the difficulty or facility of production." To explain what this means for modern industrial capitalism, Ricardo continues:

> The labour of a million men in manufactures will always produce the same value, but will not always produce the same riches. *By the invention of machinery, by improvements in skill, by a better division of labour,* or *by the discovery of new markets, where more advantageous exchanges may be made,* a million of men may produce double or treble the amount of riches, of *"necessaries, conveniences, and amusements,"* in one state of society that [sic] *they could produce in another,* but they will not *on that account* add anything to value; *for everything rises or falls in value in proportion to the facility or difficulty of producing it,* or *in other words, in proportion to the quantity of labour employed in its production.* (emphasis mine, *PPE* 182)

There are two statements in the two sentences of this passage. In the case of the second statement, the direct assertion is embedded in qualifications that almost overwhelm it. One can extract the statement from the sentence, but not without losing all the careful definitions, qualifications, and explanations that ensure the statement's claims to absolute accuracy—to truth on the Cartesian a priori model.

Ricardo's prose becomes even more grammatically contorted when he tries to explain how such an increase in riches (as that described above) can actually result in a decrease in value:

> But the value of the general mass of commodities will nevertheless be diminished; for, although the value of the increased quantity produced in consequence of the improvement will be the same exactly as the value would have been in the less quantity that would have been produced, had no improvement taken place, an effect is also produced on the portion of goods still uncon-

sumed, which were manufactured previously to the improvement; the value of those goods will be reduced, inasmuch as they must fall to the level, quantity for quantity, of the goods produced under all the advantages of the improvement: and society will, the increased quantity of commodities, not withstanding its augmented riches, and notwithstanding its augmented means of enjoyment, have a less amount of value. (emphasis mine, *PPE* 182–83)

The rigorous specificity of this passage offers Ricardo's readers a firm grasp not only on the specific (but hypothetical) scenario described but also on the basic economic principles that come into play in the scenario and on the reasons that they come into play in this instance. To glean this economic wisdom, however, the reader must be able to follow the logic of subordination through which the scenario is hypothesized. Because the scenario is modeled on a mathematical equation in which everything must be accounted for and both sides of the equation must come out equal, the opacity of the passage is doubled. The reader is simultaneously forced to think spatially rather than sequentially—a kind of thinking largely alien to the "generality of readers" in the early nineteenth century—and in addition, the reader is denied even the most minimal narrative progression on which to anchor his or her reading as he or she attempts to follow the apparent detours of the sentence's mathematical logic. In other words, the "mathematical cast" of Ricardo's reasoning demands of the reader an ability to read what is virtually an entirely new referential system, without providing any familiar signposts or semantic bridges between the foreign mathematical logic and the much more familiar narrative conventions of expository prose.

In addition to making his *Principles* uncongenial to the majority of even his educated potential readers, Ricardo's refusal to narrativize his ideas also deprives them of the rhetorical effects of conventional narrative forms. This refusal has two linked effects, both of which were significant for the theoretical and ideological development of classical economic theory. The first and more obvious of these effects is the lack of any acknowledged moral content or framework in Ricardo's *Principles*. In his introduction to *Ethical Philosophy*, Ricardo's Scottish contemporary James Mackintosh wrote, "The purpose of the Moral Sciences is to answer the question *What ought to be?*"[46] In sharp contrast, the scientific paradigm of equation and prediction that organizes Ricardo's text asks and answers the questions "What *is?*" and "What *will* be?" In other words, Ricardo argues that the questions posed by and for political economy are positive rather than normative. These positivist questions exclude not only the individual moral question of whether one should prefer riches to indolence but also more community-oriented ethical questions of "ought" or "should" addressed by many of Ricardo's predecessors and contemporaries.

These exclusions, in turn, are part of a second and even larger exclusion: in writing outside traditional narrative conventions, Ricardo also disdains the semantic devices that facilitate imaginative identification. By using abstract personifications of "labor" and "capital," Ricardo refuses his reader the opportunity to project his or her mind into the affective situation of a laborer or capitalist. These personifications are, for Ricardo, positions rather than personages, and because they are granted no affective specificity through description or individuation, there is no basis for the reader's imaginative identification between the reader and the prose actor. Without imaginative identification, there is no basis for moral sentiment—just as there is no basis for suspense or other narrative affect.

The significance of this exclusion becomes most apparent when Ricardo discusses the dynamics of wage increase or decrease and the attendant condition of "the labourer." In this, as in other passages that assume the "progress of society," Ricardo does introduce at least a minimum of narrative temporality into his prose. This temporality, however, as well as the actors who move within it, remains extremely abstract. In his chapter "On Wages," Ricardo writes:

> Labour, like all other things which are purchased and sold, and which may be increased or diminished in quantity, has its natural and its market price. The natural price of labour is that price which is necessary to enable the labourers . . . to subsist and perpetuate their race, without either increase or diminution. . . .
>
> The market price of labour is the price which is really paid for it, from the natural operation of the proportion of the supply to the demand; labour is dear when it is scarce and cheap when it is plentiful. . . .
>
> It is when the market price of labour exceeds its natural price that the condition of the labourer is flourishing and happy, that he has it in his power to command a greater proportion of the necessaries and enjoyments of life, and therefore to rear a healthy and numerous family. When, however, by the encouragement which high wages gives to the increase of population, the number of labourers is increased, wages again fall to their natural price, and indeed from a reaction sometimes fall below it.
>
> When the market price of labour is below its natural price, the condition of the labourers is most wretched: then poverty deprives them of the comforts which custom renders absolute necessaries. It is only after their privations have reduced their number, or the demand for labour has increased, that the market price of labour will rise to its natural price, and that the labourer will have the moderate comforts which the natural rate of wages will afford. (*PPE* 52–53)

I quote this passage at length because it reveals the logical progression through which the distinction between a natural and market price of labor results at some times in a "flourishing and happy" and at other times in a "most wretched" condition for the laboring population. The logical progression reveals and constructs these outcomes as inevitable, and this inevitability places these conditions outside either the moral realm of "ought to be" or the affective realm in which the reader's sympathies are engaged in "the tragedy of the human condition" (or some such narrative rendering of common emotions or even a potentially shared condition).

When Ricardo does elaborate on the conditions produced by the divergence of natural from market price, it is to link those conditions to another set of predictions—another set of inevitabilities. The "flourishing and happy" condition of the laborer results in his rearing "a healthy and numerous family"—a result that is translated by Ricardo into an increase in the number of laborers and an attendant fall in wages. In contrast, the "most wretched" condition of the laborers results in a "reduc[tion of] their number" and the consequent restoration of a balance between the natural and market price of labor. The "condition of the labourers," then, is for Ricardo less a category of suffering or happiness important as such than a quantifiable factor in a distinctly mathematical equation. As such, the condition of "flourishing and happy" is essentially interchangeable with the condition of "most wretched." Affect—whether physical or emotional—is subsumed into a naturalized economic dynamic in which the laborer's condition, whatever its content, is seen as leading inevitably to its opposite.

Despite Ricardo's evacuation of moral and affective content from his account of the laboring class, his system does provide for the possibility of some narrative progress—some mechanism through which the overall condition of the laboring class might be slightly ameliorated, even if trapped within the dynamic described here. Given human nature, the progress of society, and economic law as constituted in Ricardo's model, the one variable that can disrupt this socioeconomic seesaw is the level of "food and necessaries" that "the habits and customs of the people" establish as a social and economic norm. Ricardo notes that "many of the conveniences now enjoyed in an English cottage would have been thought luxuries at an earlier period of our history" (*PPE* 55). It is this norm of customary food, necessaries, and conveniences, along with the cost of producing food, that establishes the "natural price" of labor for Ricardo. If these customary levels are high, then the laborer will, presumably, respond to fluctuations in the supply and demand of labor before his family's "most wretched" condition is that of starvation. He and they will still inevitably be "wretched" because deprived of the "comforts" to which they have become accustomed, but that wretchedness will not necessarily mean starvation and will have the beneficial effect of prompting him to refrain from producing still more laborers. Thus, Ricardo writes, "the friends of humanity cannot but wish that in all countries the labouring classes should have a taste for comforts and enjoyments, and that they should be stimulated by all legal means in their exertions to procure them. There cannot be a better security again a superabundant population" (*PPE* 57). Significantly, Ricardo does not elaborate upon what "legal means" might effect this stimulation. It is clear, however, that in Ricardo's system "superabundant population" is a threat not only to the condition of the laborer but also to the profits of the capitalist. By calling into cultivation inferior lands, such excess population increases rent and raises wages, which then cut into the capitalist's profit: the "friends of humanity" upon whom Ricardo calls have an economic, as well as "humanitarian" or civic, motivation for encouraging a high standard of living among the laboring population. Thus, even when Ricardo seems to begin to gesture toward a wider set of criteria for social well-being, these criteria can—and must—be logically subordinated to his narrower economic analysis. This economic analysis, in turn, consistently equates social "progress" with "healthy" profit margins.

Ricardo's dispassionate treatment of the condition of the laboring class points to some of the key differences between his economic vision and that of his predecessor, Adam Smith, and his contemporary, Thomas Malthus. For Smith, one of the explicit and most important goals of national economic development was the improvement of the material *and* moral welfare of "the great body of the people" (*WN* 302) Smith's greatest reservation about industrialism, with its attendant division of labor, was its effect on the intellectual and moral well-being of industrial laborers. In other words, it was not enough for Smith that the material well-being of the poorest members of society be improved; their moral and intellectual well-being must also be attended to. And while Smith saw material improvement as a natural and inevitable product of the market system, he argued that the government must directly and proactively address the other concerns—for example, through state-sponsored compulsory education for all members of the working class. Smith's larger-than-economic definition of the laborer and the laboring classes led him to qualify and supplement an otherwise largely optimistic account of the capitalist economic system.

In contrast to Smith, Malthus had a notoriously pessimistic vision of the future of the British working classes. At the same time, Malthus's economic doctrine, even in the gloomier version of the first edition of his *Essay on the Principle of Population*, was more fully informed by an encompassing and determinative providential framework than even Smith's *The Wealth of*

Nations. For Malthus, the physical sufferings of the poor under the inevitable hardships of the population principle were always contextualized within a religious vision that provided spiritual compensations. Furthermore, with his revised second edition of the *Essay*, Malthus provided the mechanism of moral restraint through which members of the working classes could simultaneously improve their moral *and* material condition. Thus, both Smith and Malthus, though in radically different ways, viewed workers and the poor as possessing moral as well as material elements of individual subjectivities and agencies. And for both, these extra-economic human components could not be totally subsumed within or subordinated to economic aspects. The dramatic distinction between Ricardo's discursive treatment of the laboring classes and that of Smith and Malthus provides some insight into the reason for the historical success of his economic vision. By defining a distinct domain of "the economic" and then considering human agents solely in terms of their relationship to that domain, Ricardo provided the ideological groundwork and justification for dismissing all other considerations as at best irrelevant and at worst dangerous to the economic well-being of the whole community. This basic capitalist ideology, however historically "necessary" for the untrammeled pursuit of individual and national wealth vis-à-vis the marketplace, was incompatible with much of the religious, moral, and political self-definition of the emergent British middle class (not to mention the working and landed classes). Thus, it was not only the unfamiliarity and difficulty of Ricardo's prose style that might have rendered his economic writings unappealing to the broader British public but also the theoretical reductionism that Ricardo effected through that prose.[47]

Many features of Ricardo's writings that were alien and uncongenial to his contemporaries have been identified by later economic theorists as the crux of his contribution to political economy. Ricardo's abstraction and disaggregation of an economic domain constitute much of his status as the founder of modern, classical economic theory: his reification of "the economic" provided later economists with a delimited object of analysis and with the methodological tools through which to conduct that analysis. These economists, in turn, could demonstrate to lay audiences the rationality and immutability of economic laws, thereby authorizing their own area of scientific expertise and reassuring the public of the stability and comprehensibility of this new economic universe. These later classical economists, however, were able to develop their economic theories within institutional domains that were already largely authorized as at once secular, scientific, and authoritative by the social, cultural, and political structures of nineteenth- and twentieth-century Britain and America. In contrast, when Ricardo was developing his economic ideas in post-Napoleonic England, the institutional context of academic economics was not yet in existence. Even in the 1820s and early 1830s, the newly established chairs of political economy at Oxford, Cambridge, King's College (London), and Trinity College (Dublin) were occupied by intellectual figures such as Richard Whately, George Pryme, William Whewell, and Richard Jones, who were committed to studying economic theory in the context of religious thought.[48]

Without a foothold in the universities, Ricardo's theories were forced to compete for the middle-class public's confidence with the Evangelical economic theory of Thomas Chalmers; with Jones's and Whewell's theistic, inductive economics; and with Tory paternalists, Romantic writers, benevolent liberals, and other prominent cultural, religious, and political groups hostile to any scientific study of "the economy" and to any influential social role for political economists. The economic historian S. G. Checkland argues that one stage of the "Ricardian victory" may have been won behind closed doors and away from the attention of the lay public by 1821.[49] However, for Ricardo's theories to survive outside the *Encyclopedia Britannica* and beyond the relatively small audience of McCulloch's "Ricardo Memorial Lectures," the vocal, informed, and engaged Victorian lay public had to be wooed and, to at least some extent, won by the language and logic of scientific economic theory. In short, Ricardo's loyal followers had to popularize as well as propagate his economic theories.[50]

Ironically, embedded within the alien and alienating texture of Ricardo's mathematical prose was a discursive structure that could facilitate this popularizing project. By abstracting and systematizing economic knowledge within a quasi-Euclidean model, Ricardo did disaggregate "economic" from other social, historical, and political (as well as traditionally moral) concerns, an effect that he largely reinforced through the rhetoric of his prose. The very deductive and law-bound form of his system, however, also mimicked the providential assumptions of eighteenth-century moral philosophies that his text self-consciously eschewed. For eighteenth-century moral philosophers and conjectural historians, divine providence both was reflected in the "natural laws" they discussed and helped to legitimate the knowledge they produced about those laws. Ricardo imported into his text a significant trace of providentialism in the form of an unexamined assumption of a fully coherent, consistent, and law-bound economic system. Stephen Gudeman, describing the cultural form of Ricardo's economic model, writes: "The derivational model implied that 'reality' contained an innermost part which if correctly specified would provide the core from which the remainder of the economy could be derived. But this coherence of the model was only a cultural way of formulating experience; nothing outside of his discursive model dictated that Ricardo should construct a 'consistent' model."[51] Gudeman's emphasis is on the way the derivational form of Euclidean geometry is itself a cultural form, one that lends authority to the knowledge claims created by that form. I would add that part of the cultural authority of this form stemmed from its importation of associations with the more explicit providential arguments of eighteenth-century philosophers and historians. Ricardo does, explicitly, leave "providence" entirely out of his economic model, but he also repeatedly invokes "the progress of society." While not divinely authorized within Ricardo's own text, such progress had been sanctioned and insured by Christian religious belief throughout the seventeenth and eighteenth centuries. Ironically, Ricardo's secularism does not challenge the divine foundation of these terms as do the skeptical writings of Hume and, to a lesser extent, Smith. Instead, he substitutes an unacknowledged faith that internal coherence and logical consistency are a sign of "objective" veracity.

As Gudeman notes, it is the quasi-geometrical form of Ricardo's economic model that makes it "familiar and acceptable" to contemporary economists and historians of economic thought. For Gudeman, then, it is not simply Ricardo's *method*, as Joseph Schumpeter and many others have argued, but also the cultural form of his *model* that acted as a foundation moment for the constitution of modern economic science. Instead of undermining Ricardo's scientific claims, the providential structure of his economic logic provided his audience and supporters with an extremely important bridge between Christian and secular social philosophy. Despite the profound and far-reaching differences between the two systems, there was also an important similarity: both systems created order and coherence. Furthermore, both systems imagined order and coherence in such a way that present circumstances and actions constituted a predictive basis for future events. This conjunction was significant because it laid the groundwork for the reimagination of economic law as moral injunction that became central to the projects of J. R. McCulloch and Harriet Martineau.

Ricardo himself self-consciously avoids this translation of economic back into moral terms, but his popularizers were able to use the totalized coherence of his economic model as the foundation for a secular moral order. Since present economic actions and decisions were seen to have a predictable and calculable effect on the future "progress of society," the economic laws that (apparently) legislated such effects could be reframed so that they had a *prescriptive*, as well as *predictive*, authority. In the case of such normative economic laws, the ultimate consequences of one's action was not divine pleasure or displeasure, grace or damnation, but rather the secular "happiness," "well-being," and vitality of one's society. For Ricardo's popularizers, an individual's economic decision or action also had a more immediate and subjective effect: that of manifesting or reflecting upon his or her own moral character, or "virtue." In other words, one's ability to apprehend and willingness to submit oneself to *economic* law were seen as having immediate and subjective *moral* consequences (as well as more distant, "objective," and inevitable socioeconomic effects). Thus, in the writings of Ricardo's popularizers, morality is retained in the form of a kind of bourgeois virtue but is shifted from its foundational position within Christian and classical humanist discourses to a position that is derived from the self-consciously secular and amoral discourse of classical political economy.[52]

Such a shift has radical consequences for the development of both economic and moral discourse in the nineteenth and twentieth centuries. For the most part, "scientific" economic theory has followed Ricardo in eschewing morality as altogether outside its domain.[53] At the same time, such scientific theoretical narratives have continually been appropriated by other discourses and adapted into a series of moralized social narratives that celebrate a narrow, individualistic model of bourgeois virtue. This narrow model displaces Smith's justice-centered account of civic virtue in commercial society with one that privileges individual prudence above all else. Likewise, reason, self-interest, and the autonomous individual agent become the basic psychological and social structures of the moral "sentiment" derived from nineteenth- and twentieth-century economic theory, displacing the Smithian model constructed around the passions, sympathy, and the individual as a fundamentally social creature. Ricardo's popularizers do construct a "moral vision" of commercial society based on Ricardo's economic theory, but this vision is no longer one that can imagine morality as a concern not reducible or amenable to rational economic calculation. Thus, in promulgating classical economic theory, writers such as McCulloch and Martineau also popularized a new morality that was coterminous with capitalist ideology rather than in any way contesting it.

chapter two

Providential Economics: J. R. McCulloch's Nationalist Narratives

In recent years, scholars from a wide disciplinary range have explored the process through which expert scientific knowledge is disseminated to lay publics.[1] These scholars are interested not simply in the infusion of scientific terminology and imagery into the public discursive domain but also in the diffusion of scientific ideas to a range of nonspecialist publics. One of the best general studies is Richard Whitley's essay "Knowledge Producers and Knowledge Acquirers: Popularisation as a Relation Between Scientific Fields and Their Publics."[2] Whitley does not explicitly refer to Foucault's work in his essay, but his argument, like Foucault's archaeologies and genealogies, presents "meaning" as constructed by and inextricable from its discursive and institutional contexts. As the title suggests, Whitley is specifically interested in the discursive mechanisms that enable knowledge to be comprehensibly and persuasively transmitted from expert producers to lay publics. Whitley's argument is developed around two basic assertions that are crucial to understanding the development of economic theory in nineteenth-century England. First, he writes: "If, in fact, [scientific] knowledge was produced by cohesive, autonomous communities governed by their own paradigms then it is difficult to see how its communication to other audiences could fail to alter its nature since the meaning of research results would be determined by the paradigm that generated them." Whitley follows this statement with the logical conclusion that "popularization" involves much more than a simple linguistic translation of knowledge from one set of terms into another: "Any communication of knowledge claims involves some redescription which subtly alters them so that the popularisation of true knowledge to a wide audience always results in alterations to it. This is not simply a matter of 'distortion' of the true message, but is rather an inevitable concomitant of translation from *one system of discourse to another*" (emphasis mine).[3] Whitley argues that one of the major variables in determining the amount of inevitable "distortion" caused by popularization is the degree of cultural separation, real and perceived, between the producers of scientific knowledge and the "consumers" of that knowledge. For the social sciences, this distance is usually less than for the "hard" sciences such as biology, chemistry, and physics. For historical communities in which the distinction between producers and acquirers of knowledge had not yet been fully institutionalized, as in early Victorian England, this cultural distance is less than for academic sciences and popular audiences in the late twentieth century.[4]

In fact, the nineteenth century as a whole constitutes a particularly significant and complex site for issues surrounding the popularization, propagation, or diffusion of scientific knowledges. As Richard Altick and, more recently, Alan Rauch have shown, there was a virtual explosion of popularizing projects in the first half of the nineteenth century, along with a dramatic increase in the book- and periodical-reading—and -buying—public.[5] The popular economic writings of J. R. McCulloch and Harriet Martineau must be seen as part of this larger phenomenon, which included an extremely diverse range of publications. In the 1810s and 1820s, before the introduction of the affordable book trade by the Society for the Diffusion of Useful Knowledge (SDUK), the *Edinburgh Review* and *Quarterly Review* provided a format for the dissemination of emergent scientific and social scientific knowledges beyond the extremely limited printings of the books they reviewed. For example, the first edition of McCulloch's *Principles of Political Economy,* published in 1825, ran to only 1,400 copies (200 of which still remained in the publishers hands in 1829), but his *Edinburgh Review* articles during the same period averaged a circulation of 11,000 and reached an even greater audience via libraries and reading rooms. Thus, the reviews, though appealing primarily to the political and educated elite, played a crucial role in the dissemination of new knowledges. Much more self-consciously popular and popularizing than the quarterly reviews were a number of other new publishing phenomena, including the rapid growth of the encyclopedia market; the serial publications of the SDUK; the rapid emergence and proliferation of other cheap series, including reprint series such as those of the Chambers brothers and Charles Knight (after the disbanding of the SDUK); and the burgeoning market for educational texts aimed at children and adolescents.

The massiveness of this publishing boom was matched by its complexity—a complexity in the motives and means of publishers, editors, authors, and readers alike. Publishers, editors, and authors were motivated, of course, by financial considerations. At the same time, these individuals were often also driven by a sense of moral and civic mission aimed at the working and lower-middle classes. Charles Knight, for example, throughout his editorial and publishing career, intended his "cheap" publications as a positive alternative to the sensational and radical offerings that dominated the cheap press.[6]

Harriet Martineau, in addition to establishing herself as an author and contributing to her family's income, saw her *Illustrations of Political Economy* as an opportunity to instruct "the people" in the economic principles that would contribute to both the moral and the financial well-being of the British nation. McCulloch, in contrast to Knight and Martineau, seems to have been propelled by scientific and professional aspirations rather than a sense of moral or civic mission. He sought to shape public policy on the governmental and institutional, rather than individual and moral, levels, and he did so in a way that would simultaneously establish his own reputation and that of the "science" of political economy. McCulloch then used his and the science's reputation as a way to earn money. Not until 1838 was McCulloch granted a public office; before this time, his writings on and teaching of political economy were his sole sources of income. Thus, McCulloch's ability to make Ricardian principles accessible to the broader public was doubly important for his professional career: that ability helped the discourse of scientific political economy to gain a broader cultural authority at the same time that it provided the means by which he could trade on such authority.

The motives of the readers whose appetites fueled the publishing boom in the early nineteenth century were just as complex as those of the publishers, editors, and authors who fed it. Alan Rauch has shown how such readers' desire for self-education and improvement was linked to a demand for entertainment. Encyclopedias and penny magazines could meet these often contradictory desires by presenting "useful knowledge" in potpourri format with abbreviated entries that created playful juxtapositions while limiting the demand on a reader's attention span.[7] At the same time, the knowledges acquired through such reading might be valued as much for their ability to increase the reader's social status as to further his or her moral or intellectual development.[8] For many early-nineteenth-century readers, the most important factor in their literacy practices was the availability and affordability of their reading materials. Altick argues that this period introduced an entirely new class of readers who could afford some (albeit limited) financial outlay on the purchase of books and magazines.[9] The publications of the SDUK first made this market and readership visible, but other publishers soon joined the project of the society and later followed in its wake, publishing series of original texts and reprints of both nonfiction and fiction. By 1831, Altick argues, "it was not unusual to find that over half the titles issued in a given week, whether reprints or originals, belonged to one cheap series or another."[10] Many of these series, including those of the SDUK and Martineau's *Illustrations of Political Economy,* were aimed at least in part at working-class readers, but in general, this aspect was a failure because the new readership was predominantly middle class. Even at this level, Altick notes, the potential readership of books published in the SDUK's series the Library of Useful Knowledge was limited not only by financial constraints but also by level of education. Most of the texts in this series, he argues, were designed as a home university course, accessible only to the most "ambitious or brilliant students," rather than for the general middle-class reader.[11]

This question of the educational as well as financial accessibility of nineteenth-century "useful knowledge" texts points back to the issues of discursive form discussed in relation to Ricardo's writings. It also points back to problems of distortion and distance that Whitley cites in his analysis of scientific popularizations. "Scientific" knowledge about the economy in the early nineteenth century was by no means the product of a "cohesive, autonomous" community, but it did depend upon certain discursive forms and conventions that effectively functioned to *create* a certain distance between knowledge producer and consumer. McCulloch at once exploited and sought to bridge this distance through his writings and lectures. Martineau acknowledged that such a distance was inevitable in the early stages of any science but saw her own work as moving the science of political economy into a more mature stage at which such a distance was no longer inevitable, necessary, or desirable. Ironically, Whitley's discussion of the various factors that diminish the amount of distortion in the popularization of a given scientific discourse leads him to identify the development of economic thought as an example of the effects of the cultural proximity, rather than distance, between the producers and consumers of knowledge.[12] Whitley's emphasis on the proximity between aspects of Victorian culture and early economic theory is useful as a point of contrast to the popularization of other scientific theories at other historical moments. However, Whitley tends to overemphasize that closeness by contrasting it with the more dramatic two-cultures division that emerged out of such conjunctions later in the century. In so doing, he misses the opportunity to productively apply the insights of his own theory of popularization to the development of economic thought. For example, Whitley argues that popularization tends "to present current, changeable conclusions as universal, stable, and incontrovertible truths . . . owing to simplification, vividness, and absolute certainty."[13] This feature of the early popularization of economic theory is noted by both S. G. Checkland and Marc Blaug as a crucial complicating factor in McCulloch's (and for Blaug, Martineau's as well) popularizations of Ricardian economic theory.[14] By taking Ricardo's theories out of the carefully qualified scientific framework through which Ricardo constructed them, McCulloch and Martineau performed a double act of simplification. First, many of Ricardo's qualifications and specifications of his own general economic theory were lost, so that his statements and predictions were rendered more sweeping than would originally have been possible. Second, by removing Ricardo's claims from the scientific paradigm, McCulloch and Martineau removed them from the developmental narrative in which Ricardo's "truths" would fall before later research and theory, just as Smith's political economy gave way to Ricardo's. Rather, while both Martineau and McCulloch saw that the "science" of political economy had developed, they constructed that development as teleologically pointing toward and ending with a certain definitive set of economic truths.

The tendency for popular versions of scientific ideas to appear more absolute than the more esoteric theoretical formulations of scientific experts is one effect of what Whitley calls "a translation from one system [or paradigm] of discourse to another." A more specific and, for the purposes of my analysis, more significant aspect of popular translations of economic thought in the early nineteenth century involves the historically specific nature of Victorian popular discourse and the distance between the conventions of such popular discourse and those of Ricardo's self-consciously scientific discourse. I have already suggested some features of popular nineteenth-century discourse to provide points of contrast with Ricardo's prose. In particular, various aspects of narrative form seem important to the structure and accessibility of prose written for "the generality of readers," and the narrativization of political economy seems to go hand in hand with its moralization. When J. R. McCulloch and Harriet Martineau embody economic theory in narrative forms, they almost of necessity undo the separation of economic from moral concerns that was in large part effected through Ricardo's deliberately abstract articulation of his economic theories.

My support for this reading of Ricardo's popularizers lies as much with my analysis of their literary projects as with my analysis of Ricardo's mathematical and amoral prose. In this chapter and the next, I want to turn more directly to their economic writings in order to explore the ways in which Ricardo's theories are complicated and even controverted by the narrative conventions of his most loyal followers. I need to emphasize that I am using the term "narrative conventions" in a very broad sense. Whereas Harriet Martineau adopts the traditional and easily recognizable conventions of popular narrative fiction, McCulloch's writings are never explicitly framed as narrative. On the contrary, his economic writings are much more likely to be seen as expository *in opposition to* narrative. While for most purposes this designation would be accurate, I want to emphasize the narrative aspects of McCulloch's writings in order to illustrate the extent and significance of the difference between his prose and that of his "master," Ricardo.

It may seem counterintuitive to position McCulloch as a "popularizer" of scientific economic theory. Certainly, his role in this regard is complex and contradictory, since he is widely identified as the first "professional" economist. He was the first political economist to support himself primarily through his teaching of and writings on political economy. He was one of the first and most active members of the Political Economy Club. In the club, through private correspondence, at dinner parties, and in the press he entered into alliances and debates with every other major economic thinker of the early and mid-nineteenth century, including Thomas Malthus, James Mill, Nassau Senior, Robert Torrens, and Lord Overstone. Finally, McCulloch is identified by historians of economic thought as being almost single-handedly responsible for the dominance of Ricardian economic theory in Britain in the 1820s and 1830s. In fact, it is McCulloch's historic role as the dominant spokesman for Ricardian economic theory that positions him as "popularizer" as well as "professional."

Indeed, McCulloch's career and reputation demonstrate the extent to which the role of "professional political economist" depended, in the early nineteenth century, on the economist's popularity—his public voice and visibility—as well as on the skills, demeanor, and associations that we now associate with professionalism. McCulloch's public authority regarding economic issues came not from his post as professor of political economy at the London University. Rather, he earned his post largely through his public role and influence. Similarly, McCulloch constructed much of his public authority not through the more theoretical writing of his *Principles of Political Economy* but rather through his more popular periodical and encyclopedia articles, which applied economic principles to matters of practical and public policy concern. As a self-minted member of the emergent profession of political economy, McCulloch was able to command more authority and respect for his economic writings than were his female, "amateur" contemporaries, Jane Marcet and Harriet Martineau. But his public role also singled him out as the appropriate figure for satiric critique in such popular attacks on political economy as Thomas Love Peacock's *Crotchet Castle* and Thomas Carlyle's *Chartism*. Nor was it only McCulloch's contemporaries who treated him as a popular figure as well as a professional. Twentieth-century historians of economic thought, almost without exception, have treated McCulloch as a "follower," "promulgator," or "popularizer" of Ricardian economic thought rather than as an economic theorist making contributions in his own right. Hence, more than any other of the professional economists who emerged alongside McCulloch, his historical role in relation to economic discourse has been read almost exclusively as that of a popularizer of another's theories and ideas.

As the primary popularizer of Ricardian economic theory, McCulloch was most closely allied with James Mill, who was also a devoted adherent to Ricardian economics. There were, however, important differences between the two. Mill, unlike McCulloch, saw Ricardian economics as one plank of a larger utilitarian project to overhaul British society, politics, and economics along Benthamite lines. As part of this project, Mill was committed to a radical political program that was anathema to McCulloch, for although McCulloch's economic theories were radical, his politics were solidly Whig, and even at times conservative Whig. These political differences were exacerbated by the administrative and financial conflicts that emerged around McCulloch's appointment to the chair of political economy at London University in the late 1820s.

Politically, McCulloch was closer to Nassau Senior than to James Mill (and, later, John Stuart Mill). Senior shared McCulloch's general commitment to a Ricardian economic program, but Senior took a more moderate and on some points even critical approach to that program than McCulloch. His two most important critiques of the position advocated by McCulloch and James Mill centered on the Malthusian population principle and the definition of political economy as a science. The latter critique was particularly telling: Senior argued that for political economy to be a "science," its theoretical elaboration needed to be distinct from practice and policy. He echoed John Stuart Mill's distinction, in "On the Definition of Political Economy," between the "art" and the "science" of political economy. Senior's emphasis on this analytical distinction points to a different model of the professional political economist than that embodied by McCulloch. McCulloch, as we have seen, created a professional identity in which economic knowledge was frequently articulated, elaborated, and promulgated through discussions of current economic problems, policy, and practice. Senior's insistence that theory and practice be distinguished anticipates W. Stanley Jevons's later revisions of the science and suggests a model of the "professional" primarily as researcher and scientist—a producer of knowledge *apart* from the public rather than an interpretive mediator between abstract theory and public concerns.

While there were important differences between McCulloch and his allies James Mill and Nassau Senior, his most famous and significant economic antagonist was Thomas Malthus. Most of McCulloch's debates with Malthus were inherited from David Ricardo; the most famous of these debates involved Malthus's perceived "physiocracy," that is, his privileging of agriculture within the economic domain, his prolandlord position, and his consequent rejection of free trade. Malthus also, as we have seen, rejected Ricardo's abstract method. Even though McCulloch himself did not retain the rigor of Ricardo's abstraction, he *did* retain the economic principles derived from that abstraction and the analytical privileging of abstractly stated "economic laws" over "concrete facts" in the theorization of the economic system. The more important difference between Ricardo/McCulloch and Malthus for the discourse of "scientific economics," however, was the issue of the relationship between economic law and divine law. For Malthus, economic laws were part of a larger scheme of divine providence; for Ricardo and McCulloch, such laws were naturally occurring and amoral phenomena that existed independently of any religious or moral framework. McCulloch tended more than Ricardo to remoralize the functioning and the stakes of the economic system, but he did not, like Malthus, subordinate that system as a whole to religious schema.

When McCulloch does appeal to moral issues in his economic writings, it is usually through his deployment of national and cultural narratives, which retain the moral codings that Ricardo sought to elide within his own economic text. Unlike Martineau, rather than constructing original narratives in order to illustrate the workings and stakes of various principles of political economy, McCulloch tends to rely on preexisting cultural narratives, which he explains, supplements, or revises in order to reveal the logic of political economy. One of the generic narrative forms to which McCulloch returns repeatedly in his writings is the narrative of scientific development I mentioned before. McCulloch takes as his model of this genre such studies as Smith's "History of Astronomy." In Smith's story of the development of astronomy, the history of scientific thought is seen as unfolding according to its own internal logic. Although this internal logic is shown to be informed by the conjunction of a predefined human nature with various historical contingencies, in the end the plot of Smith's story seems to be primarily determined by what he calls "the real chains which Nature makes use of to bind together her several operations."[15] In this Smithian narrative, then, both the inevitabilities of divine providence, on the one hand, and the contingencies of unintended consequence, on the other, give way to the inevitabilities of physical nature.

The significance of Smith's plot structure in this narrative lies in the slippage through which his philosophical skepticism gives way to the promise of order and certainty hidden within "the reality of which we have daily experience." Whereas Smith's narrative retains elements of the tension between these two interpretations of history through its conclusion, later writers such as McCulloch focused solely on the satisfying convergence of scientific speculation upon the law-bound inevitabilities of the natural and human worlds. Through the perception of such convergences, scientific speculation was imbued with the standards of natural fact as the supreme scientific value.[16] This value often acquired the moral overtones of absolute truth even in the realm of the physical sciences, while in the realm of the human sciences, "natural truths" were often equated with providential law and translated wholesale into moral injunctions. In McCulloch's writing, the natural truths discovered by the science of political economy have both kinds of value—the metaphysical value of being "Truth" (with a capital T) as opposed to error and the moral value of being truths that constitute standards of human behavior. When McCulloch narrates the historical development of the economic science, his emphasis is on the metaphysical value of truth as an absolute.

In his *Encyclopedia Britannica* article on political economy, reprinted separately as *Outlines of Political Economy;* in his *Discourse on the Rise, Progress, Peculiar Objects, and Importance of Political Economy;* and in his "Introductory Discourse" to his edition of *The Wealth of Nations,* McCulloch begins his narrative of scientific development with an account of how the mistaken moral values of the ancient and middle ages led to "neglect of the science." This section is followed by an explanation of how mercantilism arose as an erroneous version of the science. The French physiocrats, discussed next, are accorded a bit more truth value and scientific authority than the mercantilists, with François Quesnay even given the status of first "rais[ing] it [political economy] to the rank of a science" (*Discourse* 42). McCulloch ends his discussion of mercantilist and French economical theories with the summary pronouncement that "to establish the science of Political Economy on a firm foundation, it was necessary to take a much more extensive survey, and to seek for its principles, not in a few partial and distorted facts, or in metaphysical abstractions, but in the connection and relation subsisting among the various phenomena manifested in the progress of civilization" (*Discourse* 54). Here Smith's "real chains of nature" are replaced by the law-bound progress of civilization, ironically conferring upon civilization the value of nature, and further conferring on both the value of absolute truth. This formulation sets the dramatic stage for McCulloch's introduction of Smith as the Newton of political economy. McCulloch even uses the temporizing transitional phrase "at length" to characterize the relief of scientific suspense wrought by Smith's transformative work, *The Wealth of Nations.* Through Smith's work, "the science was, for the first time, treated in its fullest extent" (*Discourse* 57). Despite the Smithian errors and inaccuracies that necessitated the further developments of Ricardo, McCulloch celebrates *The Wealth of Nations* for its accomplishment in reducing the principles of political economy "into a consistent, harmonious, and beautiful system" (*Discourse* 57). In other words, even if Smith did not succeed in grasping accurately every aspect of the science's natural truth, he did accomplish much in the way of finding the natural order into which such truths would fall.

This accomplishment accords Smith a heroic status in the developmental narrative of political economy and prepares the way for the science's other hero, David Ricardo. Where Smith succeeded in reducing the science of political economy to a "beautiful system," Ricardo's analytic powers enabled him to simplify that system even further. Thus, for example, while Smith allowed the possibility of a complicating divergence between individual and public interest, Ricardo (and, with him, McCulloch) argued that they are identical, and that the latter is only and inevitably arrived at through the former. McCulloch's introduction of Ricardo into his story of scientific development is openly celebratory. He writes: "The powers of mind displayed in [his] investigations,—the dexterity with which the most abstruse and difficult questions are unravelled,—the unerring sagacity with which the operation of general and fixed principles is investigated,—the skill with which they are separated and disentangled from such as are of a secondary and accidental nature,—and the penetration with which their remotest consequences are perceived and estimated, have never been surpassed" (*Discourse* 69). Ricardo's heroic accomplishments in the science of political economy will, according to McCulloch, "for ever secure [his] name . . . a high and conspicuous place in the list of those who have done most to unfold the complex mechanism of society, and carry this science to perfection" (*Discourse* 69). The perfection to which McCulloch refers is a perfection both of methodological form and of theoretical content. In terms of content, this perfection carries a strong connotation of absolute truth; in terms of form, the perfection is one of extreme logical rigor and abstraction (as opposed to the more digressionary form of Smith). It is clear, however, that for McCulloch these two forms of perfection are deeply involved with one another. Together they constitute the dramatic climax of McCulloch's history. This climax is followed immediately by a brief denouement admitting the virtual unreadability of Ricardo's scientifically perfect prose and pointing to the popularizers who, in the words of Harriet Martineau some years later, can "display" these truths once they have been discovered. But the Ricardian climax itself is represented as the true end point and conclusion of McCulloch's developmental narrative. There is no sense of a larger developmental scheme in which the Ricardian paradigm would eventually give way to another paradigm, just as the Ptolemaic universe gave way to the Copernican universe in astronomy. Rather, the emplottedness of economic truth leads by stages to the Ricardian "era" with its metaphysical overtones of final truth and absolute perfection; the quest for economic knowledge has been heroically completed, and there is nothing left for the storyteller but to become "displayer" or expositor of that final truth.

In addition to constructing a hierarchy of scientific discoveries leading to "Truth," McCulloch's *Discourse* also frames his explanation of economic theory with the much more explicit moral weightiness of a lengthy injunction about the duty of learning the science's true principles. McCulloch declares that "it is the duty of all who do not voluntarily choose to relinquish the noblest and most valuable privilege enjoyed by the citizens of a free state—that of expressing their opinion on the conduct of public affairs—to qualify themselves for its proper exercise" (*Discourse* 80). In this passage, McCulloch implies a link between the moral duties of citizenship, the expression of public opinion, and certain qualifications requisite for the correct or socially beneficial fulfillment of one's duty.[17] Later, McCulloch adds that the qualifications for good citizenship can by no means be satisfied by good intentions alone. In speaking of the necessity for legislators to "be well instructed in this science," McCulloch declares: "In financial and commercial legislation, it is impossible to make a single false step,—to impose a single injudicious tax or restriction,—without materially affecting the interests of every individual, and actually endangering the subsistence of many families. *Rectitude of purpose affords no security against error.* The want of acquaintance with *sound scientific principles,* has often frustrated *the best intentions;* and has rendered measures intended to hasten the progress of improvement productive only of disaster and disgrace" (emphasis mine, *Discourse* 81). Through this passage, McCulloch in effect argues for a new form of civic virtue. "Good intentions"—whatever one's religious or political framework—are at best impotent and at worst harmful if they are not informed by and wedded to "the general and fundamental principles" (as opposed to a few scattered notions) of the science of political economy. Furthermore, with his language of "progress" and "improvement" versus "disaster and disgrace," McCulloch begins to gesture toward the larger significance of this new moral injunction to scientific knowledge, for the language of progress, improvement, and their opposites suggests not simply an opposition between material well-being or hardship but also the more intangible social and moral effects of government legislation.

McCulloch's critique of good intentions is addressed specifically to the nation's legislators, but he is even more concerned with the education of the general public. In fact, he explicitly states that the public should not hide behind its legislative representatives in order to protect itself from the moral claims of the new science. McCulloch calls such logic a "poor apology for ignorance" and proclaims that "the great and increasing influence of public opinion ... renders it of the utmost importance that the public should be well informed on all the matters affecting the best interests of the state" (*Discourse* 84). This result is possible, McCulloch insists, only if "the people" know "the principal causes of national wealth and national poverty, and, ... of the circumstances which really determine their condition in life" (*Discourse* 84). After having captured his reader in this rhetorical net, McCulloch then goes on to clarify the stakes of knowledge and ignorance. On the side of ignorance are a series of fruitless wars "waged for the purpose of preserving or acquiring some exclusive commercial advantage" (*Discourse* 89). In contrast, on the side of knowledge, McCulloch beckons the reader with the following promise: "The truths [of political economy] are destined to exercise the most salutary influence on humanity—to convince mankind that it is for their interest to live in peace, to deal with each other on fair and liberal principles, and not to become the dupes of their own short-sighted avarice, or the willing instruments of the blind ambition, or petty animosities, of their rulers" (*Discourse* 89–90). According to McCulloch then, the principles of political economy are the true teachers of moral lessons. Those moral lessons constitute the "salutary influence" that will lead humanity toward peace, fairness, liberality, and other vaguely defined social virtues.

The salutary influence toward which McCulloch gestures in this and other passages enjoining economic self-education includes, of course, improvements in material as well as moral well-being. Not surprisingly, the moral aspects are usually secondary to the material aspects of human improvement, but the moral benefits of economically rational behavior are not, for McCulloch at least, incidental. Rather, they are a crucial element of the larger process that Smith, Adam Ferguson, and other eighteen-century philosophers linked to the long-term course of economic development—civilization. The process through which humankind moved from "barbarian" or "savage" states to those of higher civilization was a major preoccupation for the Scottish enlightenment philosophers.[18] In addition to the more familiar genre of "narrative, document-based history," these philosophers developed a second genre of history to which Dugald Stewart gave the name "conjectural history." Stewart identified a number of features that characterized this new form of history. First, conjectural history arose not from the study of any specific historical period but from comparisons between "our intellectual acquirements, our opinions, manners and institutions, [and] those which prevail among rude tribes."[19] These comparisons, according to Stewart, provoked the question of "by what gradual steps the transition has been made from the first simple efforts of uncultivated nature, to a state of things so wonderfully artificial and complicated."[20] Because there is no documentation about many of these steps—especially the important earlier ones—the place of historically documented "fact" is instead supplied by philosophical and historical "conjecture." In the resulting philosophical narratives, actual historical developments are subordinated to "natural" progress, and unique and particular sequences give way before the typical.[21]

McCulloch never takes upon himself the writing of a systematic conjectural history of economics and civil society, but he does incorporate many aspects of the genre into his major economic writings, such as his *Principles of Political Economy, Outlines of Political Economy,* and *Discourse on Political*

Economy. For my purposes, the significance of McCulloch's use of this genre is its interest in the causes and processes of civilization. For the eighteenth-century philosophers who developed the notion of conjectural history, the process of civilization was by no means celebrated as an unequivocal "good." Along with the development of civilization might come the decline of the martial spirit, for example, or civilization might develop through cycles of growth and degeneration. For some eighteenth-century conjectural historians, the development of civil society was ideally treated as philosophically and scientifically value-neutral. For the majority of the Scottish philosophers who developed the genre, however, civilization was more or less explicitly contrasted with savagery or barbarism as a positive outcome of society's developmental process.[22] This contrast was unproblematically adopted by less skeptical or philosophical thinkers such as J. R. McCulloch to illustrate the social and moral stakes of economic development. The reason all people have a duty to learn the true principles of political economy, according to McCulloch, is that they can then use their influential public opinion to support government policies and legislation that will facilitate, rather than retard, the civilizing economic processes of laissez-faire capitalism.[23]

McCulloch is explicit about the connection between the development of capitalism and civilization, including the latter's positive moral valence. In the opening pages of his *Discourse,* he writes:

> Neither is the acquisition of wealth necessary only because it affords the means of subsistence: without it we should never be able to cultivate and improve our *higher and nobler faculties.* Where wealth has not been amassed, the mind being constantly occupied in providing for the immediate wants of the body, no time is left for its culture; and the view, sentiments, and feelings of the people, become alike *contracted, selfish, and illiberal.* The possession of a decent competence . . . is necessary . . . to *improve the moral and intellectual character,* and to ensure any considerable proficiency in liberal studies and pursuits. And hence the acquisition of wealth is . . . indispensably necessary to the advancement of society in civilization and refinement. (emphasis mine, *Discourse* 3)

For McCulloch, civilization, moral improvement, generosity, and intellectual development are all the effects of the acquisition of wealth, and since capitalist economics as formulated by political economy was supposed to be the fastest and most effective way to amass wealth, both capitalist development and the knowledge of political economy took on an explicitly positive moral status. The narrative of the growth of capital via conjectural history thus becomes for McCulloch a narrative of civil and moral improvement.

McCulloch takes his moral claims for capitalism even further and asserts that capitalism's moral benefits are not just the unintentional result or side effect of economic change but are actually part of a providential design. At two different points in his *Discourse,* McCulloch claims that natural economic law is part of a providential design for human improvement. The first such claim occurs at the beginning of his essay and concerns the morality of individuals. McCulloch writes: "The consumption of wealth is indispensable to existence; but the eternal law of Providence has decreed, that wealth can only be procured by industry. . . . This twofold necessity renders the production of wealth a constant and principal object of the exertions of the vast majority of the human race; has subdued the natural aversion of man from labour; given activity to indolence; and armed the patient hand of industry with zeal to undertake, and patience to overcome, the most irksome and disagreeable tasks" (*Discourse* 2). While in another context it is conceivable that McCulloch intended the terms "industry," "patience," "zeal," and "indolence" to be morally neutral economic terms, his simultaneous invocation of "Providence" (with a capital P) inevitably imbues such language with moral valuation. Thanks to providence, McCulloch implies, humankind is able to overcome its natural fallen state of indolence and raise itself upon the moral pedestals of industry and patience.

McCulloch's second reference to providence in the *Discourse* refers to the morality of nations rather than individuals. In writing about free trade and what he calls the territorial division of labor, McCulloch claims that "Providence, by giving different soils, climates, and natural productions, to different countries, has evidently provided for their mutual intercourse and civilization" (*Discourse* 104). One paragraph later, McCulloch develops this providential vision of free, international commerce with the celebratory declaration that commerce is "the grand engine by which the blessings of civilization are diffused. . . . Its humanizing influence is in this respect most important. . . . By making particular people depend for the means of supplying a considerable portion of their wants on the assistance of others, it has gone far to remove a host of the most destructive prejudices, and forms a powerful principle of harmony, of union, and of concord" (*Discourse* 106). Capitalism, via commerce, is thus responsible not only for the moral salvation of individual souls through industry but also for the moral salvation of whole nations on which it providentially enforces commercial interdependence, and thus also, McCulloch hopefully proclaims, harmony, union, and concord. Likewise, the conjectural historical narrative of capitalism and commerce, when told by McCulloch, becomes deeply infused with moral values and injunctions that render it anything but scientifically neutral. By linking his explanation of political economy to a providential narrative of civilization, McCulloch succeeds in adding moral urgency to his message but undermines the universalizing authority that Ricardo had attempted to establish through the logical rigor and mathematical abstraction of his prose. Although "providence" was a highly recognized authority among many of McCulloch's readers, it was much more open to competing interpretive claims—especially religious claims—than were the apparently neutral, given, and universal "facts" of natural economic law.

While McCulloch's moralization of commercial and civil development plays a fairly minor role in his disquisitions on the science of political economy, when he turns his attention to the pressing political and economic problems of his day, this implicit narrative of moral development takes on a much more important theoretical and rhetorical role. In these discussions, McCulloch often constructs a dramatic opposition between England's past narrative of material progress and civil development and those aspects of Britain's current economic and political situation that threaten to reverse this positive process and turn Britain's national story into one of decline. Through these narratives McCulloch does not, like Harriet Martineau, construct working-class characters with whom the reader can identify sympathetically. Instead, he creates a story in which his middle-class reader is directly involved and through which that reader is personally threatened. McCulloch's conjectural historical narrative enables him to connect his middle- and upper-class audience to the working-class and poor objects of concern through a national narrative of progress or decline in which all classes must rise or fall together. In short, he constructs and builds his narratives around a complex collective human agency called "the nation" or "Britain," rather than the more personal human agency of individualized class representatives.

This narrative appeal is particularly important and powerful in McCulloch's *Edinburgh Review* articles on the Corn Laws and Poor Laws. In both cases, McCulloch's arguments against these laws tend to be constructed around narratives of economic decline, moral degeneration, and national upheavals. In opposition to these narratives, McCulloch invokes promising images of the material and cultural progress, national security, and moral strength that can be achieved only through a return to the natural economic order of laissez-faire capitalism. The implicit alignment of the opposition of civilized versus uncivilized with that of moral versus immoral, and with that of natural versus unnatural, is particularly strong in the rhetoric of these articles. In his historical narratives of economic and social development, McCulloch's economic beliefs enable him to assume the ultimate ascendancy of a positive, natural development leading up to the best aspects of contemporary British culture, but in his narratives of the future, McCulloch seems deeply fearful that such natural improvement will not be allowed to continue. Rather, because of the operations of the Corn Laws and Poor Laws, McCulloch fears that the natural processes of economic, social, and moral development will be reversed, and thus that these unnatural *economic* provisions will lead to social and moral decline and, perhaps, even the production of such perverse, unnatural monstrosities as national rebellions and civil unrest.

McCulloch makes one of his most powerful and explicit statements about these connections in an article on the rise and fall of profits. He writes of the Corn Laws: "How long this system—a system so utterly at variance with every principle of sound policy—is to be supported, we know not; but we are bold to say that no people *emerged from barbarism* ever before *subjected themselves to such a scourge.* Its effects have already been *most disastourous* [sic]; and if it be not abandoned, it is easy to see that it must ultimately affect all classes with the *curse of universal poverty, and the complete ruin of the country*" (emphasis mine).[24] While McCulloch does not explicitly say that the Corn Laws will return England to the barbarism from which it has emerged, his threat of universal poverty and national ruin certainly carries that connotation, especially coming as it does so rhetorically close to the image of past barbarism. Later in the article, McCulloch links these more general fears of social and economic degeneration to nationalist fears about England's internal security and middle-class fears about order and security of property. He writes that "mobs and popular commotions are in fact the natural and necessary consequences of a dearth of corn. . . . We have no idea, indeed, that it is possible for the corn laws and the constitution to exist together" ("Rise and Fall" 22). McCulloch repeats the first part of this assertion almost word for word in his 1826 article on the abolition of the Corn Laws, and then reinforces it by adding: "Those who are prepared to defend such a system must be prepared for the bloodshed and commotion of which it cannot fail to be productive."[25] The only way to prevent such a result, McCulloch concludes, is for the country to "rid . . . [itself] of the monstrous and intolerable nuisance of the Corn Laws" ("Abolition" 359). In this final passage, McCulloch again links an implicitly unnatural social and national unrest to the explicitly unnatural, monstrous economic processes set in motion by the Corn Laws. The passage also demonstrates how McCulloch is constructing two opposing narrative visions of England's immediate future. The natural narrative of progress will continue the processes of material and social improvement for all members of English society. The unnatural narrative will tear apart the nation by impoverishing its lowest classes and turning them against their "betters"—the middle- and upper-class readers of the *Edinburgh Review.*

McCulloch's argument about the Corn Laws is solidly based upon Ricardian economic principles, but much of its persuasive power seems to be aimed at his reader's social fears, nationalist sentiments, and unconscious assumptions that what is natural is good, while what is unnatural is perverse, monstrous, and evil. McCulloch openly proclaims that "the whole mischief to which [the Corn Laws] give rise . . . do[es] not admit of being measured by a pecuniary standard" ("Abolition" 339). This assertion allows McCulloch to argue against one of Ricardo's most fundamental economic principles in order to appeal to the landlords who are protected by the Corn Laws—the principle of self-interest. Indeed, as I mentioned before, McCulloch had criticized Smith for allowing that there could be a difference between what is best for the individual and what is best for the public. But when he turns to the landlords, McCulloch implicitly asks that they forgo the measures that are in their own best economic interest in order to consider the larger economic and social interests of the state: "It is, moreover, . . . the extremest folly to suppose, that a system, which is so essentially injurious to the other classes of the community, can really be beneficial to those who have so deep an interest in the public prosperity as the landlords" ("Abolition" 345). McCulloch tries to supplement this appeal with the economic rationale that high corn prices draw down the national rate of profits, and thus depress the economy in which the landlords must participate. But read in the context of his invocation of a larger-than-pecuniary interest, McCulloch's statement inevitably takes on political and moral aspects and suggests that he has found an exception to the law of self-interest. McCulloch would argue, of course, that such an economically unnatural appeal is necessary only in the face of such monstrously unnatural laws. However, it is significant to note that the gloomy social and political narratives McCulloch builds around the Corn Laws lead him into making his own unnatural appeal.

The structure of unnatural laws counterbalanced by equally unnatural remedies takes on a much more dramatic form in McCulloch's attacks on the Poor Laws. There his degenerative narrative seems to lead directly to a recommendation that the English government adopt artificial measures to encourage the emigration of the English and Irish poor. At the beginning of his 1828 article on the Poor Laws, McCulloch restates the narrative of causation between wealth and virtue that he referred to as "Providential" in his *Discourse:* "No one loves industry and frugality for their own sakes. They are practised, by the best of us, only as a means to an end. . . . Now, if such be the fact, is it not obvious, that if the state proclaim that all who are in indigent circumstances . . . shall be provided for by the public, the most powerful motives to the practice of industry and frugality must be wholly destroyed."[26] By taking away this providentially mandated incentive to industry, the Poor Laws interfered with the natural economic order that would have led to the moral virtue of the poor. For McCulloch, as for many of his contemporaries, poverty was not even the problem to address; it was pauperism, rather than poverty, that constituted the real political, economic, and social threat to British society. The Poor Laws were, in fact, seen as in large part responsible for this latter problem, though they had ostensibly been designed to solve the problem of poverty. Pauperism, in turn, was seen by many as a moral rather than an economic problem—a moral problem caused by unnatural state intervention. The Poor Laws, according to a "Mr. Hodges" whom McCulloch cites in an 1831 article on pauperism, have "totally changed . . . the moral character of the poor . . . within my memory."[27] McCulloch further reinforces the moral aspect of this problem by comparing the condition of those supported by the Poor Laws to the condition of slaves. Like slaves, these paupers are victims of an unnatural economic system that has reduced them to a less-than-human status.

In order to rectify this unnatural situation, McCulloch not only calls for the repeal of the Poor Laws but also suggests that emigration to the colonies is the surest way to reverse the degenerative process those laws had put into operation. He writes: "We disclaim all participation in the tender mercies of those who would persuade the labourer to continue in a state of slavery and destitution in England, when he may become free and prosperous in the colonies."[28] McCulloch's belief in the beneficial alternative of emigration is so strong, in fact, that in this 1831 article he supports government legislative intervention in the form of a bill to facilitate emigration. Thus, while he rejects the artificial action of the Poor Laws as perverse, monstrous, and degenerative, McCulloch encourages a similarly interventionist measure that would subsidize the emigration of the poor to Canada, Australia, and other British colonies. McCulloch might justify this provision as a support, rather than a transgression, of natural economic laws, since its ostensible function would be to increase the mobility of labor mandated by Ricardian theory. But his justification depends on some rather neat reasonings to explain a recommendation that certainly goes against the spirit, if not the letter, of Ricardo's extremely antigovernment model of laissez-faire economics.

In his earlier article on the Poor Laws, McCulloch transgresses both the spirit *and* the letter of Ricardian economic law when he identifies one of the worst and most current causes of English pauperism to be not the operation of the Poor Laws but the immigration and free competition of Irish labor. McCulloch's discussion of Irish immigration into England is infused with some of his strongest and most explicit appeals to the degenerative narrative he at other points associates with unnatural government intervention into the economic sphere. In this case, however, the threat of barbarism is located not only in a potential English future but also and more much more immediately in the present of England's Irish neighbors and immigrants. McCulloch writes: "Great Britain has been *overrun by half-famished hordes,* that have, by their competition, lessened the wages of labour, and by their example, degraded the habits and lowered the opinions of the people with respect to subsistence. But great as the mischief is that has already been occasioned by this *barbarian immigration,* it is trifling indeed to what we may confidently predict will be produced by it, if no efforts be made to put a stop to it" (emphasis mine, Poor Laws 327). Ironically, it is by means of the "natural" economic laws of free competition and aspects of the population principle that the Irish effect their degenerative influence on English labor. But rather than alter the operation of these laws within England, McCulloch proposes that the government intervene to prohibit the free movement of labor from Ireland to England:

> A law should, therefore, be enacted, to prevent any individual coming from Ireland to Britain, without a passport; and the custom-house officers ought to be instructed to refuse passports to all who cannot establish, by satisfactory evidence, that they belong to some other class than that of labourers, or that they have some other object in view in visiting Britain, than that of employing themselves as labourers. The same thing might, perhaps, be more easily effected by imposing a pretty heavy tax on all passengers; and making the owners of the vessels responsible for its payment. But, however the object may be attained, we hold that it is indispensable that a stop should be put to the farther immigration of paupers. When the people of Ireland have been raised to something like the same level as those of England, the freest intercourse may be allowed between the two countries. Till then, however, we must stand on the defensive. (Poor Laws 328)

This passage is striking for several reasons. McCulloch's language of "raising" the "people of Ireland" clarifies the relationship between his xenophobic recommendation and the narrative of civil and economic development outlined in his more theoretical economic writings. The passage also exposes the extent to which racial, ethnic, and national discrimination is written into the logic of classical economic law: such law can function to improve the social and economic well-being of the nation only if the cheap labor of the colonies is much less proximate and liable to importation than their cheap commodities. Otherwise, such cheap and thus implicitly degraded labor will operate to depress too dramatically "the people" of the nation, even as it enriches the nation's capitalists.

Another striking feature of McCulloch's demand for "artificial obstacles" to immigration is his suggestion that perhaps the easiest way to create such an obstacle would be to place a "pretty heavy tax" on all Irish travelers to England. While McCulloch certainly does not advertise or even acknowledge this effect, such a tax would constitute a protective restriction upon the importation of "foreign" Irish labor precisely paralleling the Corn Laws' protective taxes upon the importation of foreign corn. This parallel reinforces the "unnaturalness" of the provision McCulloch demands for restrictive legislation and the contradictory treatment of labor and commodities within economic theory. These complications of Ricardian doctrine are worsened by McCulloch's suggestion of further forms of government intervention in relation to Ireland. He appeals here, as in his 1831 article, for government support to fund the emigration of the poor to Britain's distant colonies, though in this case he is concerned primarily with the Irish poor. He also asks that the English government intervene to prevent Irish landowners from subdividing and subletting their own land. If the practice of subletting within Ireland is not ended almost immediately, McCulloch predicts, "the numbers and the misery of the population will go on increasing, until the whole country, from the Giant's Causeway to Cape Clear, be overspread with potatoe [*sic*] beds, and *hordes of half-naked and half-starved savages*" (emphasis mine, Poor Laws 329). Except for the brief introduction of an 1818 "table of paupers," this passage constitutes the last statement of McCulloch's article. The hysterical image of relentlessly spreading potato beds and invasive "hordes of half-naked and half-starved savages" is the way he closes an article that begins as an economically based critique of the Poor Laws but ends up as a paranoid attack on England's subjects, neighbors, and potential immigrants.

While McCulloch's discussion of the Poor Laws is not without its explanations of economic law and logic, it is through such exaggerated images and rhetoric that McCulloch attempts to impress upon his general English reader the urgency and implications of those "scientific truths." In fact, at several points in his article, McCulloch appeals even more overtly to the fears of the English middle classes. For example, when discussing the operation of the Poor Laws during a general scarcity of corn and food, McCulloch claims that such laws, by guaranteeing subsistence for the laborer, throw the whole pressure of any scarcity "entirely upon the other, and chiefly the middle classes" (Poor Laws 319). Even more dramatically, when speaking of the general operation of the Poor Laws, McCulloch goes on to cite an "intelligent witness" who states that he has heard his laborers frequently complain of their allowance and threaten him with, "We will marry, and then you must maintain us" (Poor Laws 321). Through such statements and reputedly authoritative quotations, McCulloch directly points his Corn Law and Poor Law articles toward the moral, social, and economic class anxieties of his predominantly middle- and upper-class readers. Such statements, however, are only slightly more pointed than McCulloch's repeated references to narratives of national civil degeneration caused by economic declines such as a fall in profits (via the Corn Laws) or a fall in wages (via Irish immigration). When McCulloch addresses such controversial political and economic issues as the Corn Laws and the Poor Laws, he seems drawn away from the seemingly neutral "rational" or scientific language of economic theory and toward social and national narratives designed to directly and *irrationally* appeal to the interests and fears to the emerging middle classes.

This slippage is particularly important because the anti–Poor Law and anti–Corn Law campaigns were two of the main vehicles through which the Victorian middle-class public learned the basic outlines of classical political economy. Those campaigns ultimately led to two of the main legislative enactments of such economic theory—the 1834 New Poor Law and the 1846 repeal of the Corn Laws. Through his written support for these political movements, McCulloch helped make Ricardian theory more visible, concrete, and immediately relevant to the concerns of the *Edinburgh Review*'s educated readers. In winning support for his anti–Poor Law and anti–Corn Law positions, McCulloch also gained a broader, popular authority for scientific economic theory—even when, as in some of the articles examined here, he explicitly subordinated his theoretical explanations and references to narrative projections of national revolution, social and moral degeneration, barbarian invasions, and class warfare. Despite the specific details of the rhetoric at the surface of his arguments, McCulloch constructs his narrative projections according to the sequential logic or "plots" of scientific political economy. This underlying economic structure at once adds authority to McCulloch's inflated rhetoric and carries with it the secondary rhetorical force of natural socio-economic inevitability.

At the same time that such linguistic conflations helped to mutually reinforce the authority of political economy and certain phantasmic social anxieties, they also placed "scientific" economic theory within a discursive context much different from that of both Ricardo's *Principles of Political Economy* and McCulloch's own economic treatises. Although McCulloch could still claim that his arguments were based on economic law, his rhetoric forged an alliance between such "universal" economic laws and the interests of discrete groups of individual and classes. Such alliances deeply problematized McCulloch's own claims to neutral scientific authority, and they also undermined the scientific claims of Ricardian economics as a whole. Because most of McCulloch's audience had never read Ricardo's writings, they would have been unaware of Ricardo's painstaking attempts to establish a narrow *scientific* authority for his economic theory. Perhaps most members of the *Edinburgh Review*'s audience would have read selections of McCulloch's more theoretical economic prose, but that prose also appeals to extra-economic forms of authority such as "Providence," literal or implied. Even if readers came to McCulloch's articles with an acquaintance with Ricardo's or even Mill's more scientific discussions of economic theory, McCulloch's dramatic alliances of that theoretical content with classist and nationalist sentiments could not fail to affect their overall conception of the nature and scope of Ricardian economics. Thus, even as McCulloch constructed the rhetoric through which he successfully popularized Ricardian economic theory, he also helped to construct the complex and nonspecialized discursive ground from which many of political economy's most prominent middle-class critics would launch their attacks.

chapter three

Sentimental Science: Harriet Martineau's *Illustrations of Political Economy*

During 1832, the same year that the first Reform Bill was passed, Harriet Martineau began to write her series of novellas titled *Illustrations of Political Economy*. Through this series, her first major literary production, Martineau simultaneously established herself as an author and affirmed the emerging science of political economy as a new providential system of natural laws and inevitable consequences. Although political economy already had such prominent spokespersons and advocates as David Ricardo, J. R. McCulloch, James Mill, John Stuart Mill, and Nassau Senior, Martineau's narrative project turned that "science" into a complex series of natural injunctions that could be used to regulate almost all elements of human behavior and to ameliorate almost all aspects of human experience. In addition, Martineau's overwhelmingly successful literary debut extended the audience for classical economic theory by rearticulating its principles within an economically and intellectually accessible form, published independently of any explicit political or social allegiances. In this chapter, I explore how the form and the content of Martineau's *Illustrations* were the basis of one of the most important extensions and expansions of scientific economic theory in the early nineteenth century. I also argue, however, that Martineau's popularizing project was riddled with tensions and contradictions that ultimately compromised its didactic message. More specifically, the very fictional forms that Martineau so successfully used to win an audience for political economy were also the source of the tensions that deformed her project.

During the nineteenth century, Martineau's popularizing project was most often compared not to that of J. R. McCulloch, the "professional economist," but to that of Jane Marcet's *Conversations on Political Economy* (1816). Marcet's text, the first edition of which actually predated Ricardo's *Principles of Political Economy and Taxation,* is interesting and important as a point of comparison and contrast with Martineau's later narrative project. First, there are several significant similarities between Marcet's and Martineau's writings on political economy. Both authors are women contributing to a traditionally masculine discursive field. Similarly, both are nonspecialists who self-consciously attempt to domesticate the "foreign" or "alien" subject of political economy for other nonspecialist readers by rewriting "expert knowledge" in more familiar and accessible generic forms. Finally, both writers see the promulgation and teaching of economic knowledge as having an explicitly moral element.

There are, then, important similarities between the two popularizing projects. The differences are equally striking and, ultimately, more significant for my purposes. First, there is the difference in timing. Marcet's work was published before McCulloch had begun to profess Ricardian economics as the teleological endpoint of political economy's scientific development, before the brief period in the 1820s when political economy was considered a fashionable rage, and before the discourse of political economy began to have a significant impact on national legislation and policy. Martineau's novellas, in contrast, were written at a time when the idea of political economy as a fashionable discourse had passed but during which political economy was self-consciously deployed in national debates about the Poor Laws, the Corn Laws, banking, the Irish question, slavery, and colonial policies.

The intended audience for each text was also different. Marcet's *Conversations* were aimed at the children and young adults of the landed and governing elite, while Martineau's *Illustrations* were aimed at adults of all classes of British society. This difference relates to a crucial difference in authorial intentions. Jane Marcet's text was one in a series of "conversations," most of which actually focused on the natural sciences, that she wrote to instruct young people in the sciences. Martineau undertook her authorial project because she identified political economy as *the* privileged master discourse of social, economic, and political life. For Martineau, political economy was not simply one science among others that should be taught to privileged children; it was the scientific discourse within which was embedded a complex template for individual moral behavior and national social progress.

This difference is reflected in the two projects' differing treatment of moral questions. In Marcet's *Conversations*, the well-intentioned but uninformed Caroline consistently articulates traditional moral principles that seem to be at odds with the principles of political economy voiced by her tutor, Mrs. B. However, through the course of the conversations, Mrs. B explains to Caroline how the two systems—that of morality and that of political economy—are not at odds. Instead, Mrs. B teaches Caroline, the principles of political economy "tend to promote the happiness of nations and the purest of morality."[1] Martineau would not disagree with this statement, but her notion of "the purest of morality" differs decidedly from that of Marcet. As the whole dialogic structure of *Conversations* stresses, Marcet's emphasis is on the reconciliation of traditional conceptions of morality with the apparently amoral—or even immoral—injunctions of political economy. For Martineau, in contrast, the injunctions of political economy *themselves* constitute the groundwork of a new moral system. The principles of political economy constitute the providential framework on which the individual novellas work out and illustrate this new moral system. Individual moral choice, within this system, has an inevitable effect upon the well-being of the nation as a whole, one that is worked out time and time again through the course of Martineau's tales. This effect is one of the reasons that it is important for Martineau to reach an audience of all classes. Morality, for her, is not primarily a private or personal matter but instead is fundamentally linked to the affairs of the nation. Via what Martineau perceives as the scientific and naturally determining "laws" of political economy, individual economic actions inevitably react upon the welfare of the community as a whole. Because of her belief in this connection, narrative becomes an ideal format for Martineau's popularizing work. At the same time that she adopts the genre of fictional narrative for her project, Martineau firmly believes that "science" is what authorizes the project. Her goal in *Illustrations of Political Economy* was to maintain political economy's claims to scientific validity while at the same time making the "science" more attractive and accessible. Published between 1832 and 1834, *Illustrations* included twenty-five novellas, each focusing on one economic principle or set of principles. Martineau selected these principles to follow the systematic unfolding of the "science," thus beginning with the basic principles of capital and labor in the first volume, *Life in the Wilds,* and ending with the principles of government taxation in the volume *The Farrers of Budge-Row.*

Martineau explains the goals of her project in the twenty-five-page Preface to the first volume. Adopting a complex rhetoric of "science," she attempts simultaneously to authorize a body of knowledge that many of her contemporaries dismissed as abstract and inhumane and to legitimate her own narrative contribution. Martineau opens the Preface with a brief survey of the wide array of "sciences" pursued "in an enlightened nation" such as her own, including theology and philology as well as astronomy and the new science of political economy. She then places these sciences in competition with each other for the status of "the most important of the world," which sets the stage for her argument that political economy, the least studied of all the sciences, is actually the most important. She asks: "Can anything more nearly concern all the members of any society than the way in which the necessaries and comforts of life may be best procured and enjoyed by all?"[2] Because political economy is so important and so understudied, education in the new science becomes a moral imperative: "Is it not [the people's] . . . duty, should it not be their pleasure, to listen to those who have observed and compared and come to a certain knowledge of a few grand principles, which, if generally understood, would gradually remove all the obstructions, and remedy the distresses, and equalize the lot of the population? Such ought to be the disposition of the people" (Preface ix). For Martineau, then, learning the principles of a "better economy" is a positive duty for the people and one that "ought to be [their] disposition" (Preface ix). The reason "the people" have a duty to learn the "few grand principles" to which Martineau alludes is inherent in the providential scheme of social amelioration outlined in the latter portion of the passage. Knowledge will allow people to obey the natural laws that govern their world, and it is only through such obedience and conformity of human law and behavior to natural law that the material and moral well-being "of the greatest number" will be attained (*MMF* 144). Thus, in effect, these laws *were* providence for Martineau.[3] According to Martineau, individual moral principles are derived from the economic system rather than influencing the shape that system "should" take; the system of natural economic laws gives those principles authority and dispenses rewards and punishments for conformity and nonconformity.[4]

In order to instill in people a sense of their duty to learn and live by economic law, Martineau needed to get people to read about political economy, which meant that she had to establish both the importance and the attractiveness of classical economic theory. This situation points to the central tension that underlies Martineau's project. She must make economic theory accessible and interesting to a nonspecialist public in order to create for herself and for it a readership. At the same time, much of the basis of her appeal to this public was the claim of scientific truth made through Ricardo's abstract systematization of economic theory. Once the precision and certitude of his theoretical model were recontextualized in terms of "common" or "familiar" issues, the scientific authority and coherence of economic theory were endangered.

Martineau is aware of this tension within her projected narratives, and in another turn of her scientific rhetoric she attempts to manage the tension with a developmental model of the sciences that accommodates both scientific abstraction and the popularization or "illustration" of such abstractions. Repeating the phrases "it is natural" or "it is perfectly natural" five times in two pages, Martineau defensively rationalizes and naturalizes as a developmental process a number of radically different moments, or "stages," within the emergence of a science. Martineau's recitation of what is "natural" and "perfectly natural" even attempts to rationalize the threateningly irrational aspects of that process, such as differences, "disputes," "contradictions," and "perplexities." Next, her developmental narrative naturalizes and authorizes "cold dry form" as equivalent with the attainment of certainty and regularity within a science. This attainment would seem to be the privileged moment of truth within the development of a science, but for Martineau the stability of certainty and regularity is not the end point of such development. Rather, this is a moment when one still looks *forward* with "hope" and expectation, for the final stage in Martineau's narrative is not simply "truth" but the "beauty" of that truth. According to Martineau, the way to "discover and display" this beauty is through the "familiar, practical form" of "pictures," "illustrations," or "applications"—precisely the form to which her narrative project aspires.

Through the historical teleology she has created, Martineau points directly to her own illustrative project and explicitly attempts to justify her use of fictional narrative to teach the science of political economy. First, Martineau anticipates and meets the objection of hidden didacticism, writing: "We trust we shall not be supposed to countenance the practice of making use of narrative as a trap to catch idle readers, and make them learn something they are afraid of. We detest the practice and feel ourselves insulted whenever a book of the *trap* kind is put into our hands" (emphasis in original, Preface xiii). What characterizes this "trap" type of narrative for Martineau, and what separates it from her own literary project, is that these works just "pretend to be stories" (Preface xiii). In other words, narrative is not the natural form of the knowledge promulgated in works of "the trap kind" but rather an unconvincing veneer over otherwise unpalatable truths. In contrast, Martineau chooses narrative form because, in her own words, she "really think[s] it the best in which Political Economy can be taught" (Preface xiii). Martineau believes that narrative, at this time, is "the most faithful and most complete" method of teaching this new "moral science." The current stage of political economy, when the "beauty" of the science is to be discovered and displayed, is implicitly privileged by Martineau as the best, or at least the most important, stage of that development.

It must be acknowledged, of course, that some of Martineau's rhetorical celebration of narrative is probably a compensatory gesture. Instead of being the "best" or "most important" form through which to promulgate political economy, fictional narrative may have been almost the *only* form through which Martineau could approach the topic and science of political economy—or at least the only form through which she, as a woman, could do so relatively safely and successfully. As it was, her harshest critics and reviewers focused on the "unfeminine" quality of her subject matter, and even her more favorable reviewers tended to emphasize the beauty of her fictions rather than the truths those fictions conveyed.⁵ However, the historically determined quality of Martineau's literary "choice" ought not to render invisible the impact of the form she chose for the popularizing project she envisioned.

Martineau's fictional narratives enabled her to humanize the theory and abstraction many saw as not only uncongenial but also un-English.⁶ In addition, by constructing images of economic principles at work among the working classes, the narrative form helped Martineau argue against the accusation that political economy represented only middle-class interests, at the expense of the laboring classes.⁷ Less contentiously, she was able to entice her readers with exotic settings and picturesque descriptions of such places as Africa, the West Indies, and Ceylon. Such far-flung settings also enabled her to imaginatively extend the rule of political economy beyond Europe and its colonies to virtually all known locations on the globe. Most importantly for Martineau, her narratives enabled her to assert or, she would say, demonstrate the significance of political economic theory for all, not only extending it with a broad geographical sweep but also penetrating all spheres and aspects of social existence. In conjunction with her materialist psychology, Martineau's political economy is shown to legislate individual morality, social order, personal psychology, character, and civility, to name just a few of the "economic" effects the novellas explore.

By 1834, Martineau's publisher, Charles Fox, was selling 10,000 copies of each monthly volume, with the whole series reaching an estimated 144,000 readers. (Compare these numbers to John Stuart Mill's *Principles of Political Economy*, which, while popular and authoritative, sold only 3,000 copies over the course of four years.) In his patronizing but generally favorable article on the *Illustrations* in the *Edinburgh Review*, William Empson declared that since their publication, "We have heard more political economy . . . than we believe was ever before heard outside the Political Economy Club."⁸ Even the unfavorable reviews testify to the importance of Martineau's work, simply because of the number of reviewers who felt compelled to respond to it.

Martineau's popularizing project, then, seems to have been largely successful. But precisely because Martineau developed such an accessible form through which to promulgate economic ideas, her narrative project invited attacks from all quarters. Moreover, her economic novellas not only suffered from the external critiques of conservative reviewers throughout the British Isles but were also plagued by internal contradictions produced by her combination of abstract, "scientific" theory with fictional narrative forms. Despite the careful, justificatory logic of her Preface, Martineau's literary project is riddled with a series of contradictions generated by her attempt to synthesize such divergent modes of discourse. Although many of these tensions overlap with one another, for the sake of clarity, I have grouped them into three sets of disjunctive effects. The first set of tensions might be described as the problems that develop when an abstract theoretical system such as Ricardian economic theory is practically deployed in a "real-world" situation with its own preexisting economic systems in place. Of course the scenarios described in Martineau's novellas are *not* the real world but rather narrative representations that deploy conventions of history, realism, geography, and travel narrative. As I shall demonstrate, however, even these realistically rendered—albeit fictive—contexts put a strain on the capitalist theoretical principles that Martineau attempts to embroider onto their background. The second set of tensions is closely related to the first—the product of differences between the dynamics or logic of a specific abstract theoretical system and the dynamics of the specific narrative forms used to "illustrate" that system. The final set of tensions concerns contradictions within the logic of the abstract theory itself. In other words, Martineau's narrative form at times exposes logical flaws within the economic theory she intends to promote, making visible disjunctions hidden by Ricardian abstraction.

Each of these tensions is important because they dramatically demonstrate the extent to which the dominant form of nineteenth-century economic thought—classical political economy—was at once made possible and undermined by the linguistic modes through which it was developed and articulated. In addition and more generally, the contradictions that open up within Martineau's novellas reveal the power of literary and other discursive forms to shape and deform the supposedly static content that they "express." For Martineau's project, the very narrative forms that enabled her to construct a much broader audience for political economic theory also changed important aspects of that theory as it had been developed by men such as Smith, Ricardo, and James Mill. Thus, the very fact of the wide circulation and readership of *Illustrations* makes it important to examine more closely the relationship between the narrative form of Martineau's project and the economic doctrine it intended to popularize.

The first set of tensions that challenges Martineau's narrative project is the gap between an abstract theoretical system, such as Ricardian economics, and the deployment of that system within an apparently referential representation of a specific and recognizable historical and geographical situation. Martineau does seem aware of potential conflicts in the application of a new theoretical system to a historical (rather than hypothetical) social situation. Though not in these terms, Martineau's narratives regularly foreground the gap between precapitalist or noncapitalist economic models and contemporary models of nineteenth-century industrial and commercial capitalism. In one of her most striking stagings of such a gap, for example, Martineau's *A Manchester Strike* represents an alternative economic consciousness that understands but rejects marketplace logic. The characterizations of the novella's protagonist, Mr. Allen, and his wife point to the powerful presence of alternative economic models existing alongside and competing with industrial capitalism.

Importantly, it is not the striking workers in Martineau's tale who most vividly represent these competing economic modes. Although the workers' strike is doomed to fail, the rationale that drives their strike is largely marketplace logic: they want to withhold their labor now, to increase demand for it, and thus, they hope, to increase their wages. The progress of the plot proves the mistakenness of their economic rationale and thus "educates" them in the "correct" principles of wages and the wage fund. From an early point in the narrative, the workers' rationale is resisted not only, as expected, by the masters but also very emphatically by the workers' wives. In their first discussion about the possibility of a strike, one of the workers accuses those resistant to the idea of a turnout as being "afraid of their wives" and declares "that they might wait long for a strike if it was necessary to refrain till the women voted for it, since there was never a woman yet who did not hate a turn-out as she would the plague" (*MS* 23–24). The reason the women hate a turnout is, among other things, that it brings immediate hardship to the household economy and creates potentially long-term uncertainty about future household income. The strike leader, Allen, must meet and quiet his wife's resistance to his acceptance of that public role, even though he is doing it for the good of the larger community. Likewise, when economic hardship begins to pinch the strikers, Allen's wife, Mary, begs him—on the basis of his family's welfare—to leave the strike and accept work from the masters. Women in *A Manchester Strike*, it seems, have a very nearsighted, family-based view of community and economic good. Thus, when the children who had continued to labor despite the strike are locked out by the masters, the strike committee "shook their heads over this weighty additional item of weekly charge," but the children's mothers "stroked their . . . heads and smiled when they wished them joy of their holiday, and bade them sleep on in the mornings without thinking of the factory bell" (*MS* 110). The response of these mothers to their children's unemployment suggests that the domestic unit in *A Manchester Strike* is never solely an economic unit but also, importantly, an affective one. As an affective or sentimental unit, the domestic sphere of the novella is shown not as a complement to the marketplace logic of the workers' and masters' public sphere but rather as having a symbolic economic logic of its own, in conflict with the more abstract reckonings of husbands and strike committees.[9]

Although it is mothers and wives who represent and speak for a kind of sentimental economics within most of *A Manchester Strike,* there are several narrative moments in which the *reader* is implicated in resisting the supply-and-demand logic of the striking workers, the masters, and Martineau's didactic narrative itself. In terms of the reader's sympathetic identification, the sentimental heroine of this novella is not Allen's wife but his daughter, Martha. Early in the story, in a scene that is incidental to the plot of the striking workers, the reader follows Martha to work one night in the factory. Through this extended scene of sentimental hardship and intimacy, the narrative binds the reader to this young character:

> The little girl repaired to the factory, sighing at the thought of the long hours that must pass before she could sit down or breathe the fresh air again. She had been as willing a child at her work as could be till lately: but since she had grown sickly, a sense of hardship had come over her, and she was seldom happy. She was very industrious, and disposed to be silent at her occupation; so that she was liked by her employers, and had nothing more to complain of than the necessary fatigue and disagreeableness of the work. She would not have minded it for a few hours a day; but to be shut up all day, or else all night, without any time to nurse the baby or play with her companions, was too much for a little girl of eight years old. (*MS* 64)

From its opening sentence, this passage offers numerous details to facilitate the reader's sympathetic identification with Martha, including the understated assertion that she had "nothing more to complain of than the necessary fatigue and disagreeableness of the work," which suggests the child's own exhausted and anything-but-youthful acceptance of her situation. It is the final sentence, however, that cinches the knot of the reader's sympathies—the phrases "all day," "all night," "without any time to nurse the baby or play with her companions," and, finally, "a little girl of eight years old" are piled one on top of the other, constructing an increasingly accelerated pitch of sentiment.

While the reader's sympathy for the child laborer creates some dissonance from the main plot of the strike, it does not directly contest the logic of that plot. The workers are striking for increases in their own pay rather than against child labor, and the narrative constructs the children themselves as willing laborers—injured not by the fact of labor but by its conditions. During a later series of scenes, however, the sympathetic identification the narrative has forged between Martha and her readers works as an indictment of the marketplace logic of both men and masters. Martha's one possession, regular companion, and joy throughout the story is her pet bird, Billy. As the economic hardship from the strike becomes extreme, Martha's father approaches her as she plays with her bird:

> "Martha, do you think you could bear to stay at home without Billy?"
> Martha's countenance fell.
> "You see, my dear child, we have sold almost everything we have; and when we can scarcely get food for ourselves, it does not seem to me right to keep animals to feed. This was why I sold the dog so many weeks ago." (*MS* 116)

Trying to keep up with her father's economic logic, Martha responds:

> "But, father, it is only just a halfpenny now and then. Mother has always found me a half penny now and then for Billy." (*MS* 116)

Martha's reasoned response is met by another turn of the economic screw:

> "A halfpenny is to us as much now, child, as a guinea is to some people; besides we could get money by Billy. Ah! I knew it would make you cry to say so."
> And he left her and walked about the room *in the way which it always frightened Martha to see*. She sobbed out a few words,—
> "I can't—I can't help crying, father, but I don't mean—I wish you would take Billy and sell him." (emphasis mine, *MS* 116)

In this scene, we see the reverse of the process Gillian Brown describes as structuring Harriet Beecher Stowe's *Uncle Tom's Cabin,* in which alienated market commodities are affectively transformed into sentimental possessions.[10] Rather than commodities being recuperated as sentimental possessions, Martineau shows us a sentimental possession being transmogrified into a commodity. Equally significant is the fact that this process is performed not by the villain of the story but by its hero. Nor does it seem as if little Martha has been rationally won over to her father's commodified view of her pet; rather, her "reconsideration" seems to be based on the sentimental blackmail that makes Martha want to stop her father's frightening pacing. Martha even accompanies her father to the bird fancier's, appealing to her father that "nobody could make Billy sing all his songs so well as herself"—and thus, implicitly, no one could sell him for so much (*MS* 117). Thus, Martha helps her father sell her bird, though as long as the bird remains in the shop, she lingers longingly by its door. When one day she repairs to the shop to find

Billy gone, sold to a "country customer," she returns melancholically to her house and ceases her daily watching.

This is the last that Martha or the reader hears of her pet bird. And to the extent that this scene is intended to register the futility of the strike, it seems to have served its purpose. However, to the extent that the scene has sympathetically implicated the reader in a domestic or affective economy, Martha and her bird linger beyond their didactic economic role to create an emotional indictment of the economic system and logic that have separated them. In other words, when the narrative invokes an alternative, domestic economy through its sympathetic imbrication of the reader in Martha's plight, then Allen's exchange of his daughter's pet for a small sum of money—or any sum of money, for that matter—seems a very unequal exchange, a very bad deal. Allen's rhetoric and logic of economic need, tested against little Martha's sentimentalized plight rather than against a hypothetical scenario, comes out seeming violent and perverse to the very readers it was intended to impress.

The reader's sympathies are even further confused by the narrative's representation of yet another alternative economy within the narrative of *A Manchester Strike*. In this case, the reader is positioned to sympathize with Allen against the pleadings of his wife. In honor and gratitude for his leadership, the strike committee has given Allen the gift of a new suit of clothes. But when the people turn against his leadership, Allen returns the clothes to the committee with a sense of high honor. As hardship pinches the community and recourse to the pawnbrokers becomes a regular mode of subsistence, Allen's wife requests that out of love for and duty toward his family, Allen retrieve and sell this suit of clothes. When he fails to accede to her request, she goes secretly to the committee, asks for the clothes in her husband's name, and sells them to the pawnbroker on the way home. Allen discovers this transaction during an embarrassing scene in front of the strike committee when the people accuse him of having openly rejected, but secretly accepted, the suit of clothes. Allen is finally enlightened that his wife is, in his own words, "the dishonest person [who] has used [his] name to obtain possession of the clothes," and when he returns home he tells his wife "his unalterable will that not an article should be purchased by her beyond a bare supply of daily food till the clothes were brought back again and restored to the Committee" (*MS* 124, 126).

Most of the lingering sympathy the reader may have felt for Mary's desire to get money for her family's maintenance is cut off by the ways the narrative stages Allen's public embarrassment and discovery. The reader is left free to sympathize unreservedly with Allen's noble intentions and disgrace. Thus, when Allen receives unexpected money from his friend Bray for caring for Bray's daughter, the reader celebrates with him that he now has the opportunity to buy back the suit of clothing. The narrative closes this subject with the following statement: "[The clothes] proved a dear bargain; but that was a secondary consideration, poor as Allen was. He went to rest that night, satisfied that his *honour* was redeemed, and that his wife would scarcely venture to *put it in pawn* again" (emphasis mine, *MS* 132). What is striking about this subplot is the extent to which Martineau's narrative seems to support Allen's rejection of a primarily monetary understanding of the suit of clothes. In this set of transactions, the mother's domestic economy is positioned as much closer to a standard market economy than Allen's and the union's gift economy. Allen is rewarded for his allegiance to this older, precapitalist gift economy by yet another gift, which allows him to redeem the suit of clothes, and with it his honor.

This narrative turn is striking in a story that is explicitly intended to illustrate the omnipresent and omnipotent principles of political economy. It is even more striking when placed alongside the narrative's refusal to grant a similar reprieve for the sentimental, domestic economy of Martha's pet bird. However, there is yet another important factor involved in the story's "clothes plot": the fact that Allen's friend Bray—the one whose gift allows him to redeem his honor—is a proscribed worker who now earns his money as a strolling player. Thus, Martineau's narrative not only sympathizes with and approves of Allen and his noneconomic aspirations toward honor but is, in fact, so committed to the fulfillment of those aspirations that it resorts to the pockets of a strolling player—the character perhaps furthest from the capitalist economy that dominates the story's main plot—in order to secure the fulfillment of those aspirations.

Through this subplot, Martineau's story of labor laws and strike futility is deformed from its stated didactic purpose. It is as if Martineau has tried to write that story of free labor and market economics on top of a world dominated by the alternative economic systems of sentimental possessions and gifts. In the first instance, Martha's bird, the novel's plot remains committed to market economics even as readers may wish for the alternative system in which Martha's bird could never be reduced to, and disposed of for, shillings and pence. But in the second instance, the gift economy operating between Allen and the strikers is so compelling that the novel's plot—and its sympathies—makes a swerve away from the mandate of capitalist economics that underwrites the entire project of the *Illustrations* to allow Allen to redeem his precious honor. This redemption is somewhat mitigated by Martineau's return to the cold, hard facts of capitalist economics at the story's conclusion, where the reader finds that Allen has himself become a proscribed worker who can earn money only by hauling a water cart about Manchester. The subplot of Allen's honor and his clothes may, indeed, be Martineau's consolation prize to Allen and the reader for this harsh narrative conclusion. At the same time, it seems that this narrative concession ends up undermining, rather than reinforcing, the fictional message it was meant to support.

The second set of tensions that riddles Martineau's didactic narrative project appears similar to the first but is different in significant ways. Rather than the contradictions that arise from the confrontation of an abstract theoretical model with a resistant, if fictively rendered, reality, this second set is related to the clash between two explicitly discursive systems. The contradictions that emerge are more specific to the historical cultures in which those discursive systems were developed. Already, in the narrative of Martha and her pet bird, we have seen one such conflict. As we have seen, part of the narrative dissonance caused by Martha's story is related to the imposition of abstract economic theories onto the sentimental economics of the home. The narrative is also disrupted by tensions between the logic of a specific theoretical system—classical political economy—and the logic of a particular narrative form—sentimentalism. Because of Martineau's use of a series of sentimental conventions in her representation of Allen's daughter, the reader sympathizes with Martha and desires to see her difficulties relieved through the resolution of the story. When instead the reader is forced to accept the "facts" not only of the sale of Martha's bird but also of her return (followed by all of her younger siblings) to factory labor after the strike, the reader is prone to be dissatisfied.

Martineau herself conceptualizes one of the problematics of her tales as a potential tension between readers' sentimental expectations and what she considers to be the "truths" of economic and social law. In the Preface to *Demerara,* one of her earliest economic tales doubling as an antislavery story, Martineau explicitly invokes sentimentalism as a potential liability in the "correct" reception of her narrative. Rather than rejecting sentimentalism, however, Martineau attempts to revise sentimental conventions so that they can accommodate the various imperatives of political economy. She begins by rejecting the idea that her slave characters would command more sympathy and interest if they were uniformly innocent and virtuous; instead, Martineau writes:

> That [slaves] command our sympathies by their injuries alone, that they claim our compassion by their vices yet more than by their sufferings, is a statement the force of which their adversaries cannot gainsay. . . . If I had believed, as many do, that strong feeling impairs the soundness of reasoning I should assuredly have avoided the subject of the following tale, since SLAVERY is a topic which cannot be approached without emotion. But, convinced as I am that the reason and the sensibilities are made for cooperation, and perceiving, as I do, that the most stirring eloquence issues from the calmest logic, I have

not hesitated to bring calculations and reasonings to bear on a subject which awakens the drowsiest and fires the coldest. (*DM* v–vi)

This statement is a manifesto for the revision of sentimentalism to accommodate reason and its mandates, including, as the story shows, the mandates of an economic law that judges the institution of slave labor impractical, inefficient, and doomed to self-destruct. Rather than being antithetical faculties, Martineau argues, true sympathy and reason should work together and reinforce each other. Martineau wants to reinvent sentimentality through her story so that she can harness its emotional power without sacrificing the reasoned logic of economic law.

Perhaps the most dramatic example of Martineau's attempt to revise the sentimental rhetoric of traditional abolitionist literature is her characterization of a young slave girl, Hester, and her slave guardians, Robert and Sukey. Ten-year-old Hester is in most ways a typical sentimental child. She is constantly misunderstood, underfed and underclothed, beaten, and neglected. Rather than representing Hester as persecuted by her white slave masters, however, Martineau makes Hester's most immediate tyrants her slave guardians. It is through them, Martineau insists, that a little slave girl like Hester is liable to experience the worst tyranny of slavery, rather than through the blows or persecutions of her owners. Martineau writes of Hester's guardians: "If Robert had to lead a horse . . . anywhere, he was sure to beat and torment the animal to the utmost by the way. If his wife found a reptile in her dwelling, she killed it as slowly as she dared, and as cruelly as she could. It would have been well if their power had not been extended beyond beasts, birds, and reptiles; but it was not only shown, by their example, that slavery is the school of tyranny, but, in the instance of the poor little sufferer [Hester] who lived with them, that the most dreadful lot on earth is to be the slave of slaves" (*DM* 46). In the case of Robert and Sukey, since Martineau draws them as largely unsympathetic anyway, there is no apparent tension between the reader's sympathy for Hester and her feelings toward her guardians. Through them Martineau makes her rather lugubrious argument that sentiment must be combined with reason: there is no point in blaming the most immediate villains, Robert and Sukey, for their behavior because they themselves are the victims of a system that corrupts all whom it touches.

In contrast to the lengthy characterization of their tyranny, Martineau constructs one brief scene between Hester and her slave hero, Cassius. Passing by Cassius's provision ground just as he discovers he has been robbed, Hester approaches him to find out what has happened and to offer comfort. But Cassius turns on her violently, shaking her, accusing her, and threatening to beat her if she doesn't tell him who robbed him (information she does not have). Although Cassius soon controls himself and retracts his accusations and threats, his brief outburst presents the reader with a more challenging lesson in sentiment. Through Hester, the reader is forced to see even the heroic, "good" Cassius as so deeply tainted by the system of slavery that he will victimize the young neighbor whom he normally protects and befriends. Thus, Martineau reinforces her point that our sentimental heroine, Hester, is tyrannized not by bad, immoral individuals but by a bad, immoral system. To right the wrongs done to poor Hester, the reader must understand and attack the entire system under which she lives; the characters of Robert and Sukey are simply the most prominent and unambiguous narrative scapegoats through which this lesson is taught.

Martineau makes a series of similar revisionary gestures toward sentimentalism in her novella *Weal and Woe in Garveloch*. The first involves Ella of Garveloch—one of the provident heroines of the tale—instructing her eldest son that he must no longer give away the shells he gathers to the hungry children who besiege him at the shore. This scene is immediately followed by one in which Kenneth goes down to the shore to gather shells and has to turn away the children who have come to rely on his sympathetic generosity. Kenneth's new resolve to keep his own shells is represented as a form of self-denial rather than a selfish gesture. Because of the demand for food at home, Kenneth as an individual can no long afford the luxury of sentimental generosity outside the home. Kenneth is not unsympathetic to the children, and he continues to help them protect their own shells from raids and thievery, but Kenneth's sympathy is now guided by the reasonings of his mother that instruct him to protect the welfare of his immediate family first.

At a later point in *Weal and Woe,* the sentiment of maternal anxiety for their children is said to have rendered Ella and her friend Katie "peculiarly qualified for seeing the truth when placed before them . . . and there remained not a doubt, after calculating numbers and resources, that there must be some check to the increase of the people" (*WW* 104). According to Martineau, then, analytical reasoning and mathematical calculation are actually products of maternal sentiment rather than being anathema to such sentiment. This passage becomes even more striking when it is placed in the context of a long conversation on Malthusian principles of population growth that takes place at the sickbed of Ella's soon-to-die youngest child. Through this scene and the two mothers' conversation, the reader, like Kenneth, is instructed in a rationally informed sentimentality—one that will highlight and reinforce, rather than subvert, the "true" principles of political economy.

Although Martineau repeatedly attempts to harness and control the effects of sentimentality, there are many points throughout at which the traditions of sentimental narrative come into direct conflict with the economic theory that functions as providential determinism in her novellas. The sale of Martha Allen's pet bird and her return to grueling factory labor are two such instances of narrative dissonance in *A Manchester Strike*. Another significant moment of conflict between theory and sentiment deforms *Weal and Woe*. Near the beginning of that story, the narrative sets up a romance plot between Ronald, Ella's brother, and the widow Katie, whom Ronald has loved since well before she was married. For the first portion of the narrative, Ronald postpones his declaration of love and his marriage proposal out of deference to Katie's recent widowhood, and by the end of the narrative, Ronald renounces his romantic love for Katie because of the shortage of food in Garveloch. Out of respect for the population principle, he will remain single and be to her as a brother, and to her children as an uncle. While Katie and Ronald appear to be content with this outcome, readers schooled in the sentimental tradition of romantic love are liable to rebel against this narrative dictum and its denial of their sympathetic desires for romantic fulfillment.

Such a standoff between the reader's sentimental desires and the courses determined by economic law recurs throughout the *Illustrations*. By evoking the narrative desire and expectations inherent in sentimental conventions and then refusing to meet them, Martineau subjects the reader's own sentimental impulses to a kind of narrative violence. Because she does so in the name of inevitable economic laws, those laws themselves appear to be the source and instrument of that violence. The result of these sets of dense discursive contradictions between economic law and sympathetic identification is a deformation of Martineau's narrative project.[11]

In *A Manchester Strike* and *Weal and Woe*, it seems to be Martineau's sentimental narrative that suffers most from the conflict between literary conventions and the logic of political economy, but there are other moments where Martineau's use of sentimental conventions results in the distortion of the abstract theory she wants to profess. The reader's sense in *A Manchester Strike* and *Weal and Woe* that economic law has become a kind of negative providence is a general example of such an effect. But there are other points in the *Illustrations* where political economy seems to be more immediately and specifically distorted by its encounter with sentimental conventions. In part 2 of Martineau's two-part novella *Berkeley the Banker*, for instance, the narrative's villain combines the language of political economy with the language of sentiment in order to manipulate and take advantage of his innocent young wife.

Edgar Morton marries Hester Pardon early in part 1 and then whisks her away to London. All her village friends think she has made a wonderful match, but when she reappears in part 2, the reader discovers that the opposite is the case—in fact, Hester is the sentimental heroine victimized by her own husband.[12] The purity of the reader's sentimental identification with Hester is soon tarnished, however. When her selfish husband suddenly does an about-face, hands her a stack of large-denomination bank notes, and hurries her off to Haleham for two weeks, the reader is immediately suspicious of Edgar's intentions and begins to guess that the bank notes are forgeries that he intends for her to pass unwittingly. Hester, however, is completely taken in and overwhelmed with gratitude.[13] Even after she returns to London and becomes aware of her husband's motives, she remains so devoted to him that she becomes his willing pawn in passing forged notes through the London shops. Hester's own sentimental reading of her marriage, then, results in her complicity in the forgery project that leads her husband and his male companions to the gallows.

While Hester's excessive sentimental susceptibility forces the reader to distance herself from full sympathetic identification with the heroine, it is Edgar's own use of sentimental rhetoric, in tandem with the rational logic of political economy, that results in the mutual contamination of both discursive systems. When Hester discovers that Edgar is a forger, she confronts him and begs for his confidence. In response, Edgar justifies his actions by using a perverted version of economic rationale to justify his occupation. According to Edgar, he is providing much-needed currency in a suddenly contracted economy, and thus actually aiding the people of Haleham by passing his notes to them. Later, Edgar also begins to use sentimental language in order to disguise his coldhearted exploitation of his wife. As Hester begins to collapse emotionally and physically under the strain of her occupation, Edgar repeatedly prods and manipulates her back to her employment through a feigned concern for her welfare: "She had often asked whether she could give assistance upstairs [on the forgery presses], instead of passing notes: but Edgar always put her off with speeches about staining her pretty fingers with printing ink or hurting them with the rollers" (*BB2* 90–91). The effect of Edgar's easy manipulation of the language of sentiment is to cast a shadow of distrust over the reliability of such language. When the reader sees Edgar using the language of political economy in precisely the same ways that he has misused the language of sentiment, the reader's wariness is liable to be turned against that language as well. Of course, Martineau intends for the reader to see through Edgar's misuse of both rhetorics—even as Hester herself sees through it at times—but the very fact that the reader must approach such language with caution weakens the strength of Martineau's sentimental and economic claims. While Martineau seems quite conscious that she is exposing the literary language of sentiment to distrust, her parallel disclosure of the weakness of the rhetoric of economic theory seems beyond her intended narrative effect. If figures such as Edgar Morton and Mr. Cavendish, whom we meet earlier in the story, can manipulate the language of economics in the same way that Edgar manipulates the language of sentiment, then how is the reader to trust any economic account as straightforward and authoritative?

Martineau's use of sentimental conventions contaminates her narrative project in *Berkeley the Banker* in yet another way. Early in the story, the narrative promises a romance between Melea Berkeley and the curator, Henry Craig. Because of the currency crisis and the crash of the Haleham and D— banks, the courtship is suspended at the end of part 1. Unlike the lovers of *Weal and Woe*, who are forced to totally renounce their romantic love at the end of that volume, Henry Craig's words of hope close part 1 of *Berkeley the Banker*. While the reader is busy following the sentimental trials of Hester in part 2, the currency cycle turns its course so that Melea and Henry are again economically acceptable candidates for marriage, and part 2 concludes with the very happy ending of a double wedding between this young couple and the older Mrs. Pardon and Mr. Pye. In some ways, the whole melodramatic plot of forgery and abuse that emerges around the figures of Edgar and Hester seems like a narrative distraction or stalling tactic to allow enough economic time to have passed for these two marriages to be economically provident as well as sentimentally fulfilling. While the reader of just *Berkeley the Banker* might be satisfied with this narrative sleight of hand, the reader of the whole *Illustrations* series cannot help but compare the middle-class fates of Melea and Henry to the working-class or peasant fates of Ronald and Katie in *Weal and Woe*. Where the one couple is narratively rewarded for their economic providence, the other couple is, in effect, narratively punished. Furthermore, because the main difference between the two couples is class, the economic theory Martineau has hoped to defend from accusations of class bias actually seems to reinforce those accusations. If a character is a member of the working class, he or she must trust to "future generations" to realize a happy ending. On the other hand, if she is a member of the middle class, Martineau's narrative will carry her through the currency cycle and leave her at the point of economic stability that can result in immediate marriage and happiness. Likewise, where Martineau seems bound to an extremely rigid and literal interpretation of the population principle in the story of Katie and Ronald, her tale of currency and banking economic laws seems altogether more malleable: Mr. Cavendish can enrich himself by playing the system and banking irresponsibly, Edgar Morton can use economic logic to convince himself that his forgeries benefit society, and the narrator can mold a sentimental narrative of male persecutor and female victim into an "economic" story of forgery so that it will carry the reader forward through time until Henry and Melea, the hero and heroine of part 1, can be married. In other words, it seems as if Martineau allows her own and her projected reader's sentimental desires for the conventional resolution of a middle-class marriage plot to distort the didactic project so that economic theory, rather than being universal and immutable, seems at least in this case to be in the service of middle-class sympathies and desires.

Whether we read such deformations of Martineau's theoretical model as local textual effects of that model's encounter with sentimental conventions or whether we read those apparent distortions as an accurate manifestation of the deeper logic of classical economic theory depends on our own critical and theoretical model. Both the linguistic instability of Edgar's economic rhetoric and the class bias of *Berkeley the Banker*'s narrative resolution can be read as either unintended textual effect or inevitable theoretical contradiction and slippage. The third and final set of narrative effects that I want to trace seems to fall more decidedly within the latter category of literary repercussions. In these instances, contradictions within political economy itself are exposed by Martineau's contextualization of economic theory within narrative form. Just as Edgar's simultaneous manipulation of sentimental and economic rhetoric can be seen as revealing the linguistic instability of all discursive forms, so other and even more dramatic aspects of Martineau's *Illustrations* function to disclose the gaps, inconsistencies, and contradictions of the supposedly authoritative science.

One of the more didactically damaging instances of this kind of narrative exposure of the fallibility of classical economic theory emerges as an all-too-visible backdrop to *Berkeley the Banker*'s story of economic stability restored, marriages consummated, and justice served (for Edgar is, in the end, executed, thus violently liberating Hester from his tyranny). The Mr. Berkeley of the title is a provident and responsible country banker who is pulled down along with the unprincipled and irresponsible Mr. Cavendish in the currency crash of part 1. In this way, the plot of the novella seems parallel to that of *Weal and Woe,* where all—provident and improvident—suffer the downturn of the economic cycle together. However, there are significant differences between the way the narratives treat the "good" and "bad" characters. First, Mr. Cavendish and his wife actually seem to suffer little for their immoral and felonious financial management. The reader watches the Berkeleys shift quarters from their luxurious mansion to a small garden cottage and watches the two Berkeley daughters depart to become governesses, whereas Mr. Cavendish simply closes the doors of his bank and slips away from his chaotic household when the crash comes. It is not until the end of part 2 that Berkeley pays back all he owes—and even then, that payment is a reflection of the spirit rather than the letter of England's bankruptcy laws, for his creditors accept that he has paid back the "real value" of his debts rather than the face value of the inflated currency he originally borrowed. Cavendish, on the other hand, reemerges as one of the thriving forgers of part 2. Only with the noneconomic intervention of justice in the form of a kind of secret but omniscient police is Cavendish finally, the reader presumes, punished alongside his coconspirator, Edgar. For the first portion of the novella, then, the ill-principled banker, Cavendish, actually seems to fare better than the wholly responsible Berkeley. In part 2, Cavendish is punished, but he seems to meet his fate not through the working out of inevitable economic laws but rather through a kind of special dispensation of narrative providence. Berkeley, while restored to solvency, is never rewarded for his correct economic principles and dealings by a return to his former wealth.

The reason for this unevenness in the narrative's treatment of the two bankers lies in the slipperiness of the very economic principles Martineau wants to illustrate. Throughout the eighteenth and nineteenth centuries, economic theorists debated and attempted to rationalize the principles of money, circulation, and banking. The ostensible message of Martineau's story about these issues is that Ricardian economics and a gold-based currency hold the key to the stabilization of the country's currency system, but this message is repeatedly contradicted by the speeches and plot developments of her novella. After the D— bank crash in part 1, for example, Melea's reflections reveal that she has lived her entire "happy" middle-class childhood in the shadow of her father's financial ruin: "For Horace [her brother] she felt most; for Fanny [her sister] and herself least: for Fanny, because she was another self in her views of life, in capacity for exertion, and preparation for that reverse of fortune with which they *had occasionally been threatened from the days of their childhood*" (emphasis mine, *BB1* 144). Soon after the crash, Mr. Berkeley pessimistically warns his daughter and Henry Craig against marrying at all because marriage simply means incurring economic responsibilities that one will not ultimately be able to fulfill. Similarly, toward the end of part 2, Mr. Berkeley turns to his young nephew, Lewis, and says: "'Poor Lewis must be taken better care of now. . . . We must look about us to see how he is to be settled in life. What shall we do with you, Lewis? *Choose anything but to be in a bank,* my boy. Choose anything else, and we will see what we can do for you'" (emphasis mine, *BB2* 140). Each of these passages professes a different kind of currency law than that purported in Martineau's "Summary of Principles" at the end of the narrative. They tell of inevitable economic instability via the system of credit, currency, and banking on which capitalism depends—an instability that is inevitable *despite* political economy's "correct" currency principles. Martineau's narrative blames the crash of Berkeley's bank and the emergence of bubble banks such as Cavendish's on the government's faulty currency policy, but it makes no such excusing linkage in the case of the inevitability of the future crises it predicts. What results is a significant narrative irresolution at precisely the point where the narrative was intended to provide the reader with saving, solid principles.[14]

Classical economic theory's account of scientific principles of money and banking, when articulated in the form of Martineau's realistic and sentimental narrative conventions, is exposed as fundamentally inadequate. It cannot account for the dramatic cycles of inflation and deflation that plague Britain's currency cycle no matter what currency policy the government adapts, yet Martineau's narrative seems obliged to represent the extremes and the persistence of those cycles. This obligation, in turn, seems to stem both from the representational demands of the emerging social realist narrative tradition and from the sentimental conventions that dictate that the nuances, as well as the broad outlines, of narrative situations must be registered through the affective responses of characters and readers. The result of these narrative imperatives is that one half of Martineau's didactic project—its engaging and accessible narrative form—comes into direct conflict with the second half—the persuasive diffusion of correct economic doctrine to a wide, general readership. Furthermore, the explanatory power of Martineau's economic theory is rendered less than adequate, and what seems to render it inadequate is not simply the individual sympathies of the reader but rather its ability to order "reality."

Berkeley the Banker unintentionally makes visible an important theoretical slippage or failure within scientific political economy. This failure, the inability of mathematical certainty to account for and quantify the irrational, "human" elements of trust and desire at the center of the capitalist system of money or "circulating credit," weakens the authority of the Ricardian economic model as an explanatory and prescriptive social and economic tool. The claims of classical political economy are problematized at an even more fundamental level in Martineau's story *The Hill and the Valley*. In this novella about definitions of capital and labor, Martineau opposes old Mr. Armstrong, a hoarder, with the young capitalist factory owner, Mr. Wallace, in order to argue for the wisdom of transforming wealth into productive capital. In addition to these extreme models of the management of individual wealth, is a third, even more exaggerated character model—the figure of Paul the miser. Through the characterization of Paul, Mr. Wallace is actually opposed to the extremes of both "hoarder" and "miser" as a happy and healthy, if unsuccessful, medium. Where Armstrong refuses to turn any of his wealth into productive capital, choosing instead to keep it safe but unproductive as a bag of gold, and Mr. Wallace represents an almost ideal balance between the relatively unproductive enjoyment of his wealth (especially via his overindulgence of his wife) and its investment in the form of capital, Paul is a character who cannot even enjoy his wealth in the form of the necessities of food and clothing but must rather translate all his earnings into new forms of productive capital.

When he is first introduced, Paul is repeatedly mistaken for a beggar because of his ragged clothes. When he begins to speak, however, his self-assurance and education prove him to be something very different. He asks for and accepts work at Mr. Wallace's mill and predicts that he will be among Wallace's hardest laborers, despite his enigmatic background. The next narrative report of Paul comes through his landlady, who tells Mr. Wallace of Paul's habits. With his earnings from the mill, Paul has started three separate independent businesses. He has learned cobbling, and by four o'clock in the morning he is up doing cobbling work for his neighbors. Then, after a full day of hard labor for Mr. Wallace at the mill, Paul returns to his lodgings to cut out corks for a local druggist by the light of a single weak tallow candle. On the weekend, Paul goes to the fair to trade in cattle and sheep as yet another source of income. Keeping back only enough physical energy, time, and money for the absolute barest of physiological necessity, Paul transforms the entire remainder of his physical and economic capital into new means for producing wealth.

Because of his exclusive dedication to the acquisition and production of wealth, Paul would seem to be the precisely the kind of ideal economic man projected by scientific theories of political economy. He seems to be the model of the figure described in J. S. Mill's essay "On the Definition of Political Economy": "[Political economy] is concerned with [man] solely as a being who desires to possess wealth. . . . It makes entire abstraction of every other human passion or motive" (321). Like Mill's economic man, Paul seems to have no other human passion or motive than the desire for wealth. Because of this, he embodies the highest moral virtues derived from political economy: industriousness, thrift, and self-denial, all combined with, as well as motivated by, an intense, insatiable desire for wealth as an object in and of itself. With such characters as Paul's, Ricardian economic theory predicts, humankind will reach its greatest material productivity and development; with such characters as Paul's, Martineau's illustrated version of Ricardian theory would seem to predict, humankind will attain its highest happiness and virtue as well as material well-being.

In sharp contradiction to such a narrative extrapolation, however, Paul is represented as the saddest and most futile character in *The Hill and the Valley,* precisely because his desire for wealth has obliterated every other "human passion or motive." Paul describes the "misery" of his lot to his friends Armstrong and Wallace: "'Sleepless nights, when I lie cold and hungry and weary, fancying all the mischances that may happen to my earnings: incessant self-reproach when I think I have lost an opportunity of making profit; teazing [sic] thoughts of pounds, shillings, and pence, when I would now and then think of other things;—all these are evils are they not? I cannot listen to a running stream, or sit watching the fieldfares in a clear winter day, or follow the sheep-track amongst the heath on a summer's evening, with the light heart I once had; for I always have the feeling that I am wasting my time, *since these things can bring me no gold*" (emphasis mine, *HV* 82–83). The desire to produce and possess wealth has become so strong in Paul that he has become incapable of enjoying, or even indulging, any other set of needs or desires. Although Paul recognizes the unhappiness and futility of his situation and pursuits, he remains, in his own words, enslaved to his way of life. Paul may closely resemble Mill's scientific definition of economic man, but he certainly doesn't resemble Martineau's prefatory and narrative definition of a happy and healthy "economic" man elsewhere in *Illustrations*. Rather, he is, again in his own words, a "warning." He is one of Martineau's negative exemplars rather than a positive model or ideal such as Mr. Wallace or Ella of Garveloch.

Martineau's narrative even suggests that Paul's example involves a warning about morality and virtue as well as individual happiness and well-being. When the factory owners and their wives pay their visit to Paul's lodgings, Mrs. Sydney asks of Mrs. Jones, with whom Paul lodges, "whether he was a pleasant inmate and a kind neigbour." Mrs. Jones's reply is telling. She says: "So far as he was sober and regular . . . he was a valuable lodger; but he did not often speak or smile at the children; which would . . . have been the best way of gaining her" (*HV* 68). Mrs. Jones readily acknowledges that Paul is an economically valuable lodger, but the emphasis of her assessment lies on his disregard for her children. It is not that Paul is unkind to them; rather, she implies, he simply takes no notice of them, so focused and intent is he upon his projects for making money. Mrs. Jones's response splits precisely along the line of her double identity as landlady (economic) and mother (sentimental). At the same time, her reserve—almost confusion—in responding to Mrs. Sydney's question seems to be a product of a significant area of overlap between these two spheres of identity—an overlap that might be described as the social, the psychological, or even the moral. In Mrs. Sydney's words, Paul's miserliness prevents him from being not only "pleasant" but also "kind."

Because Mrs. Jones's reservations about Paul are represented as primarily maternal, they are implicitly coded as sentimental and thus, by extension, fairly individualized and internal. Paul may not please this mother, but he might still be a basically good man by other, more broadly based standards of morality and virtue (compare the treatment of Allen and his wife, Mary). This possibility seems to be borne out by his noble, self-sacrificing behavior during the workers' rioting and arson, but the closing pages of the novella return the reader to a darker vision of Paul's overly provident character—and this time that vision is explicitly marked as threateningly antisocial as well as sentimentally hard-hearted. Paul reveals to Armstrong and Mr. and Mrs. Wallace that his financial goal is to earn enough money to buy back the paternal estate he lost through his youthful gambling and indulgences. Mr. Wallace questions this goal by asking Paul: "'Do you think you should be able to enjoy your property if you got it back again? . . . Or, perhaps, there is some family connexion to whom you wish to restore it by will?'" Paul's response again reveals that self-knowledge cannot free him from his money-centered plight: "'Neither the one nor the other. . . . I have not a relation in the world; and I see as clearly as you can do, that I shall be by that time too confirmed in my love of money to enjoy the pleasures of a fine estate. I shall screw my tenants, and grudge my venison, and sell all the furniture of the house but that of two rooms'" (*HV* 135). In this statement, Paul makes a direct connection between his love of money (the Millian desire for wealth) and a character that is misanthropically selfish, hard-hearted, and antisocial. His desire for money will contaminate all his social relations and, implicitly, cause him to despise many of his social obligations. Ironically, it is his very love of money, fostered under the guise of his "provident" virtues of industriousness, thrift, and self-denial, that renders Paul such a socially and sentimentally negative character. Insofar as Paul seems to be an ideal representative of scientific political economy's "economic man," then, "economic man" seems to be incapable of also being a moral man, at least according to Martineau's schema of morality. Similarly, as a logical, even natural, production of capitalist economics, the character of Paul proves a very problematic basis for a capitalist society. Even in economic terms, Paul is a problematic character, for his very productiveness depends upon other people indulging the needs and desires he so abstemiously denies himself.

In the end, then, Mr. Wallace seems to be a much more socially and economically viable model of capitalism's and political economy's "economic man." Yet the qualities that make Wallace a more viable economic agent are precisely the sentimentalized, noneconomic qualities that characterize his indulgent relationship with his wife.[15] Just as political economy's conception of money and banking stumbles over the nonquantifiable features of trust and desire in *Berkeley the Banker,* so in *The Hill and the Valley* political economy's basic element—economic man—ends up requiring the noneconomic, nonquantifiable, and nonrational elements of sentiment and passion. In both of these novellas, Martineau's narratives end up unwittingly exposing the logical or "scientific" gaps within political economy's own theoretical system as well as the more sentimental gaps created by the theoretical system's incorporation into fictional representational forms. Furthermore, it is highly significant that in both cases, it seems to have been political economists' determination to render economic theory precise, quantifiable, and calculable that resulted in the system's logical flaws.

The early-nineteenth-century narrative forms that Martineau utilized in *Illustrations* were apparently able to embody certain kinds of "truth" that escaped the scientific calculations of Ricardian economics. In other words, through her fictional narratives, certain important cultural values were effectively represented as naturally or self-evidently true in ways that had the capacity to strengthen the scientific authority of classical economic theory. The central irony of Martineau's popularizing project was that the very conventions that she so effectively mobilized to "humanize" political economy also contained the affective, moral, and even rational logics that could undermine the truth claims of the science. It is impossible to gauge to what extent Martineau's readers registered the unintentional effects of her economic narratives, but those narratives constitute a compelling testimony to the complicated course through which classical political economy attained its powerful political, economic, social, and cultural authority in early- and mid-Victorian England.

One of the novellas, *A Manchester Strike*, begins with the following prefatory claim that seems to encapsulate the theoretical difficulties of Martineau's narrative project: "Notice: The author hopes that as she has no acquaintance with any one firm, master, or workman in Manchester, she will be spared the imputation of personality. Her personages are all abstractions." While it is obvious that Martineau's disclaimer is intended to protect her and her narrative from the imputation of any particular *historical* personality in her story of the strike, her disclaimer also signals the impossibility of any simple success for her fictional popularizing project. Decidedly *not* mathematical or scientific abstractions, the fictional personages and events of Martineau's *Illustrations* cannot be determined solely by the economic logic of political economic theory. Rather, the narrative conventions that she uses to construct those personages and events show themselves to have the power to determine and disrupt the economic ideas they were meant to merely "enliven" or serve.

chapter four

Revaluing Money:
Dombey and Son's Moral Critique

Early in Charles Dickens's novel *Dombey and Son*, little Paul Dombey confronts his father with the question, "What is money?" Mr. Dombey is taken aback by this abrupt interrogation, which interrupts his own musings about the "complicated worldly schemes and plans" he entertains for his small son—who has inherited his name, and who he imagines will also inherit and augment his commercial firm, his wealth, his worldly arrogance—in fact, his social and economic identity. As he looks down at his son, the narrator describes Mr. Dombey as "in a difficulty": "He would have liked to give him some explanation involving the terms circulating-medium, currency, depreciation of currency, paper, bullion, rates of exchange, value of precious metals in the market, and so forth; but looking down at the little chair, and seeing what a long way down it was, he answered: "Gold, and silver, and copper. Guineas, shillings, half-pence. You know what they are?"[1] Little Paul assures his father that he does know what they are but dismisses this simplified answer to his question, as, his next question implies, he would have dismissed the more complicated answer as well. For Paul is interested not in the purely economic character of money—whether that character be construed as "circulating medium" or "guineas, shillings, half-pence"; rather, he wants to know, "What's money *after all?*" or, as he elaborates for his father, "What can it do?" Nor is Paul content when Dombey expands his definition to include the social universe of Victorian capitalist society, saying that "money, Paul, can do anything . . . money cause[s] us to be honoured, feared, respected, courted, and admired, and ma[kes] us powerful and glorious in the eyes of all men" (*DS* 77–78).

Paul counters with sly innocence, making the entire conversation look like a setup: "Why didn't money save me my Mama? . . . It isn't cruel, is it?"(*DS* 78). Here Paul not only shifts the terms away from the economic (and the social defined by capitalist economics) but introduces a whole new set of terms that radically qualifies the original definitions offered by his father.

Paul's final question places money in a moral and psychological universe where the economic value of "guineas, shillings, half-pence" must be measured against an idealized standard of maternal affection. Paul's strategy in this conversation parallels Dickens's strategy in the novel as a whole. In Mr. Dombey and his commercial firm, Dickens creates an image of a totalizing, unqualified system of monetary and economic value and then places that image within a system of moral value and influence idealized and largely represented by Dombey's daughter, Florence.[2]

Dickens uses this strategy to stage his entrance into a set of contemporary debates about the nature of value, in particular about the nature of the monetary form that value takes under capitalism. Dickens's critique of the monetary form of value focuses the larger critical project of the novel—the contestation of the cultural authority of scientific political economy. While not explicitly critiquing any one political economist or school of political economy, Dickens uses his characterizations of Dombey, Carker, and Edith (to name only the most central figures) to mirror what he sees as the social, psychological, and moral distortions wrought by classical political economy's definitions of human nature. Specifically, Dickens's characterizations suggest that the process that political economists claim to be simply a *separation* of the economic is, in fact, a *totalization* of that category; instead of existing alongside moral and ethical considerations, economic concerns replace those considerations. The result, according to Dickens, is Mr. Dombey, Mr. Carker, and the havoc they wreak on themselves and those around them.

Dickens's solution to the crises he associates with political economy is to assert an alternative form of value—the moral value embodied in the character of Florence. The significance and contemporary relevance of Dickens's idealized alternative becomes apparent when we reinsert Dickens's novel into the debate over the nature of value. Between political economists' purely economic definition and Dickens's moral definition of value lies a set of texts that assert the inextricability of moral and economic value. These texts—responses to the 1844 Bank Charter Act—argued that individual moral integrity, rather than precious metals or convertible paper moneys, was the only stable basis for economic value. Dickens's novelistic exploration of the conjunctions between morality and economics can be read as part of a debate about the nature and stability of value that crossed what seem to the twenty-first-century reader to be fundamental generic and discursive boundaries, linking novels to financial legislation and economic argument to moral injunction. Dickens's assertion of the importance of moral values was not an isolated, impotently literary crotchet but part of a public discourse in which generic authority, like economics, was still a contested terrain.

In his book *Sacred Tears,* Fred Kaplan argues that Dickens's invocation of idealized moral value is an appeal to the moral sentiments theorized by eighteenth-century moral philosophers, including Adam Smith. But like Victorian sentimentalism more generally, Kaplan suggests, Dickens's appeal was part of a "late and occasionally shrill stage in a vigorous rear-guard action to defend human nature from further devaluation."[3] In *Dombey and Son,* Dickens specifically identifies the source of this devaluation with economic science and the false values that he saw it fostering in the British social, commercial, and, ultimately, moral worlds. In other works, however, Dickens links his critique of political economy to a broader analysis and criticism of utilitarian philosophy, rational and scientific hubris and narrow-mindedness, and selfishness. In *Oliver Twist,* for example, Dickens criticizes the 1834 Poor Law, with its Malthusian rationale, and parodies the entire administrative apparatus of the Poor Laws through his characterizations of Mr. Bumble, the beadle; Mrs. Bumble; and the workhouse itself. With the novel's first introduction of its eponymous hero as an "item of morality," it targets the scientific, mathematical, and statistical languages associated with utilitarian philosophy and the Malthusian population principle. Dickens goes on to expose the dehumanizing logics that accompany this language, as Oliver's existence is registered by the Poor Law and its administrators only in terms of the economic cost of his maintenance, a perspective that leads both experimental philosophers and Poor Law guardians to starve their "charges" in an attempt to discover the optimum—i.e., least expensive—level of material sustenance for them. Later in the novel Dickens uses the transparently facetious language of Fagin's thieves to indict the political economic language and logics of "enlightened" self-interest in commercial transactions.

While *Dombey and Son* focuses on the moral and psychological harm caused by and effected in the name of rationalist and materialist philosophies, *Oliver Twist* links the moral cost of such philosophies more directly to their social—and cross-class—consequences. The antidote to such dehumanizing discourses and logics in *Oliver Twist* is the simple and incorruptible goodheartedness of Oliver and Rose as well as the benevolence of Rose and Mr. Brownloe. Unlike the novelistic world of *Dombey and Son,* in which virtually all of the "goodness" of the novel is referred back to, and thus depends upon, the figure of Florence Dombey, Dickens's earlier novel distributes the ideals of moral sentiment among several major characters. *Oliver Twist* examines the evils of self-interested rationalism at work in a broader range of sites, but it also suggests a less concentrated analytical lens than is found in *Dombey and Son.*

The most famous of Dickens's attacks on utilitarianism and materialist rationalism occurs in his 1854 novel, *Hard Times.* Like *Oliver Twist, Hard*

Times examines the logic and effects of these philosophies in terms of their broad social effects across the classes. *Hard Times* also opposes the evils of these philosophies with multiple characters who can counteract it, but its world differs significantly from the worlds of *Oliver Twist* and *Dombey and Son* because of the association of all of its "touchstone" characters with the fanciful world of the circus. Sissy Jupe is the most significant of these idealized carriers of moral virtue, but even her feminine sensitivity and selfless generosity are inextricably tied to the influence of her circus upbringing. Likewise, Louisa's moral failures are linked as much to the suppression of her imagination as to the denial of her feminine desire for love (rather than for calculated "advantage") in her married life. What Dickens suggests in *Hard Times*, then, seems to be that the moral virtues of the individual, even idealized feminine virtue, must be fostered by a social community and that that community, in turn, must recognize—if not construct itself upon—the values of fancy and the imagination.

Dombey and Son also associates moral value with the powers of the imagination. The Wooden Midshipman shop, like Sissy's circus, fosters Walter's imagination at the same time that it fosters his capacity for love, loyalty, and compassion. Likewise, little Paul Dombey's life and, even more so, his death are associated with a vivid imagination as well as with his passionate love for his sister. Such linkages make sense because both affect and the imagination are opposed to the quantitative and materialist definitions of values developed by political economy, and because the sentimental philosophy on which Dickens draws identifies affect, especially compassion, as a direct effect of the human capacity for imaginative identification with others. Sympathy, as we saw in Smith's *Theory of Moral Sentiments*, is a product of humanity's imaginative capacity. Significantly, however, Florence Dombey is not herself associated with fancy and the imagination. In fact, Walter's imagination is not an entirely positive force in the novel. Unlike in *Hard Times*, Dickens maintains some space between his ideal of moral value and the imaginative capacities that sentimental philosophy saw as the source of the moral sentiments, possibly because, as various characters in the novel demonstrate, the imagination itself can be perverted by the economic logic of capitalism and political economy. Indeed, the characterizations of Mr. Dombey and Mr. Carker demonstrate the ways in which an individual's imagination can fuel egotistical self-assertion. Whereas in *Hard Times* Dickens treats the imagination as fundamentally antagonistic to the quantification and materialism of utilitarian philosophy, in *Dombey and Son* he seems to recognize a more ambiguous relationship between economic logic and imaginative powers. Instead of linking Florence's moral value to imagination and fancy, Dickens associates that value with maternal love and turns Florence into a static embodiment of the moral worth that can *ground* the wayward imagination and serve as a moral beacon toward which all the other characters in the novel can direct "good" intentions. Structurally, Florence serves the same role in Dickens's novel that the 1844 Bank Charter Act constructed for the nation's gold reserves in the British economy. This structural equivalence leaves open the question of whether the moral logic of the novel can serve as an effective antidote for the instabilities (and immoralities) that beset Britain's economic universe. By examining the journalistic debate surrounding the Bank Act, we can see how Dickens's novelistic critique of economic discourse fits into this national discussion and makes its own claims for a moral solution to problems of monetary and economic instability.

The British economic historian S. G. Checkland writes that "the leading theme of central banking history from 1815 to 1914 was the search for a principle capable of serving as a guide to the control of money and credit."[4] Sir Robert Peel's 1844 Bank Charter Act was designed to embody and enact just such a principle. The central provision of the Act set up a "simple rule" that would legislate note issue through a new definition of "convertibility." As of the 1844 Bank Act, convertibility of Bank of England notes was defined as, and was meant to be insured by, the limitation of note issue to no more than fourteen million pounds in excess of notes covered by gold holdings.[5] This new convertibility calculus was, in Checkland's words, the "crux of the Act"— the focal point for the hopes of the Act's supporters and for the criticisms of the Act's detractors. With the Bank of England's note issue limited to its gold holdings plus fourteen million pounds, its ability to rediscount bills and thus to extend credit was strictly and definitively limited. This limitation was meant to ensure that the nation's credit would never too far exceed its capital base of gold bullion, thereby ensuring bank liquidity and, hopefully, economic stability.

The provisions for convertibility represent the victory of the Currency School over the Banking School in the debate leading up to the 1844 Act because "principle" triumphed over banker "discretion" as the foundation of solid banking practice.[6] By legislating in favor of "principle," the 1844 Bank Act was in line with—was, in fact, an institutional embodiment of—the larger philosophical and ideological trend of scientific political economy. Along with the 1846 repeal of the Corn Laws, the 1844 Bank Act was one of the two most important legislative victories for Ricardian economic theory in the 1840s.[7] The *kind* of currency regulation envisioned by the Act was essential—to allow for the "natural" regulation of the money supply. In other words, the Act attempted to create an *institutional* structure through which *natural* economic law could assert itself.

The definition of "natural," or of natural economic law, depended, in turn, upon a conception of the economy as a distinct entity or sphere of agency, with a specifically delineated "inside" and a just as specifically excluded "outside." Only those things that were inside were seen as natural agents working in harmony with natural law, while anything defined as outside, if it obtruded upon the sphere of the natural, was perceived as disrupting the internal self-regulation of the economic system. This logic of an autonomous, self-regulating economic sphere lay behind the 1844 Bank Act's explicit exclusion of the discretionary agency of bankers. The Act was also intended to curtail another type of extra-economic agency, an agency invoked not by the Act itself but by much of the official discourse surrounding it. For example, when the Act's convertibility principle was suspended owing to the 1847 commercial crisis, the Chancellor of the Exchequer announced the government action in the following words:

> "Gentlemen,—Her Majesty's Government have seen with the deepest regret, the pressure which has existed for some weeks upon the commercial interest of the country, and that this pressure has been *aggravated by a want of that confidence which is necessary for carrying on the ordinary dealings of the trade.*
>
> "They have been in hopes that the check given to the transactions of a speculative character, the transfer of capital from other countries, the influx of bullion, and *the feeling which a knowledge of these circumstances might have been expected to produce,* would have removed the *prevailing distrust.*
>
> "These hopes, however, have been disappointed, and her Majesty's government have come to the conclusion, that the time has arrived when they ought to attempt, by some extraordinary and temporary measure *to restore confidence* in the mercantile and manufacturing community." (emphasis mine)[8]

"Confidence," "feeling," and "distrust"—these are terms that could characterize social or commercial relations. In both contexts they describe psychological states that, even when widespread (as in the "prevailing distrust" of the letter), reside essentially within the individual. Here these terms are invoked in their commercial or economic sense, but they nonetheless retain traces of individual psychology—a psychology whose agency takes the form of affect rather than action, an affect whose essence is unpredictability. Thus, despite all the positive economic circumstances enumerated in the letter, and despite the government's hopes and predictions about the "feeling" that the knowledge of such circumstances would produce, the affective reactions of individual agents seem to have taken a course based on some different calculation. And while the suspension of the Act was another attempt to anticipate and channel such reaction—in fact, its measures were calculated to "restore confidence"—still, this very framing of the suspension's recuperative mission suggests that its advocates were grappling with some factor external to the Bank Act's intended "economic" terrain.

In the context of the Act's suspension, this "confidence" factor is associated with economic crisis: even if the crisis, or "pressure," stems primarily from commercial and financial causes, it is "aggravated by a want of . . . confidence." But though the feeling of "prevailing distrust" cited by the Chancellor of the Exchequer is seen as contributing to and complicating economic problems, feeling itself is enfolded into normal, nonproblematic economic functioning as well. Thus, the confidence that is said to be wanting is precisely "that confidence which is *necessary* for carrying on the *ordinary dealings* of trade" (emphasis mine). Significantly, the awareness of this factor came not only in time of crisis, when the Act's economic principles had to be suspended, but even in the very introduction of the new legislation. In Peel's speech calling on the Parliament to pass the 1844 Act, he claims that its provisions "shall inspire *just confidence* in the medium of exchange [that] shall put a check upon improvident speculation" (emphasis mine).[9] If the primary goal of the Act was to stabilize the medium of exchange through the action of economic law, that primary goal was linked in Peel's speech to a different, secondary goal. The secondary goal involves "just confidence" and "improvident speculation"—terms that inject into the predictable economy elements of individual psychology and morality whose agency complicates such calculations. Though the words "just" and "improvident" invoke a stable scheme of judgment and order, these phrases expose within the economy's predictable order a noneconomic variable whose agency must be either repressed or managed. The Bank Act, to some extent, did both. It repressed individual psychological agency by establishing and putting its own "trust" in a monetary principle that operated solely according to economic law. At the same time it represented an implicit attempt to manage this psychological factor by linking it to the very stability of the currency that the monetary principle was meant to effect.

Critics of the Act attacked on both fronts, at once foregrounding the importance of the "confidence factor" within the economic system and arguing that this factor could not be controlled by the Act's monetary regulations. One of the reasons that critics of the Act saw the psychological aspect of monetary value as inescapable was their belief that the health and vitality of the British economy was inextricably linked to credit.[10] By attacking credit moneys, the Bank Act, according to these writers, attacked the foundation on which all commercial transactions were based—national commercial confidence. In particular, the Act could have the "trickle-down" effect (and this *was* an intended effect)—by limiting the legal tender in circulation—of making all bankers more cautious about granting credit to their commercial customers, and even of making commercial men more cautious about accepting each other's credit. In this scenario, commercial confidence could be equated with "the state of credit" and would be linked, deleteriously, to the Act's gold-based monetary principle.

This effect was highly undesirable in the minds of most men of business, but the Act's critics argued that it also had another effect—one not intended by the Act's framers, and even more detrimental to the strength of the commercial system. This effect was "apprehension," and its danger lay largely in the fact that it operated independently of any principle. For apprehension, rather than being a response to monetary scarcity, was seen as having the power to create such scarcity.[11] The apprehension of shortage leads to hoarding (associated with barbarism), which in turn results in the failure of money to circulate. This "suspension" of circulation has exactly the same disastrous effect as if the Bank withdrew millions of pounds worth of banknotes from circulation: credit is contracted and commerce slows or ceases.

For the Bank Act's critics, then, the role of "confidence," "trust," and "feeling" within the economic sphere was inescapable: as long as business transactions were effected through the medium of credit moneys rather than direct and immediate payments in gold (or legal tender fully convertible to gold), then the commercial system would not be able to ground itself in any self-acting economic rule. That is, once Britain's economy had (necessarily) left behind the sluggish and regressive use of gold as the basis for its commercial transactions, "confidence" had to be included as an important factor in "economic" calculations. According to the writers we have been following, the way to include and stabilize this enigmatic aspect of financial transactions was to redefine commercial man himself. Rather than trying to stabilize the system via natural economic laws, self-regulating principles, etc., they focused their "currency reform" on the individual commercial agent.

In particular, these writers argued for the need to moralize individual commercial men. If the system could not depend solely on economic law, then it should incorporate another system of laws—moral laws that would direct the economic agent and link the variables of confidence and trust to something more stable than individual impulse or market whim. Thomas Charles Banfield begins his *British and Foreign Quarterly Review* article on the Bank Charter Act with the assertion that "the history of trade is the history of money." He goes on to offer this startling definition of "money" and the currency system: "Every man, as far as his credit goes, is his own banker, and keeps his own mint. It would be a much surer method of enriching the country to teach every trader how to cultivate and direct this source of wealth, than to lead him to think that his fate depends upon either miners or bank-directors in town or country. Where the trader is true to himself, there can be no over-issuing even of notes."[12] For Banfield, in other words, money is nothing more than credit, and a man's credit depends on his moral integrity—on his being "true to himself." Precisely what this means in terms of commercial behavior is defined later in the article: "What all parties to bills [of exchange] require to be assured of is that they represent *real transactions*. It is therefore no fraud when one parcel of goods is drawn against twenty times, provided that twenty transfers have taken place between the drawing of the first and of the last bill. If the last be duly paid, every intervening drawer can receive his amount from the other" (emphasis in the original).[13]

As well as providing a definition for individual moral integrity, this passage functions to create an image of a complex commercial community bound together by faith in one another's integrity, and equally dependent on each individual's integrity. If any link in the chain of "twenty transfers" is weak, the chain could be broken and the loss, rather than any profit, transferred to all the remaining links. This would be true no matter what form of money those bills of exchange represented, but by "banking" on individual moral and commercial integrity, the community can build a truly secure basis for its credit, and hence also for its strength and growth. Thus, while the Bank Act functioned to take discretionary agency away from bank administrators, the Act's critics advocated that a similar form of agency be adopted, not simply by bank directors but by all commercial men. The real solution to the problems of monetary instability, in particular, and of economic stability, in general, was neither reliance on impersonal natural laws nor even the earlier reliance on a few selected individuals' discretion but reliance on each individual's own moral accounting.

While these writers rejected the stabilizing oppositions set up within the Bank Act—natural law versus individual judgment, and convertible versus inconvertible notes—their own "moral" solution also relied on a set of stabilizing oppositions. Banfield initially writes that all the trader must do is "be true to himself." This injunction implies a measure of moral self-knowledge—the ability to distinguish the true from the false impulses of the self. But the trader must also be able to distinguish between "real" and "unreal," or fraudulent, commercial transactions. This ability involves more than his own "true" commercial self-representation, for even if he engaged unwittingly in a fraudulent transaction, he would pass that "unreality" on to the next purchaser of the bill, and so forth. Likewise, in order for the merchant not to trade "under false pretenses," he must be able to differentiate between "property really in existence" and "imaginary property"; or, in a slightly different version, he must be able to distinguish "goods in possession [i.e., real goods] . . . at their fair value [i.e., real value]."

In other words, while arguing the need for credit moneys, the Bank Act critics still attempted to maintain an absolute distinction between real and fictitious value. The problem with this stabilizing opposition is that the Victorian capitalist economy actually depended upon a certain amount of slippage between the opposed terms. This slippage was exemplified and "writ large" via the problems of speculative booms, but it inhered even during periods of "normalcy" and "health," when values appeared fixed, stable, and real. "Credit" itself was to some extent a function of the slippage between real and fictitious forms of value, for it involved the imagination or anticipation of future value. Thus, even if the individual commercial agent were to be "true to himself" in terms of his moral impulses, he would still be confronted with an impossible injunction: the criterion of his moral integrity—his ability to maintain the false distinction between real and fictitious values—would constantly shift its ground. On such terms, moral failure was inevitable, and any economic stability supposedly based on moral integrity was impossible.[14] Thus, because of the progressive demands of the system he was meant to support, the best-intentioned moral individual, as conceived by the Bank Act critics, became no more eligible as a base for the economic system than were the gold reserves mandated by the 1844 Act.

The Bank Act critics began by arguing that the economy was not an autonomous system regulated solely by natural economic law. They were especially critical of the Act's attempt to base the entire monetary and commercial system on gold as a "natural" embodiment and store for real commodity value. "Value," they said, depended on confidence and opinion, and thus the economic sphere had an individual and psychological element that could be stabilized only by individual moral reform. Yet these writers, even while perceiving the limitations of solutions based on the conception of a closed system, ended up re-creating just such a system. At the center of their definition of moral integrity—the factor that was supposed to stand outside and ground the economic system—lay what was in effect an economic criterion: the distinction between real and fictitious value. The category of the moral, rather than linking the economic to a different and more stable order of agency and value, was itself absorbed into the sphere of the economic. The result was that the moral ended up simply reenacting at another level the contradictions and instabilities inherent in the capitalist economic system.

Dombey and Son, like the writings of the Bank Act critics, attempts to ground economic value in an ideally more stable moral value, but Dickens's attempt differs from those of the Bank Act critics in two crucial ways. First, there is much more at stake in Dickens's vision of a moralized system of value: the consequence of moral failure is not simply economic crisis but psychic collapse and social dysfunction. Second, Dickens's novel specifically locates the basis of moral value outside the economic sphere—gendering it female and placing it in the domestic sphere. By locating the moral basis of the novel outside the masculine economic sphere, Dickens attempts to avoid the kind of destabilization that undermines the moralized economy of the Bank Act critics. At the same time, because he sees purely economic definitions of value as having negative consequences in the psychological, moral, and social spheres, as well as the economic, there is a lot more riding on success or failure than merely commercial or financial crisis.

Dickens's solution to the problem of economic value depends on the oppositional logic through which, in Victorian capitalist society, gender difference could be used to stabilize individual subjectivity—specifically, the subjectivity of the male commercial agent. In *Dombey and Son*, Dombey's daughter, Florence, is both a symbol and an agent of moral value. Through her feminine character and idealized moral image, Dombey is rescued, Toots is ennobled, and Walter is rewarded and marked as "hero." But Dickens's novel also reveals the insufficiency of the gendered opposition as solution—its failure to fully realize the stabilization of masculine identity it was meant to effect. Even as her image works to bring about one set of resolutions, Florence's feminine difference is absorbed into the threatening logic of competition, sameness, and violence that she was supposed to counteract. In other words, Florence herself, rather than being an alternative to capitalist economics, is to some extent absorbed into the logic of that system.

In response, the novel turns toward another set of stabilizing differences—the cultural differences articulated in imperialism. By sending Walter to the West Indies (and later, with Florence beside him, to China), Dickens's narrative turns to the solution of colonization and racial difference that was becoming increasingly available to and significant for Victorian capitalist society. When this set of differences, too, is revealed as internal to the logic of capitalism, it contaminates the very moral ideality it was intended to shore up and exposes the fundamental failure of Dickens's moralizing project. Dickens's idealized, feminized moral value, that is, is revealed to be just as implicated in economic categories as was Banfield's image of the moral, commercial agent.

The primary contest in the novel is the tension between the moral and economic spheres of agency externalized as conflict between Mr. Dombey and his daughter. Dickens presents that conflict as the result of Mr. Dombey's inability to perceive any form of value other than monetary. The narrator describes the words "Dombey and Son," the name of the family firm, as "the one idea of Mr. Dombey's life," then goes on to elaborate: "The earth was made for Dombey and Son to trade in, and the sun and moon were made to give them light. Rivers and seas were formed to float their ships; rainbows gave them promise of fair weather; winds blew for or against their enterprises; stars and planets circled in their orbits, to preserve inviolate a system of which they were the center" (*DS* 2). The firm is described as having the same significance for Mr. Dombey as critics argued the economic sphere had for political economists. The terms of the passage are a similar, though inflated, version of political economy's assertion of the centrality of wealth in the definition of (economic) man. As "the *one idea* of Mr. Dombey's life" the firm is also the organizing lens through which he perceives the world. When he turns from his newborn son and heir (and son *as* heir) to his young daughter, Dombey sees her only as part of the one unhappiness his marriage has suffered during its first ten years—the unhappiness of having had, "until this present day . . . , no issue": "To speak of; none worth mentioning. There had been a girl some six years before. . . . In the capital of the House's name and dignity, such a child was merely a piece of base coin that couldn't be invested—a bad Boy— nothing more" (*DS* 2). A girl simply does not signify within Dombey's firm-centered family: she is not worth mentioning. Dombey's own economic metaphor toward the end of the passage suggests a different manifestation of this feminine insignificance. No issue worth mentioning becomes "a piece of base coin." "Base coin" acts as a hinge because a base coin, while having no intrinsic value of its own, can actually have a negative effect on "true value" by circulating in the stead of "real" coin. "No value" thus becomes "negative value," just as the "girl" becomes "a bad Boy." Thus, the girl who Dombey thinks is not even worth mentioning, and definitely not worth including in his calculations, becomes through this metaphor a thing that can disrupt the stability and balance of the "inviolate" system.

Dombey's metaphor of the base coin functions to prefigure the disruptive role that Florence will have within the system of value that denies her significance. In the final scene of the first chapter, Florence begins to act out this role when, as her father watches nervously, her mother reaches out to her, and her alone, for a last, dying embrace. Even though Dombey recognizes in this "closing scene" some value and meaning in which he has no part, it does not prompt him to alter his own calculations of value. Rather, Florence's role in it leads him to place her in the role of threatening scapegoat—the role she plays for Dombey through almost the entire course of the narrative.[15] Dombey remains the primary voice and agent opposed to Florence, but his view is contradicted by that of the narrator and a series of major and minor characters who make it clear that the implicit conflict between Dombey and Florence is one of incompatible systems of value rather than simply personalities or interests. The most dramatic and overt articulation of this conflict is Susan's confrontation with Dombey: "'Miss Floy,' said Susan Nipper, 'is the most devoted and most patient and most dutiful and beautiful of daughters, there an't no gentleman, no Sir, though as great and rich as all the greatest and richest of England put together, but might be proud of her and would and ought. *If he knew her value right, he'd rather lose his greatness and fortune piece by piece* and beg his way in rags from door to door, I say to some and all, he would . . . *than bring the sorrow on her tender heart* that I have seen it suffer in this house!'" (emphasis mine, *DS* 514). Florence's value is of such a high order, Susan insists, that it outweighs "all the greatest and richest of England put together." It outweighs this greatness and richness so far that the total economic debasement of beggary would be better than the moral and emotional debasement represented by "bring[ing] sorrow on her tender heart."

Florence's alternative form of value is defined not only in opposition to Dombey and his money but also through a series of pairings and oppositions with the novel's other female characters. Florence is aligned most notably with Harriet Carker, the gentle and self-sacrificing homemaker for her brother, Mr. Carker, Jr. Harriet is first introduced in a chapter that favorably contrasts the plain simplicity of her small home with the empty, false, and costly surfaces of Mr. Carker the Manager's home. Though poor and poorly situated, Harriet's home is "inhabited" by her "redeeming spirit": that spiritual presence is the true carrier and signifier of value within a household. Harriet herself is characterized in terms of depths rather than surface: she is described as having a "retiring beauty that must be sought out, for it cannot vaunt itself." In fact, her beauty actually depends upon its essence of hidden depth, for the narrator goes on to explain that if her beauty were to vaunt itself, "it would be what it is, no more" (*DS* 398–99). Such beauty cannot exchange itself for the commodified beauty of attractive surfaces without losing or destroying the very essence of its value.

Harriet's value stands in stark contrast not only to that of Carker the Manager but also to that of Edith and Alice, who sell their beauty or have their beauty sold. Yet both of these female characters, even in their degradation, are conscious that their "true" value was destroyed through these commercial transactions. Their identities are divided between the contradictory values of surface and depths, a situation that marks them out for the distinctive novelistic role of banishment and salvation. They are banished from the novel (through death or expatriation) because they have been indelibly tainted by the stain of prostitution—the translation of their feminine value into a commodity available for monetary exchange—yet both are finally saved, even in their banishment, because they recognize and bow their heads before the true, uncontaminated value of hidden depths—from which they themselves are alienated—embodied in Harriet and Florence, their "redeemers."

The characters who are not saved, and who are actually more like Carker the Manager (who is also not saved) than either Alice or Edith, are the mothers of these two women. The reason that they cannot be saved is that, unlike their daughters, they do not recognize that they are lost. They are creatures of pure surface who recognize no other value than that of money—of that which can be bought with money and that which can be sold for money, including most infamously their daughters' external beauty. Their sale of their daughters makes "Cleopatra" and "Good Mrs. Brown"[16] into dark, feminized parodies of the same capitalist system of values represented by the more powerful and dangerous characters of Mr. Carker the Manager and Mr. Dombey. Their willingness to exchange their daughters for money only demonstrates more radically than other commercial transactions the inherent logic of the system—its destruction of true values via the transmutation of all objects, entities, and qualities into the false, exchangeable surfaces that are for Dickens the counterpart to money's abstract and quantifiable form of value.

The destruction of moral value through exchange is not, however, the only danger that Dickens locates in the capitalist, commercial system of value represented by Dombey and Carker. The monetary standard of value also has a series of social and psychological effects whose threat is more mediated, but of equal concern. One of these problems appears in Dombey's reaction to the difference between his own and Florence's ability to evoke affection and regard, especially from little Paul. Dombey's reaction is not just a general hostility; rather, it is the particular hostility generated by frustrated competition. These terms are set up even before Dombey is aware of Florence as a potential rival. When Paul is still an infant, Dombey accepts the weak Miss Tox as a godmother because he perceives in her character and subordinate social position no possibility of her "stepping in between" him and his son. Because Dombey's firm-centered system of value recognizes no other form of value than a monetary one, his desire for devotion from Paul, and later from Edith, takes the form of a desire for a limited commodity. Because for Dombey all human relations are modeled along the lines of economic relations, he imagines even "emotional" relations as subject to the commercial logic of competition for wealth. This misreading of emotional relations produces two related effects. Most obviously, it collapses all forms of value into monetary value. This collapse results in competition because it renders all desire a desire for the same, for the abstract form of value represented by money, and once everyone desires the same kind of value, competition inevitably results.[17] Thus, because of Dombey's inability to recognize the difference of Florence's feminine value and influence, she becomes for him not a domestic complement to his commercial success but rather a competitor who threatens to close him out of his chosen markets.

In fact, Dombey views as a competitor anyone who expresses an interest in or evokes a response from the object of his jealous desire. So, when Dombey, soon after Paul's death, encounters Mr. Toodle wearing a slight token of mourning, he greets him with the anger of a rival claimant and later reflects: "So! From high to low, at home or abroad, from Florence in his great house to the coarse churl who was feeding the fire then smoking before them, every one *set up some claim or other to a share in his dead boy, and was a bidder against him!*" (emphasis mine, *DS* 235). Florence is most frequently and fully the figure who has "step[ped] in between" Dombey and his son; both her position within his household and the nature of her character—the very things that should make her the perfect "angel in the house"—lead to her occupation of the primary role in Paul's affection, and thus to Dombey's identifying her as the main "bidder against him."

Florence takes on her role as Dombey's scapegoat through Dombey's identifying her as his main rival, and through his sense that only such competition prevents him from obtaining sole possession of or control over the objects of his desire. This scapegoating works in effect to organize and expose the effects of competition within the novel. One result of Dombey's competition with Florence (for even if she is not, in fact, competing with him, he competes with her) is his growing sense that she is his nemesis; this notion produces a state of ever-increasing anxiety. Even near the beginning of the novel, soon after Florence's bonding embrace with her dying mother, Dombey has the sense that "she watched and distrusted him. As if she held the clue to something secret in his breast. . . . As if she had an innate knowledge of one jarring and discordant string within him, and her very breath could sound it" (*DS* 25). But with the frustration of his desire to dominate the regard first of Paul and then of Edith, this vague, creeping sense develops into full-blown paranoia: "Who? Who was it who could win his wife as she had won his boy! Who was it who had shown him that new victory, as he sat in the dark corner! . . . Who could it be, but the same child at whom he had often glanced uneasily in her motherless infancy, with a kind of dread, lest he might come to hate her; and of whom his foreboding was fulfilled, for he *did* hate her in his heart. . . . She had crossed him every way and everywhere. She was leagued against him now" (*DS* 470). The narrator traces the psychological effects of Dombey's competition with the daughter who could and should have been, as Dombey himself once briefly glimpses, "the spirit of his home" (*DS* 423). But such internal effects are not the only result of this competition, as scapegoating itself implies. Dombey's paranoia results not merely in a kind of self-induced misery and anxiety; it also results in the hostility toward Florence noted earlier. This hostility, in turn, leads to violence—at first primarily the emotional violence of constant rejection and neglect, but in the end even the physical violence of a forceful blow.

When Dombey strikes Florence, he murders "that fond idea [of her father] to which she had held in spite of him" and, by forcing Florence to flee from him, he also destroys the last redeeming vestige of "home" within his grand house (*DS* 557). Dombey's violent act, in effect, has destroyed all boundaries between the domestic sphere and the marketplace. Of course, this boundary is not one Dombey has ever recognized—that is precisely the problem, and the source of his competitive scapegoating. But with the full, physical manifestation of competition's latent violence, which is the effect of Dombey's firm-centered worldview, the separate space of a moralized domestic sphere cannot be maintained. At least, it cannot be maintained within Dombey's own household; instead Florence flees, and goes to inhabit the upper regions of the decidedly noncommercial Wooden Midshipman shop.

Dombey's violent attack on Florence suggests that there are extreme manifestations of commercial logic that even Dickens's feminine spirit cannot withstand or redeem. At the same time, the attack functions within the novel to expose the violence inherent within that logic itself. Just as Dombey's purchase of Edith works to reveal the otherwise naturalized tendencies of capitalist commodification, so his violence against Florence makes visible the inevitable effects of "normal" capitalist competition. The desire for the same limited commodity (usually money, or "wealth") that political economy defines as natural and on which capitalism depends must inevitably lead to competition; that competition, the novel suggests, is not the healthy, self-adjusting mechanism portrayed by economic theorists. Rather, as the Evangelical moralist George Fisk also pointed out, competitiveness leads to "mutual aggression . . . keen, cutting, and restless competition . . . between commercial men."[18]

The final effect of Dombey's paranoid reading of Florence as rival is his utter failure to perceive his true rival—the character who actually is "leagued against him," competitively scheming to acquire Dombey's wife and as much of his wealth as possible. It is Carker the Manager, not Florence, who desires the same thing as Dombey, and who is thus engaged with him in a relationship of "mutual aggression." Dombey cannot see this relationship both because of his obsession with his daughter and because he views Carker only as a subordinate tool. The difference that separates Dombey from Carker is the only difference that the former can perceive, since it falls within the hierarchical order of the firm and, more broadly, the social and economic hierarchies of the capitalist system. This difference is naturalized for Dombey, who thinks that because he is the head of the firm, his relationship to Carker is as fixed and immovable as the relationship of the sun to one of its orbiting planets. Dombey does not perceive that this economic difference is a specious masking of what is actually the same—until it is too late and Carker has escaped with his wife and much of the wealth of the firm. Once Carker has unmasked his hostility and his desires through these actions, all the suppressed violence of the two men's competitive relationship emerges. Through his elopement with Edith, Carker acts out the secret hate he had earlier imputed to all other employees of the firm: "'There is not a man employed here . . . who wouldn't be glad at heart to see his master humbled: who does not hate him, secretly: who does not wish him evil . . . and who would not turn upon him, if he had the power and boldness. The nearer to his favour, the nearer to his insolence; the closer to him, the farther from him. . . . There's not one among them, but if he had at once the power . . . would scatter Dombey's pride and lay it low, as ruthlessly as I rake out these ashes'" (*DS* 536–37). This verbal rampage is obviously a reference to Carker's own feelings, pointing to himself both in his emphasis on those "nearer to his [Dombey's] favour" and in his image of himself raking out the ashes, as it were, of Dombey's pride. The construction "the closer to him, the farther from him" also links the hateful virulence of these feelings to a closeness of competition. Though Carker repeatedly refers to Dombey's pride and insolence as a justification for these (his own) emotions, these attitudes of Dombey's are constructed as the inevitable or "natural" product of his commercial success, combined with his money-centered system of values. Carker's intense hatred can be seen as the inevitable product of his close and longtime competition with Dombey—a violent excess (and instability) generated by the system itself.

The means Carker chooses to scatter Dombey's pride, as well as to rob him of Edith (the symbol for both of them of masculine social power), is to strip him of his commercial enterprise. For this end, overt robbery is not necessary; all Carker needs to do is expand the firm's enterprises, embarking on "prodigious ventures resulting in enormous losses" (*DS* 627). Through this means he is able both to "speculate to advantage for himself" and to "undermine the stability and credit of the Firm" (*DS* 627). All this Mr. Morphin explains to Harriet, Mr. Carker's rejected sister, ostensibly to exonerate him from the onus of having (like his older brother, John) "taken money" from the firm. This exoneration actually functions more forcefully to indite Carker, Dombey, and ultimately the whole capitalist commercial system for the sins of speculation. For if the effects of Carker's speculations and ventures are the same as the effects of overt theft, then the difference maintained by Mr. Morphin is only a legal distinction set up for the support of the system itself.

The ultimate consequences of these speculative enterprises are expressed most significantly in the novel in terms of the impact on Dombey's character of the firm's collapse into bankruptcy. For Dickens's narrative is not concerned only with the various "guilts" of the capitalist system of values—violence, hatred, robbery, hubris. These guilts, while ultimately self-destructive, register their most immediate and emphatic effects on the social or commercial community at large. The narrative is also interested in exploring the fundamental "internal" effects—specifically the effects on male subjectivity—of constructing identity wholly around the desire for and acquisition of wealth. Dombey's paranoia in relation to his daughter is one such effect, one that is explored as a kind of ongoing and progressive destabilizing of the masculine subject in relation to the narrator's version of reality. Dombey's paranoiac scapegoating functions to protect his own view of himself and his world from the signs of its mistakenness that increasingly impinge upon it. The novel's most dramatic representations of the internal liabilities of wealth-based masculine subjectivity come when crucial aspects of this worldview can no longer be protected; in particular, when narrative events confront the subject with the realization that the very basis of his identity is illusory. This confrontation happens to Dombey in the face of his bankruptcy. But it happens first to Carker when he discovers that he has been deceived by Edith—when the deceiver realizes that he himself has been deceived.

Just as Dombey's implicit belief in the hierarchical difference between himself and Carker prevents him from seeing the sameness of their desire, so Carker's perception of himself as "deeper" than Dombey prevents him from realizing the fundamental sameness not just of their desire but of their very identities. Even though Carker does recognize that Edith and wealth are shared objects of desire for himself and Dombey, that recognition of likeness is concomitant with a belief in the differences established by competition—specifically, for Carker, a belief that by "winning" Edith he can establish his superiority to his opponent. What happens when Edith, after having already "betrayed" and abandoned Dombey, betrays and abandons Carker as well is that Carker is placed in exactly the same position as the man to whom he had thought himself superior. They are both, it turns out, tools and dupes, each of whom Edith has used to wreak her revenge on the other. This shared position, more than the shared desire that is its counterpart, has the power to expose the two characters' common identity because it destroys the structure of competition that depends on and manages that desire.

This revelation of Carker's shared identity with Dombey leads to the former's hysterical reaction. In effect, Edith's abandonment confronts him with the artificiality of the grounds of his individual identity, of the boundary between himself and the other, in this case Dombey. Carker's hysteria reveals the contradiction that is suppressed in the normal functioning of the Victorian commercial man—that his identity depends as much on being able to differentiate himself from others as it does upon his being exactly like others. He must be exactly like others, of course, because it is that similarity that makes the system operate, but he must perceive himself as different enough to participate in and to support the competitive hierarchies of the capitalist commercial and social systems—he must believe in the difference of "the top" to want to raise himself to it. It is competition that quite literally makes the individual man, giving him an identity apparently different from that of all other men. Yet for critics of the system such as Dickens, this system appeared to be an inadequate foundation for masculine identity, since the differences it relied on were merely versions of the same: the "differences" of competition were artificial, based solely on the abstract, artificial counters of money or wealth. For Dickens, moral rather than monetary distinctions were "real" and therefore provided a stable basis for identity. Thus Carker, in denying any moral hierarchy of values, has left himself vulnerable to a radical collapse of identity.

Once Edith has exposed the artificiality of the boundaries he has used to differentiate himself from his competitor, Carker finds it impossible to draw any protective barrier around himself. He can neither think nor act because there is no stable "inside" from which to reflect upon his past or to plan his future; his existence becomes an extended present of flight from thoughts and threats over which he has no control. Even though he realizes that such flight is "cowardice," he cannot stop himself: "He could have laid hands upon himself for his cowardice, but it was the very shadow of his defeat, and could not be separated from it. To have his confidence in his own knavery so shattered at a blow . . . was like being paralyzed. With an impotent ferocity he raged at Edith, and hated Mr. Dombey and hated himself, but still he fled, and could do nothing else" (*DS* 646). It is as if, by fleeing from Dombey, Carker could distance himself from the realization—and therefore from the consequences—of their common identity. But he would not need to flee if those consequences had not already overtaken and "mastered" him. Because Carker's panic precedes and determines his flight, a simple fear of Dombey's vengeance is not its sole cause. If it were, he would probably attempt to lose himself amid the crowds of France or Italy; instead, he returns directly to the familiarity of England. He is afraid, the narrator says, "of being hunted in a strange remote place, where the laws might not protect him." In fact, "the sense that it *was* strange and remote" seems in itself a threat to Carker at this point. In England he feels that "at least [he] shall not be alone, without a soul to speak to . . . or stand by [him]" (*DS* 644). The boundary between England and France becomes important here as a replacement for the boundary between self and other. Since the integrity of Carker's individual identity has been destroyed, he seeks to shore up and protect his shattered subjectivity with the boundary between the domestic and the foreign—Carker registers the foreignness of France as a threat only when the boundaries that distinguish his own subjectivity have been exposed as radically inadequate.

The journey away from the strange remoteness of foreign lands and back to the familiarity of domestic England, however, cannot reverse the movement of Carker's collapse. The journey is transformed by his collapse into a "vision, in which nothing was quite real but his own torment" (*DS* 647). The attempt to reinforce the boundary between the inside and the outside of the self with the boundary between England and France is undermined by the collapse of another boundary—the boundary between what is real and what is illusion, between what has a real existence in the external world and what is only the internal product of a tormented mind. In this visionary journey, "long roads," "morning, noon, and sunset," and "a host of beggars" all take on the unreality of phantoms. At the same time, Carker is beset by "some visionary horror" that is "quite removed from this [real terror] of being pursued" (*DS* 643). When this terror first comes upon him while he is still in France, the narrator describes it thus: "Some visionary horror, unintelligible and inexplicable, associated with a trembling of the ground,—a rush and sweep of something through the air, like Death upon the wing. He shrunk, as if to let the thing go by. It was not gone, *it had never been there,* yet what a startling horror it had left behind" (emphasis in original, *DS* 644). When Carker arrives at a depot in England, the boundary between inside and outside, reality and fancy, becomes even more confused, for what was in France a "visionary horror [that] had never been there" becomes in England a "fiery Devil" with "two red eyes," no less horrifying than that vision, but also "now, indeed, no fancy" (*DS* 651). The train is "no fancy," but it takes the shape of what had earlier been "only" a fancy. Its massive reality is absorbed into the logic of Carker's psychic collapse. First it rumbles by him as if to demonstrate the failure of his flight from foreignness, the nearness of Dombey's pursuit, and the utter collapse of his ability to maintain any boundary between "what was quite real [and] his own torment." Then, in the brief moment during which Carker meets the eyes of Dombey—"the man from whom he had fled," who is "emerging from the door by which he himself had entered there"—the train rushes upon him. The train acts out the critical moment of absolute recognition, and in that moment of recognition, Mr. Carker is "beaten down, caught up, and whirled away." All that is left after this moment of vision are the "mutilated fragments" of what was once Carker the Manager; in the face of "the other" that is "the same," what was once "Mr. Carker" flies apart, leaving behind only the mutilated fragments of his masculine subjectivity.

The form of Carker's ultimate demise also suggests the form of Dombey's crisis—the problem of self-fragmentation or self-division. When the male subject can no longer maintain the boundaries between inside and outside, neither can he maintain any integrity within himself. For Dombey, the collapse of boundaries is figured by the permeability that befalls his house after his bankruptcy. In preparation for the auction, "Jew and Christian" penetrate to all corners of the house—"There is not a secret place anywhere" (*DS* 696). In the face of this penetrating onslaught, Dombey retreats to his study, venturing out only when he is sure he will encounter no one. Yet while no embodied assailant penetrates that sanctuary, its walls are inadequate to shore up the identity shattered by loss of fortune and of fortune-based status. Within the confines of his sanctuary, Dombey's self-division emerges and develops into suicidal proportions.

Psychologically, Dombey's self-division takes the form of self-recrimination, a split between his past actions and identity and his present awareness of "that which he might have made so different in all the Past . . . that which he could so easily have wrought into a blessing, and had set himself so steadily for years to form into a curse" (*DS* 701–2). The lost potential blessing, of course, is Florence. The loss of his fortune makes Dombey realize what the losses of Edith and Florence could not—the emptiness of monetary value and the fragility of an identity grounded on that value. This awareness is not itself regenerative. Rather, it leaves Dombey with two incomplete selves that he cannot bring together to form a whole. His present realization is impotent to retrieve his past actions, and thus to re-create his identity around Florence's newfound value, but that realization, like his financial bankruptcy, has also created an unbridgeable chasm between his past identity and his present consciousness. The novel symbolizes this psychic split as a dehumanizing disjunction between Dombey's person and his mirrored image, the "spectral, haggard, wasted likeness of himself" that broods over the empty fireplace (*DS* 704). For several paragraphs after introducing this spectral likeness, the narrator describes only it, rather than Dombey himself. Supposedly, Dombey is sitting in his chair observing "this picture," but when the likeness actually rises and walks about, passes into the next room, and thinks about the details of its suicide, there is a sense that Dombey himself is the haggard specter. No longer a man, even a shattered man, Dombey has been reduced to the status of a nonhuman "it."

This sense of the identity of Dombey's "likeness" is confirmed when, at the very moment of its intended suicide, the specter is suddenly arrested by the appearance of Florence, and just as suddenly, the narrator changes his pronouns from "it" and "its" back to "him" and "his": "It sat down, with its eyes upon the empty fireplace, and as it lost itself in thought there shone into the room a gleam of light; a ray of sun. It was quite unmindful, and sat thinking. Suddenly *it* rose, with a terrible face, and that guilty hand grasping what was in *its* breast. Then *it* was arrested by a cry—a wild, loud, piercing, loving, rapturous cry—and *he* saw *his own* reflection in the glass, and at *his* knees, *his* daughter" (emphasis mine, *DS* 705). This transformation marks Dombey's salvation—his rescue from suicide, his return to humanity, and his incorporation within the moral community of the novel. Florence's reappearance functions for him, it seems, to turn back time, to rewrite the one aspect of his past that really matters. More essentially, Florence's rescuing return marks the transformative and recuperative power of her own moral value. In fact, it is the unchanging essence of that value, an essence repeatedly associated with her character, that allows the apparent turning back of time. "Unchanged still," the narrator exclaims, in sympathetic identification with Dombey. "Of all the world, unchanged. Raising the same face to his, as on that miserable night. Asking *his* forgiveness!" (emphasis in original, *DS* 705). Thus, while Carker is condemned to death by the narrative, acting out the most extreme logic of a competition-based male subjectivity, Dombey is retrieved from the brink of such extremity, thereby demonstrating the regenerative powers of Florence's unchanging depths.

There is a problem with this almost magical reconstitution of Dombey's male subjectivity that is suggested by the passage quoted here. Though Florence raises "the same face" to Dombey as on "that miserable night" in which his competitive paranoia burst forth into violence, she is at the same time asking his forgiveness, insisting that she knows her duty better now than when she fled, and pleading with him that she can change. She is, it seems, denying the violence that led her to flee her father; this denial necessitates an alternative explanation for her "abandonment" of him, an explanation that she finds in insistence on her own guilt and failure of duty. In order for Florence to play the role of the unchanging ideal for Dombey, it seems that she must absorb his violence and guilt into herself. And even though the narrative suggests, as does Dombey, that he rather than she needs to be forgiven, it nonetheless participates in her erasure of Dombey's violent act. "That miserable night" is as close as the narrator or any of the characters ever comes to mentioning it, and after that oblique mention the blow is never even indirectly referred to again. The narrative, in other words, seems to need to deny that violence in order to see Florence as a true savior. Her insistence on her own guilt is the only remaining trace of Dombey's violent blow: she becomes a martyr not to real physical violence but to the self-obliterating tendency that Dickens associates with feminine worth.

The narrative's denial of the competitive violence it earlier unleashed suggests that there is something inassimilable about that moment. One reason it is inassimilable, it seems, is that Dombey's blow embodies a threat to Florence as the human incarnation of Dickens's moral ideal. Whether as a real physical threat or as a symbolic spiritual (or ideological) threat, Dombey's violence is something Florence can meet only with flight. It is, finally, his bankruptcy rather than her beneficent influence that leads to his repentance; her role as spiritual savior begins only after all violence (except self-violence) has been crushed out of him. The failure of Florence truly to resolve the problem of competitive violence is also suggested by the "new" Dombey's complete retreat from the world of the capitalist marketplace. Rather than return, regenerated, to practice a new kind of moral commerce, Dombey remains within the bosom of the family for the rest of the novel. The moral and commercial, then, at least in terms of Dombey's personal narrative, seem to remain antagonistic, even mutually exclusive, polar opposites, with a suspicion lingering that the latter force in certain situations remains more powerful than the former.

One reason for this anxiety lies in the possibility that the antagonism between the moral and economic forms of value may result not so much from the essential difference between those forms but rather from Dickens's failure to define his moral form of value as different *enough*—his failure to imagine a moral frame that is structurally different from the monetary form of value. This anxiety about the potency and difference of moral value is focused on the figure who embodies that value, the idealized character of Florence. It becomes most apparent in regard to the question of desire, and the possibility of a similarity between the desire for wealth and the desire for Florence. If desire for Florence, as the ideal embodiment of moral value, is the same as the desire for wealth, then that desire would lead just as inevitably to a competition between the same, though now between those who desire *her*, rather than those who desire the abstract social value embodied by money. Yet such competition seems to be absent from Dickens's narrative. It emerges only to be mocked in Mr. Toots's self-dramatizing jealousy of Walter Gay, and the potential violence even of this parodic competition is siphoned off from these two central male characters and located instead in the marginal figure of the Game Chicken. Because of this displacement, even the parodic version of male competition and violence can be easily banished simply by banishing the Game Chicken.

There is a more sinister aspect to the relationship between the Game Chicken and Mr. Toots. The displacement of male competition into a marginal character, one who can be excluded from the narrative without apparent loss, suggests that humor and parody themselves are not strong enough tools to distance the threat that the narrative appears so lightly to entertain. Instead, the narrative can be seen as adopting the same kind of scapegoating gesture so fatal to Mr. Dombey's clear vision. Nor, finally, is the narrative simply displacing its anxieties about intraclass male rivalry onto an otherwise neutral figure of its own creation; rather, it is implicitly resolving those anxieties by scapegoating a character who represents a different and lower class. The Game Chicken's competitiveness and violence are represented as products of his difference—his ignorance, crudeness, and generally low horizons—rather than of his gendered sameness.

The Game Chicken, then, can be read as a trace of the narrative's anxiety about the version of desire it has constructed—specifically about whether it is truly an alternative to the mutually destructive desire of competitive capitalism. Perhaps the most powerful sign of this anxiety is the absence of any direct competition between those who desire Florence rather than its presence. If we look specifically at the organization of such desiring characters within the novel, we find a pattern of intense but carefully staggered relationships. First, of course, there is Florence's relationship with Paul. Though she does love her father and care for Walter at the same time as she devotes herself to Paul, both of the former are distanced—Dombey by his own willful blindness and Walter by social and geographical space. Thus, Paul receives Florence's virtually undivided attention and reciprocal desire. When Paul and Walter meet, they are friendly and brotherly, with no signs of competition. In fact, Paul's desires for the future—to live in the country with Florence, implicitly to have Florence all to himself—are in direct conflict with Walter's equally preemptive desire to win Florence as a wife, but these mutually exclusive desires for Florence-filled futures never come into conflict. It is obvious that one reason Paul must die is to avoid growing into the adult identity his father imagines for him, but it is almost equally apparent that his death is necessary to allow the fulfillment of Walter's desires without raising the specter of competition and violence.

Walter does not win Florence immediately after Paul's death. Instead, there is a period in which Florence's desire is focused mainly on her father, followed by a brief interlude in which she is torn between an unrequited love for her father and the requited affection for his new wife, Edith. This is an interlude of conflict among all three characters, but the source of that conflict is Dombey's misplaced competition *with* Florence, rather than *for* her, as well as Florence's own misplaced loyalty to her father, which results in her internal conflict of affections. The latter conflict is resolved for Florence when both Dombey and Edith become for her mental ideas or shadows, allowing her to reconcile her conflicting loyalties in the protected space of her own mind. During this time, Walter is even further distanced, for soon after Florence returns from Brighton to London, he is removed from London to the oriental seas. This distance is important because though Florence's primary love objects are "only" mental figments, they must still be protected from any competitive threat based in the real. This necessity is apparent retrospectively because it is only after Edith's betrayal of her marriage has destroyed her shadow reality, and after Dombey's violence has banished the very idea of him from Florence's mind, that Walter can return from abroad to claim his bride. Without the competing image of her father (or her brother) to deter her, Florence can now give her "woman's heart" to Walter Gay.

As if in a gloss on this story, the narrator comments that "the confidence and love of children may be given many times, and will spring up in many places; but the woman's heart of Florence, with its undivided treasure, can be yielded only once, and under slight or change, can only droop and die" (*DS* 674–75). More critically, one might paraphrase this statement by saying that Florence has been married and sexualized, Dickens needs to restabilize her character by fixing her loyalties wholly to one relationship; the transference of her loyalties at this point would be disastrous. The staggering or serializing of desires that foreclosed competitive conflict earlier in the novel can no longer be used as a solution once Florence is spiritually and legally wed. So when Dombey's object of desire is suddenly transformed from money to Florence, the narrative is again confronted with the threat of male competition. Of course, one could argue simply that there is no threat: Dombey is father and Walter is husband; these are two different kinds of desire, and Florence can accommodate and satisfy both. The way the narrative unfolds, however, suggests that this is not the case, and, in fact, by its attempts to manage this potentially dangerous triangulation, the narrative actually confirms the presence of a latent anxiety.

The narrative negotiates this situation in two ways. First, from the moment Florence appears to reclaim her distraught father, Walter is discussed as her husband but does not appear physically in that role. He appears in the final chapters only once, basically to give his spousal approval for Florence's visit to Edith. There is no occasion for competitive conflict between him and his father-in-law, for the two never meet as such. Second, and even more significantly, we discover in the final scene of the novel that the narrative provides a *second* Florence, a child with no presworn allegiances. Rather than running the double risk—the risk to her integrity and the risk of their competition—of dividing Florence's affections between two male characters, the narrative generates a second Florence who can be (and is) claimed as Dombey's sole province: "But no one, except Florence, knows the measure of the white-haired gentleman's affection for the girl. That story never goes about. The child herself almost wonders at *a certain secrecy he keeps in it. He hoards her to his heart.* . . . He is fondest of her, and most loving to her, when there is no creature by" (emphasis mine, *DS* 734). With this closing metaphor, the narrative comes close to acknowledging its own failure to produce a true alternative to the system of monetary value it has set out to critique. The novel may have created in Florence a different kind of desire, one focused on mothers and morality rather than money, but this alternative desire cannot avoid duplicating the structure of the original desire. Moral value, at least its feminine embodiment, is too much like monetary value. The problems of competition, violence, and psychic instability remain, although within the fictional world of the novel they can largely be managed.

Dickens does offer an alternative, or at least an attendant, solution to the problems inherent in a social system centered around monetary value. Although she is the ideal of moral value in the novel, Florence is not its only carrier. In the character and career of Walter Gay, Dickens also explores a vision of how a moralized male character can survive, or even thrive, within the sphere of commercial and monetary values. Here is a character raised to cherish the romance of the sea rather than the business of the City, who pledges and gives unwavering allegiance to Florence from the first moments of their meeting. On his initial entrance into the commercial sphere, he takes up an inferior position within Dombey's firm. There he seems stuck, in terms of commercial success, unable to raise or distinguish himself, and with his moral and romantic character continually alienating the firm's "Head." At the same time, the narrative reiterates the risk to his character of even this minor position within the merchant's den. Carker, Jr., sees in Walter an image of himself long ago—an image of the self that ruined its commercial prospects and, more importantly, tainted its moral future through the act of theft from the firm. He watches Walter with anxiety for signs that he is tending in the same disastrous direction, and the narrator seems to watch as well. But the sense of the narrative seems to be less a concern that Walter will steal from the firm to become like Carker, Jr., than that he will capitulate to its values to become like Carker the Manager. The repeated invocations of Carker, Jr., as dark double for Walter suggest the even darker double of the morally depraved brother, the double of the double.

As long as Walter remains within the London firm, this foreboding continues, creating an atmosphere of moral hazard around Walter's commercial role. His banishment to the West Indies dissipates this atmosphere and, soon afterward, puts in its stead the more manly and morally beneficial hazards of seafaring adventure and risk. Dickens's strategy for managing the violence and aggression of competition, in other words, is imperial expansion, albeit a specific and highly romanticized version. By sending Walter Gay off to the West Indies, and later to China, the narrative adopts a solution generated and embraced on a much broader scale by Victorian culture as a whole. Economically, empire and imperialism were solutions to the problem of commercial competition because they generated a whole new set of markets for consumption, beyond the supposedly overcrowded markets of Britain and Europe. This commercial expansion into a colonial or "other" space outside Britain effected a displacement of the ideological problem of competition at home. For although imperial expansion still depended for its success on competition, one was in competition with another group of people rather than another commercial Englishman. Hence, imperialism could be described as and made to look like something other than competition, with its attendant train of violence and aggression; it could be understood instead as the natural superiority of the Englishman. When British commercial men took over the markets of colonial peoples and places, they were seen as bringing civilization and prosperity to those peoples as well as to themselves. Thus, rather than the mutual destruction wrought by competition at home, "competition" with peoples abroad brought mutual benefit.

Although Dickens adopts the general framework of the imperialist solution for Walter Gay, he modifies it in significant ways. This modification appears necessary because of Dickens's consciousness of a form of violence implicit in the structure of imperialism, despite the veil of natural superiority. It is the violence of domination, an oppression of the weak by the strong in the name of any form of hierarchical superiority. Apparently the inverse of competition between the same, this form of violence is in fact simply another manifestation of the aggression generated by that competition: the exploitation of colonial others presumes their possession of or access to certain values that can be translated into the abstract value of money or capital—values that may therefore profitably be appropriated by imperialist venture. Susan Nipper explicitly associates this form of violence with Walter's imperialist voyage as she bemoans his departure: "'Goodness knows,' exclaimed Miss Nipper, 'there's many we could spare instead, if numbers is a object, Mrs. Pipchin as a overseer would come cheap at her weight in gold, and if a knowledge of black slavery should be required, them Blimbers is the very people for the sitiwation'" (*DS* 220). Whether in the form of the selfish and spiteful domination of a Mrs. Pipchin or of the more benevolent but equally misguided and destructive domination of "them Blimbers," Susan perceives that oppression and oppressors are the essential demands of such commercial ventures as that upon which Walter is to be launched.

It may be for this reason that Walter is never allowed to reach his first destination. Instead, his ship is wrecked, and he is thrown into a very different kind of adventure. His story of the wreck and his survival is a story of a manly and heroic struggle against the odds and the elements. Rather than through oppression of the dark, colonial other or violent competition with his "own kind" in England, Walter Gay is allowed to gain his manhood and his (small) fortune through communal struggle *with* other Englishmen against the violence of nature—facing the risk neither of moral contamination nor of financial loss but rather of the loss of life itself. Of course, after Walter (alone) has survived this risk and adventure, he goes on to join in another imperialist commercial enterprise, and there he actually begins to establish his commercial identity as well as a small savings of capital. But this portion of his adventure is not related or followed within Dickens's narrative. It remains "offstage," thus allowing Walter to profit from his commercial encounters with the empire without confronting the implications of those encounters for his character.

Finally, even the minimal difference of unrepresented imperial adventure fails to stabilize the oppositional structure of capital logic. For though Walter's imperialist experiences are never directly represented within the text, empire itself seems to pervade Dickens's novel, its traces reemerging repeatedly within the descriptions and symbolism of English characters, situations, and institutions. A severe case of "the return of the repressed," these repeated interpolations of imperialist images take the form of that which the novel must deny in order to embrace the solution of empire. This solution includes not only the violence of imperial domination and oppression but also the despotism and idolatry that supposedly characterize the "inferior" colonial peoples but that in Dickens's novel are aspects of English capitalist society as well. In the case of each of these characteristics—violence, despotism, and idolatry—the metaphorical vehicle though which it is invoked is an oriental or imperial image, while the image's tenor is an Englishman (or -woman), or English society more generally. Because of this metaphorical structure, the "inferior" cultures of the colonial empire seem to be contaminating "superior" English culture, eroding and undermining the very superiority on which its imperial self-justifications depend.

Usually these contaminating images are associated with those aspects of British culture and society that the narrative openly critiques. Thus, for example, Perch's sycophantic deference to Dombey is described in terms of idolatry and oriental despotism, and Carker is described as "Grand Vizier" to Dombey's "Sultan." Once incorporated into the text, however, these metaphors set up a pattern of imagery that threatens the very essence of Dickens's moral solution as well as challenging the supremacy of British commercial culture. To understand how this threat unfolds, we must return to Florence. I have repeatedly referred to Florence as a moral ideal. She functions this way not only within the large ideological structure of the novel, as a static symbol and embodiment of the moral value Dickens opposes to capitalist commercial and monetary values, but also as an agent and marker of the progress of that positive value within the plot. When Dombey finally embraces "true value," it is in the form of Florence, and Walter is rewarded for avoiding the pitfalls of commercial competition by marriage with Florence. For both men, their relationships with Florence promise the end of their masculine self-division and instability by providing them with a stable moral value on which to base their identities and an object of desire that is outside the circuit of commercial competition. I have already described how Dombey is saved from a dehumanizing and suicidal self-division by the reappearance of a Florence who is "unchanged still. Of all the world unchanged." In addition, it is clear that part of Florence's power to effect this regenerative transformation is the absolute stability—even stasis—of her character. She becomes quite literally the only fixed point on which Dombey can base his identity, the only constant that can allow for the carrying of the shattered subjectivity of the past into the new, whole subjectivity of the future.

The fixity of Florence's character is elaborated most fully in terms of Walter's relationship to her. Earlier in the novel, long before he has finally "won" Florence, Walter explicitly locates the source of his moral strength in Florence herself—even the *image* of Florence. Torn by conflicting fantasies and desires about the still young Florence, expressed in the form of contradictory narratives about her future development, Walter comes to the realization that "to reason with himself about Florence at all, was to become very unreasonable indeed; and that he could do no better than preserve her image in his mind as something precious, unattainable, unchangeable, and indefinite—indefinite in all but its power of giving him pleasure, and restraining him like an angel's hand from anything unworthy" (*DS* 183). This passage suggests that as Walter's moral ideal, Florence's role is necessarily less that of a character with her own narrative and development than that of a sacred image. Like that of a sacred image, Florence's function depends on her unchanging representation of certain values, a certain irreducible distance (here marked as unattainability), and a vagueness or lack of any distinct characteristics but those of her symbolic raison d'être. Thus, in many ways—and almost entirely at certain points in the novel—Florence's character becomes virtually iconic in its static, moral ideality. For example, when a somewhat older and more mature Florence appears to bid Walter good-bye before his sea voyage, the touch of her hand calms and inspires rather than excites him: "Its touch [did not] awaken those old day-dreams of his boyhood that had floated past him sometimes even lately, and confused him with their indistinct and broken shapes." Rather, seeing "the purity and innocence of her endearing manner" and remembering her recent attendance on her brother's deathbed, he pledges himself "in the solemn presence he had seen there . . . to cherish and protect her very image, in his banishment, with brotherly regard; to garner up her simple faith, inviolate; and hold himself degraded if he breathed upon it any thought that was not in her own breast when she gave it to him" (*DS* 221–22). Here Florence's "simple faith" functions in exactly the same way as her "sacred image" did in the earlier passage, and in the earlier part of this same passage. In fact, the antecedent of "it" in the last two clauses is somewhat indefinite, so "it" could refer to "her very image" as well as "her simple faith." Thus, the same aspect of her character that signifies her moral depths, her simple but unwavering faith, also works to create the effect of a spiritualized surface, an iconic image or symbol of "true value."

I have examined these passages in such detail because I want to illustrate the centrality of Florence's iconic ideality to Dickens's attempt to construct her as an alternative to, and thus also a solution for, the problem of capitalism's and political economy's totalizing system of monetary value, including the resulting instability of Victorian male subjectivity. These passages suggest that in the process of creating a character who embodies the pure depths of moral and spiritual value, Dickens has also inadvertently created a form of idolatry. Florence's role as ideal representative, regardless of the content she represents, effectively structures her as a creature of pure surface, as frozen, static image. Rather than being the opposite of a character of false surfaces such as Cleopatra, Florence's character ends up sharing with such figures many of the qualities she was meant to oppose. This sharing implicates her not only in the imagery of implicitly false surfaces and false values associated with characters such as Cleopatra, Carker the Manager, and Dombey himself but also in the idolatry associated with the "inferior" civilizations overtaken and dominated by British commercial imperialism. Such idolatry is precisely the worship of surface images and the assignment to those images of magic powers over the fates and fortunes of the humble earthly beings who worship them. The novel never confronts, or even acknowledges, this inherent threat to its moral solution; in fact, by emphasizing Florence's image as "sacred" and "angelic," it implicitly invokes the domesticating framework of Christianity to contain and naturalize Florence's iconic effects. Nevertheless, once the network of oriental and imperial imagery has emerged within the novel, Florence's character cannot be immunized against its contaminating signification. Florence may represent moral value, but she represents it in a form that undermines that value's claim to difference—its difference from the English alternative of monetary value and, even worse, from the colonial alternative of savage idolatry.

Ironically, the reappearance of savage, colonial otherness within Dickens's privileged carrier of moral value parallels the Bank Act critics' attack of the Act's convertibility principle. Though the Bank Act critics failed to generate a viable alternative to the Act's convertibility calculus, they did effectively expose the regressive and, in their words, "barbaric" logic behind its return to the gold standard. Gold-based currency, they argued, would mislead bankers and commercial agents into thinking that gold, rather than credit (or commodities), was the true carrier of economic value. This situation would result in hoarding and put an end to the progressive economic development that separated England from its colonized counterparts—counterparts, they argued, whose "barbaric hoards" England had easily "won" through its expansive, imperial enterprises. By attempting to fix moral value onto the static figure of Florence, Dickens ends up reduplicating the regressive gesture of the Bank Act's gold standard, thus even further belying his claims for the difference of his feminine moral value.

The blurring of both of these differences leads directly back to the linked problems of sameness, competition, and violence that Dickens's moral critique identifies but cannot fully escape. The emergence of the structure of idolatry within Dickens's own moral vision chips away at the natural superiority that could justify imperial expansion—that could construct imperialism as a real alternative to the competitive violence of capitalist England. The inherent violence of Walter Gay's colonial ventures may remain offstage with the colonies themselves, but the contaminating effects of such ventures reemerge within the very image that was supposed to symbolize Walter's successful escape from the competitive threat. Through the erosion of cultural difference marked by this contamination, imperialist violence is granted a structural presence as simply another form of capitalist competitive violence that the novel's narrative silences attempt to deny. Thus, Dickens's moral solution to the problems of the monetary form of value is doubly compromised. It is Dickens's narrative strategy, rather than Florence's moral value, that manages and "resolves" the threat of competitive male desire within the novel. Yet the texture of the narrative itself exposes that management as inadequate, suggesting evasion rather than resolution and eroding the moral basis for the attendant vision of empire as escape.

chapter five

The Economics of Working-Class Masculinity in Mayhew's Letters to the *Morning Chronicle*

In a letter to the editor of the *Morning Chronicle* in February 1850, Henry Mayhew wrote of his investigative project into the London laboring poor: "I made up my mind to deal with human nature as a natural philosopher or a chemist deals with any material object; and, as a man who had devoted some little of his time to physical and metaphysical science, I must say I did most heartily rejoice that it should have been left to me to apply the laws of the inductive philosophy for the first time, I believe, to the abstract questions of political economy."[1] While Mayhew's claim to originality in applying the "laws of the inductive philosophy" to the "abstract questions of political economy" is disingenuous given the long history of debate upon the issue of what method was best suited to the new science, his statement of his aspiration exposes an extremely important and often unremarked aspect of his work: his self-conscious engagement with classical economic theory. Furthermore, his opposition between the implicitly concrete aspects of an inductive investigation and the abstract "laws" of a deductively formulated science point to one of the central tensions of his work—the tension between particulars and generalities, between the recording of concrete details and the derivation of abstract truth statements from those details, and between the proximity of immediate, direct engagement with his investigative subjects and the mediated distance of a scientist analyzing his data.

The cultural historians Anne Humphreys and Regenia Gagnier see this tension as a fundamental structure of Mayhew's work on the London laboring classes.[2] The tension operates at two different levels. First, there is the tension between the specific abstract claims made by classical political economy and the "data" that Mayhew produced through his investigations. As both Humphreys and Gagnier explain, the further Mayhew pursued his "inductive" research into the relationship between "labor" and "poverty" in London, the more he became convinced of the inadequacy of the dominant classical formulations of the "laws" that regulated wages, labor, and price. Mayhew's solution to this problem—one that he pursues increasingly in the letters and, later, in the wrappers to his *London Labour* series—is to develop his own alternative theory of wages and labor. Though Mayhew does make some headway in this endeavor, his success is hampered by a second level of tension between the unmediated recording of details and the mediated derivation of abstract truths. As Humphreys and Gagnier explain, Mayhew's determination to produce an alternative theory of political economy is continually undermined in his written work by his observation of, fascination with, and commitment to recording the material and subjective specificities of his investigative subjects. At the same time, both critics argue that it is precisely his textual engagement with such material and subjective specificities that constitutes Mayhew's most significant achievement—as a social investigator, as a critic of classical political economy, and as a critic of the capitalist social and economic organization theorized and rationalized by classical economic texts.

Whether the value ascribed to this aspect of Mayhew's writing is described as ethnographic, humanistic, or literary, it suggests that simply reading *through* the textual details of Mayhew's work in order to derive the alternative economic theory he sought to produce is not an adequate interpretive strategy. At the same time, since Mayhew did seek to develop such a theory, his gestures in that direction demand attention. Thus, my reading of Mayhew's journalistic project is informed by the same tension between concrete and abstract, particular and general, that structures Mayhew's work. In this chapter, I examine Mayhew's letters to the *Morning Chronicle* both for their explicit critique of classical economic theory and for his more indirect assertions about the evils of a socioeconomic order organized according to classical economic theory. By developing a "literary" reading of his journalistic text, I show that one of the most subtle and effective of Mayhew's discursive strategies is to link the situation of the laboring classes to a series of middle-class anxieties about working-class morality, prostitution, and masculinity.

Henry Mayhew's letters to the *Morning Chronicle* (1849–50), while less well known than his four-volume *London Labour and the London Poor*, served as both the basis and inspiration for the larger study, with some of the letters incorporated into *London Labour* virtually word for word. Despite this overlap, the focus of the two works is very different.[3] While Mayhew's observations about urban street sellers and costermongers fill most of the pages of the later study, Mayhew's focus in the *Morning Chronicle* letters is fixed steadily on the working poor of London's more traditional laboring trades. Assigned to be the "metropolitan correspondent" for a series of articles examining labor and poverty in the period immediately following the cholera epidemic, Mayhew moved steadily through the course of the series toward seeing the two terms—"labor" and "poverty"—as inextricable and often mutually constitutive. In examining the conjunction of these terms, Mayhew's letters staged his intervention into the cultural debate over the authority and terms of economic discourse. Though Mayhew did continue to pursue the object of an alternative political economy in *London Labour and the London Poor* (1861–62), his work there is, with the exception of the opening section of volume 4, much less directly engaged with the problems and language of classical political economy.[4] In the later text, rather than focusing on the working poor as a class, Mayhew's fascination with the myriad varieties of London street sellers leads him to develop a generic model that tends to erase the very category of class, as Regenia Gagnier has shown.[5] This erasure, of course, constitutes its own critique of the discourse of political economy, but that is a critique that has been ably elaborated by Humphreys and Gagnier.[6] Furthermore, in shifting his focus away from the poor as a laboring *class,* Mayhew also shifts his attention away from the specific anxieties about domesticity and female labor that pervade his *Morning Chronicle* letters and form a crucial part of their critique.

The significance of this critique should, at least in part, be measured by the responses it produced. E. P. Thompson notes that Mayhew's letters raised an outcry from political economists, philanthropists, and free-traders alike, even while it was, at its peak, highly popular with the general reading public.[7] Mayhew's increasingly outspoken critique of free trade ultimately led to a dispute over censorship with the paper's editor and toward an abrupt termination of the series. In 1851, after leaving the *Morning Chronicle,* Mayhew continued to publish his investigations through a series of pamphlets titled *London Labour,* the wrappers of which became a vehicle for his regular replies to the letters of his smaller, increasingly working-class reading audience. On those wrappers, in the "Answers to Correspondents," Mayhew began to draw more conventionally formulated economic conclusions from his investigations.[8] Mayhew also began, in November 1851, to publish in parts a longer study called *Low Wages, Their Causes, Consequences and Remedies.* This longer study provides a much more coherent formulation of Mayhew's investigative "findings" and a much more sustained and extended address to contemporary political economists than the *Morning Chronicle* letters. It is, in effect, more "conclusive" than the letters. There is, however, a very different kind of conclusiveness about Mayhew's letters than that offered by the more "scientific" prose of *Low Wages.* Rather than a closure that involves the summary of a problem and suggestion of a solution, the conclusiveness of the letters is implicit in the subtler, narrative patterns of repetition, echoing, subtexts, and metaphor that make up a complex web of signification. The championing of trade societies that emerges within the letters as Mayhew's overt "solution" to the problems his investigations have uncovered is just one part of that web; the web is also connected to the working-class ideology of the family wage and to middle-class anxieties about prostitution among impoverished needlewomen.

By examining the *Morning Chronicle* letters as a discrete text with its own investments and internal economy, in relationship to a complex historical and discursive context, my reading allows me to explore a central concern that has been overlooked in previous readings of Mayhew's investigative work.[9] That concern, and the link that fuses all the patterns mentioned above, is the image of an autonomous working-class masculinity that Mayhew often indicates by the term "artisan," and that looks very much like middle-class Victorian masculinity. On the surface, this image involves a man's ability to support his family in comfort and to provide the family with a solid center of moral integrity and self-development. Underneath that surface, but linked inextricably to it, the image demands a certain independence and psychic integrity that is heavily implicated in the male worker's relation to the material and social world outside the family bounds.[10] Mayhew's "conclusion" involves the specter of the destruction of that autonomy and integrity by the working conditions of the competitive trades; much less explicitly, Mayhew's text asserts the need for domesticated working-class women who, rather than competing with their husbands in the marketplace, will shore up men's masculine identities by remaining dependent and at home.[11]

In his letters Mayhew reveals a multitude of evils suffered by the workers in these urban trades. The focus of his investigations, however, is the role of the competitive capitalist system in creating these evils. Further, Mayhew presents the essential threat posed by competition as the erasure of the differences that distinguish the "honorable" from the "dishonorable" segments of the trades. The main economic distinction between these two segments was that the wages of the former were regulated by custom—at least to a large extent— while the wages of the latter were determined solely by "free-market" competition.[12] Mayhew's concern was not solely with the almost uniformly bad conditions for workers in the dishonorable sections, in contrast to the relatively good conditions of those in the honorable portions of their trade. Rather, his concern crystallized around the erosion of the features that distinguished the honorable portions of the trades, for he saw how both laborers and masters in such trades were forced either to adopt practices used in the dishonorable portions or to lose their work through the competition presented by the dishonorable trades. Mayhew identified this erosion as the central threat to the moral and physical well-being of the urban working classes.

Mayhew's diagnosis of the evils of the metropolitan trades was distinctly different from the accounts of his middle-class predecessors and contemporaries. Classical political economists and those influenced by political economy explained the causes and effects of poverty among the working classes through three different, but interrelated, concepts. Two of these concepts—a natural, subsistence wage rate and supply and demand—are present in Ricardo's opening statement of his theory of wages in his chapter "On Wages." Ricardo writes:

> Labour, like all other things which are purchased and sold, and which may be increased or diminished in quantity, has its natural and its market price. The natural price of labour is that price which is necessary to enable labourers, one with another, to subsist and perpetuate their race, without either increase or diminution.... The market price of labour is the price which is really paid for it, from the natural operation of the proportion of supply to the demand.... However much the market price of labour may deviate from its natural price, it has, like commodities, a tendency to conform to it.[13]

According to this definition, poverty would be a relatively temporary phenomenon during which the market price of labor falls below its subsistence, or natural, price. Such a fall, in turn, is generally attributed to an increase in the population of the laboring class, creating an excess supply in labor. The economic historian Oswald St. Clair succinctly sums up the connection between these two classical economic concepts: "Thus in the view of Ricardo, and also of Malthus, it is in every country *the labourers themselves who determine what their standard of living shall be*" (emphasis mine).[14]

The third Ricardian concept, the wage fund, leaves behind the idea of a natural, subsistence wage altogether. In its place it constructs a theoretical fiction of an absolutely fixed fund of capital out of which wages can be paid during a given period, usually one year. This fixed fund of capital now constitutes the "demand" side of the supply-and-demand equation, once more leaving it in the hands of labor to control its own "supply," and therefore its market price. The concept of the wage fund uses the "natural" balancing of the law of supply and demand, but it was developed to explain shorter-term alterations in the balance than those that could be explained by the Malthusian principle of population.[15] The diagnostic effect of the theory of the wage fund was, however, precisely the same as the Malthusian principle in placing all responsibility for low wages with the laborers themselves. It had the further effect of rendering any demand for higher wages irrational and inevitably ineffective: the wage fund was fixed, so there was no way for masters and capitalists to augment wages, even if they wanted to; only a decrease in the supply of workers could bring an increase in the price of labor.

Competition, the diagnosis offered by Mayhew and many of his working-class interviewees as the cause of poverty wages, was not even a term applied to questions of labor and wages by most political economists. As a term implicit in the law of supply and demand, competition was seen as natural, inevitable, and therefore good. The term became explicit only in relation to "producers." There it was contrasted positively to price-inflating monopolies, and thus discussed as something to be sought in its purest form. Only under the terms of free competition could the market operate properly and naturally, ensuring the consumer the lowest possible prices—which were the "natural" prices—for commodities.[16] In stark contrast, Mayhew's letters, like Dickens's novel *Dombey and Son,* identify competition as the root of the evils they unfold. Also like Dickens, Mayhew presents the essential threat posed by competition as the erasure of differences he considers to be crucially important. Among these foundational differences is that between the honorable and the dishonorable trades. In Mayhew's texts, however, the erasure of difference results not primarily in a moral or psychological crisis for middle-class commercial males but in a broader cultural crisis for the working classes, particularly for the working-class male.

Mayhew's first step in textually constructing the central opposition between honorable and dishonorable trades is to reformulate the culturally dominant distinction between the laborer—including the laboring poor—and the pauper. This distinction had a long history in England but was newly and powerfully inscribed in the New Poor Law of 1834. With the criteria of "less eligibility" and the workhouse test, the New Poor Law used "scientific" principles to widen the moral gap between the economic categories of self-supporting and non-self-supporting members of the lower classes. Implicitly, the self-supporting were considered the respectable and relatively comfortable working classes, while the paupers' inability to support themselves was viewed as moral failure. Pauperism entailed laziness, drunkenness, and thriftlessness and was to be discouraged and implicitly punished by the harsh conditions of the new workhouse.

The New Poor Law's opposition between laborer and pauper, however, obscured the presence of another category—the poor.[17] The poor often labored but were never "comfortable," as the definitions of the New Poor Law implied that they would be. Despite long hours and hard labor, the laboring poor were unable to earn enough money to support themselves— either as individuals or as families. One of Mayhew's central critical strategies in the letters to the *Morning Chronicle* is to focus on the plight of "the laboring poor"; by so doing, he exposes the incompleteness of the categories defined by the New Poor Law. Mayhew begins with the category of poverty and then links it at every point to various relationships to work. As Anne

Humphreys notes, in this regard Mayhew's letters formed a sharp contrast with those of Angus Reach, the provincial correspondent for the *Morning Chronicle,* who kept the categories of labor and poverty separate in his series.[18] Thus, in describing "the task" in his first letter to the *Morning Chronicle,* Mayhew begins with a definition of poverty: "Under the term poor I shall include all those persons whose incomings are insufficient for the satisfaction of their wants—a want being, according to my idea, contra distinguished from a mere desire by a positive physical pain, instead of a mental uneasiness, accompanying it."[19] By basing his distinction on the criterion of "positive physical pain" Mayhew attempts to fix his definition of poverty to something almost objectively observable, while at the same time removing it from moral categories by relating it to something physical, as opposed to mental—"a mere desire."

As Mayhew goes on to develop his definition of poverty, it seems as if he is returning to the implications of the laborer-versus-pauper opposition by using the terms "honest" and "dishonest."[20] But as he elaborates these terms, the relationship of poverty and the laborer to work comes to predominate: "The large and comparatively unknown body of people included in this definition I shall contemplate in two distinct classes, viz., the *honest* and *dishonest* poor; and the first of these I purpose sub-dividing into the *striving* and *disabled*—or in other words, I shall consider the whole of the metropolitan poor under three separate phases, according as they *will* work, they *can't* work, and they *won't* work" (emphasis in original, *UM* 102). The urban poor whom it is Mayhew's task to investigate, then, are defined in terms of their relationship to work. Mayhew's study and interviews of 1849–50 deal almost exclusively with the "honest" poor—those who work and continue to strive for an independent subsistence but are nevertheless unable to obtain sufficient incomes to meet their bodily necessities.

Mayhew, then, focuses his study of the urban working poor on the independent laborer—the artisan—whether that laborer works for an honorable or a dishonorable trade. "Independence" is a crucial term informing Mayhew's investigations, used both by Mayhew himself and by the laborers he interviews. Sonya Rose explains the significance of the term for the Victorian working classes in relation to an early-nineteenth-century artisanal culture that claimed its independence through its "property" in skilled labor. This culture also linked masculine "independence" to the ideals of female domesticity and the male breadwinner.[21] Mayhew's use of the term "independence" seems at once to draw upon its working-class definitions and to play upon the similarities between the emergent gendered ideology of the working class and the bourgeoisie's separate-spheres ideology. Thus, while his entire study is a critique of the capitalist labor system, Mayhew adopts as a norm a model of masculinity that in many important aspects resembles the masculinity of the Victorian middle classes, which profited from that system.[22]

Independence is the key for deciding questions of morality for the working-class male, as it is for the middle-class male. Just as the male pauper is seen as immoral because of his dependence, the male worker who retains his economic independence is seen as implicitly more moral, at least when defined against the pauper. When Mayhew turns toward the opposition between honorable and dishonorable trades, and with that opposition to the question of working-class morality, he carries into his investigation the ideology that privileges masculine independence. The honorable segments of the trades are regularly noted for maintaining the male worker's independence in relation to the process of production and traditional middle-class or artisan-class moral values, while what middle-class writers and working-class speakers themselves identify as immoral behavior or situations is almost without exception found in what Mayhew calls the dishonorable section of any given trade. Thus, in Mayhew's letters, questions of morality—at least among men—are read in terms of the economic system.[23]

The honorable-versus-dishonorable distinction also governs the organization of Mayhew's letters. As he studies each trade, his first move is to break it up into these two factions—not really halves because in every case the number of workers in the dishonorable part of a trade far exceeds that of those in the honorable portion. He begins with the honorable part, as if to set up a standard of decency or normalcy, and then moves on to the dishonorable part, allowing the sharp contrasts between the former and the latter to indict the competitive system. In all his investigations Mayhew explores the laborers' conditions of work and living, but the main force of the interviews emerges when Mayhew focuses specifically on the conditions of a worker's family life. In the honorable trades Mayhew and the workers he interviews repeatedly draw a picture of the family that resembles the Victorian middle-class ideal. The structure of an independent, working husband and a dependent, domestic wife (and children) was advocated by many middle- and working-class writers as the appropriate familial structure for the English working class.[24] For the middle class, this structure was called the "domestic" or "separate-spheres" ideology; for the working class, it was called the ideology of the "family wage." This ideology either erased female labor or marked it as a sign of deviance—deviance either of the individual woman or of the system that forced her to work outside the home. Maintaining a family wage thus becomes for Mayhew, and for many of the laborers he interviews, a marker of membership in the honorable, rather than the dishonorable, segment of a trade. It signified the ability of a worker to support his family while simultaneously constructing women and children (in contrast to working-class men) as dependent, and as "dependents" who needed male support in order to live out their proper and "natural" roles. The economics of this familial organization is, in turn, endowed with an aura of "true" domesticity. For example, in an interview titled "A carpenter working for the best prices," the workman follows an account of his money wages with the claim that "I have always been able to keep my family, [my wife not] having to do anything but the house-work and washing" (*UM* 342). And of cabinetmakers in the honorable trade, Mayhew writes: "The great majority of the cabinet-makers are married men, and were described to me by the best informed parties as generally *domestic* men, living, whenever it was possible, near their workshops, and *going home to every meal.* They are not much of play-goers, a Christmas pantomime or any holiday spectacle being exceptions, *especially where there is family*" (emphasis mine, *UM* 367). In this passage, Mayhew constructs an image of the cabinetmakers as prototypical family men. At the same time, the passage repeatedly places "the family" at home, within the domestic sphere. The worker goes home to every meal, implicitly, because his family is already there. Likewise, the exceptional holiday outing noted in the final sentence creates the normative image of a family at home.

The full power of the family image comes into play in the contrast Mayhew sets up between family conditions in the honorable and dishonorable trades. This juxtaposition is drawn by one of the dishonorable workers as he contrasts the days when his trade had no dishonorable segment to the trade's present condition. Mayhew describes an elderly man with a "heavy careworn look," at work making tea-caddies with the assistance of his wife and daughter. This situation of joint familial labor is thrown into stark relief by the mechanic's account of how the trade had changed over the past forty years:

> I have been upwards of 40 years a fancy cabinet-maker . . . making tea-caddies and everything in that line. When I first worked on my own account I could earn £3 a week. I worked for the [honorable] trade then. . . . There was no slaughter-shops in those days. And the good times continued till about 21 years ago, or not so much, I can't tell exactly, but it was when the slaughter-houses came up. *Before that,* on a Saturday night, I could bring home, after getting my money, *a new dress for my wife* . . . and *something new for the children when they came,* and a *good joint for Sunday.* Such a thing as a mechanic's wife doing needlework *for any but her own family wasn't heard of then.* . . . *There was no slop needlewomen in the wives of my trade.* It's different now. *They must work* some way or other. (emphasis mine, *UM* 383)

For this worker, the degeneration of his trade—as well as his own passage from its honorable to its dishonorable sector—is marked by his loss of the ability to support his wife and children as well as to keep them comfortable (i.e., to provide the new dress, the good joint, etc.). The emergence of a dishonorable sector within the cabinetmaking trade is signaled by his frequent references to slaughterhouses, a type of warehouse business that gave out work to laborers but paid very low wages and produced low-quality goods. Not only is this worker poor financially and in terms of his conditions of life—such as housing and food—he is also poor in terms of his family life: he has been robbed of his ability to support wife and daughter, who, though they do work within the home, are engaged in long hours of waged labor, which his work requires.

This impoverished worker belongs to the same trade—cabinetmaking—that employs the honorable member who testifies to the domesticity of his class. It is not primarily the trade, then, but rather the line between honorable and dishonorable that demarcates the artisan and family man from the beleaguered laborer. The external factor that delineates honorable and dishonorable in the cabinetmaking trade is membership in the trade association, which is mentioned briefly in Mayhew's statement about honorable cabinetmakers as family men. Mayhew discusses the trade association more fully in a section called "The truth about trade unions." Here he deplores the general misinformation about the function of trade societies—particularly the public's sense that they are organized solely to extract "an exorbitant rate of wages" from employers and that they are necessarily involved in strikes. After explaining why these ideas are mistaken, Mayhew offers an alternative picture of the trade society: "The maintenance of the standard rate of wages is not the *sole* object of such societies—the majority of them being organized as much for the support of the sick and aged as for the regulation of the price of labour" (emphasis in original, *UM* 377). Next follow calculations of the number of trade societies in England, Scotland, and Ireland; the numbers of their membership; and the amount they collect and distribute annually in support of their own poor, aged, and disabled. At the end of these calculations Mayhew proclaims that "the working people of this country . . . contribute therefore to the support of their own poor nearly five millions of money every year" (*UM* 377).

After this high praise of the ability of workers' associations in the honorable portions of the trade to support their poor, he turns his attention to the dishonorable trades: "It is the slop-work of the different trades—the cheap men, or non-society hands—who constitute the great mass of paupers in this country. *And here lies the main social distinction between the workmen who belong to society, and those who do not*—the one maintain their own poor, the others are left to the mercy of the parish. The wages of the *competitive men* are *cut down to bare subsistence,* so that, being unable to save anything from their earnings, a few days' incapacity from labour drives them to the workhouse for relief" (emphasis mine, *UM* 378). What Mayhew here claims as the "main social distinction" between workers in the honorable versus the dishonorable trades seems to differ from the distinction made by the workers themselves, for they emphasize their relative abilities to support not their own poor but their own families. Yet Mayhew's criterion for distinguishing the different sections of the trade in this passage so precisely parallels the criterion invoked by the workers—and often by Mayhew himself—that it seems as if he is constructing the trade associations as extensions of the male-supported working-class family. Just as the honorable artisan can maintain his own family independent of the labor of wives and children, the honorable trade society can maintain all its members and all its families (including the families of its widows) when circumstances shift them into the category of dependency. In contrast, workers in the dishonorable portions of the trade fail to sustain not only their families but also themselves. The trade society, then, represents an expanded moral as well as economic family: it not only supports the structure of the worker's immediate family by helping to keep up wages but also provides an infrastructure that can keep its members from falling into the dependent and morally denigrated category of pauper.[25]

Even when workers in the dishonorable trade manage to avoid crossing the line between laborer and pauper, they testify repeatedly not only to their inability to support their families but also to what they see as the perversion of their family relations—the ideal of which was constructed retroactively as "traditional" by proponents of the ideology of the family wage. These workers claim that their "natural affections" for their families are being undermined by the extremity of their poverty. One man says: "I can't say what I thinks about the young uns. Why you loses your nat'ral affection for 'em. The people in general is ashamed to say how they thinks on their children. It's wretched in the extreme to see one's children, and not be able to do to 'em as a parent ought" (*UM* 114). This Spitalfield silk weaver belonged to a working population infamous for the deterioration of its trade in early- and mid-Victorian England. But such sentiments are not expressed solely by those in such notoriously debased trades. A worker in the woodworking trade tells Mayhew that most of his colleagues marry early and have large families because they need their own children's labor to make enough to survive. Because of the importance of their labor, he proclaims, having children becomes more like "breeding slaves" than "raising a family" (*UM* 395).

These references suggest that the beleaguered workers see their own children as a "free" source of labor that allows them to scrape out a bare subsistence and avoid the workhouse. For such workers, the labor of their children at once jeopardizes and protects their independent masculine subjectivities. But other workers see child labor as explicitly and exclusively threatening, for it lowers wages even further. These speakers see child labor as competition—a nonunionized, cheap form of labor that forces grown men to accept children's wages. It is not just "child labor" in general that is seen as a competitive threat but more specifically the labor of a man's *own* children. A tailor says: "By such means the regular tailor is being destroyed; indeed *a man's own children are being brought into competition against himself,* and the price of his labour is being gradually reduced to theirs" (emphasis mine, *UM* 188).[26]

By forcing children—those who would normally be dependents—into competition with their fathers, the capitalist marketplace radically perverts the family on which these male laborers' identities depend. One of the results of such "perversion," as this passage exposes, is the loss of prestige for the male worker within his own family. When he can be driven out of the market by his own children, he loses the ground of his familial authority and his status as an autonomous, independent agent among dependents. According to this logic, the worker who can support his family without the aid of their labor is more of a man than the worker who must rely on his wife and children; the worker who makes the family wage retains more authority within the household than the man who has to rely on the financial contributions of his wife and children.[27] Barbara Taylor writes revealingly of the working-class controversy about whether women should work at wage labor outside of the home: "The wage-earning wife, once seen as the norm in every working-class household, had become a symptom and symbol of masculine degradation: it 'unsexes the man and takes from the woman all womanliness,' as Engels wrote of the Manchester working population in 1844."[28] Taylor's account suggests that for the male worker, having a wage-earning wife could be almost as degrading as being forced into the workhouse and becoming a pauper. In addition, Taylor reveals that, in contrast to the question of child labor, the issue of female waged labor was a point of contestation within the working class itself. While this contestation remains invisible on the surface of Mayhew's text, the anxieties it provoked for both this middle-class writer and his working-class subjects are intertwined with the text's more overt anxieties about competition and working-class masculinity.

The destruction of the male-supported working-class family in the dishonorable trades is the most frequently mentioned moral evil that results from unrestrained competition. It is also the most often-invoked marker of whether a worker belongs to the dishonorable or honorable section of a trade—it constitutes a moral measuring stick against which Mayhew judges not the workers but the conditions of their labor. However, Mayhew's text incorporates another marker that indicates the extreme end of the competitive dishonorable trades. This marker is prostitution: prostitutes are not simply women working but women working by selling their own bodies. While Mayhew's explicit investigation of prostitution is confined to his discussion of needlewomen and female slopworkers, the image he creates permeates his entire text. For Victorians, the prostitute was an image of virtually unrivaled cultural and imaginative power. Lynda Nead writes that "the prostitute stood as the symbol of the dangerous forces which could bring about anarchy and social disintegration" and that "prostitution was a powerful metaphor for the problem of working-class demoralization and radical opposition."[29] Discussed early in his series of letters, Mayhew's needlewoman-turned-prostitute haunts his text and his other speakers' words and carries with her a set of meanings otherwise largely invisible in the interviews.

Even before he presents his study of prostitution among needlewomen, Mayhew offers the comments of a "female operative," a seamstress who concludes a discussion about the state of her trade with the following assertion: "A mother has got two or three daughters, and she don't wish them to go to service, and she puts them to this poor needlework; and that, in my opinion, *is the cause of the destitution and prostitution about the streets* in these parts. So that in a great measure, I think *the slop trade is the ruin of the young girls that take to it*—the prices are not sufficient to keep them—and *the consequence is they fly to the streets* to make their living. Most of the workers are young girls who have nothing else to depend upon, and *there is scarcely one of them virtuous*" (emphasis mine, *UM* 121). This passage links prostitution to physical destitution rather than to moral degradation. The seamstress's assertion blames this destitution on the system of labor—the slop trade—under which these women work. Further, it suggests a connection between prostitution and the destruction of the working-class family by noting that most of these workers have nothing else to depend on—a statement that, since it refers to working-class women, implicitly translates as, "They have no male worker to support them." Finally, the closing statement in its vague all-inclusiveness— "scarcely one of them virtuous"—opens up the image of a pervasive, perhaps even choleric, miasma of immorality threatening not only the laboring classes but the entire city of London.[30]

Prostitution as a contaminating evil was not a new cultural image for Victorians. But a prostitution that was linked to physical want rather than immoral sexual desire, in the same way that poverty was linked to want rather than desire in Mayhew's opening statement, was not a common configuration in mid-nineteenth-century England. Other writers often ostensibly set out to explore the "environmental"—as opposed to "moral"—causes of prostitution, such as poverty, but their accounts inevitably ended up collapsing these two categories.[31] In contrast, Mayhew's interviews of needlewomen-turned-prostitutes repeatedly link the women's "fall" to extreme physical want. At the same time, Mayhew allows the women's testimonies to humanize them, even while demonizing prostitution itself. For Mayhew, it is prostitution and the conditions that force needlewomen to it that are inhumane; "prostitution" and the "prostitute" are not identical terms. Indeed, as we shall see in the interviews and testimonies of Mayhew's needlewomen, "prostitution" is itself an extremely broad and flexible category, including everything from living unmarried with a man to solicitation and streetwalking—in short, any female sexuality that manifests itself outside marriage.[32] The broadness of this definition makes Mayhew's collapsing of all these needlewomen's stories into *the* story of prostitution all the more significant: he is, in effect, implicated in creating the category of prostitution even as he excoriates it.

Mayhew creates this category primarily to indict the economic system he sees as having created it. For example, one of Mayhew's interviewees turns out to be the daughter of an independent preacher. Mayhew writes that in his "nearly ten-mile" trek to confirm her story, he hears from two of her former employers (where she had been in service) "in the highest terms of the girl's honesty, sobriety, industry, and *of her virtue in particular*" (emphasis mine, *UM* 149). It is as if by verifying her former "virtue," Mayhew can separate her from the taint of prostitution, even though the power of her story, and of his retelling of it, depends precisely on that taint. Likewise, Mayhew quotes another needlewoman as saying that she "was virtuous when [she] first went to work" and that she "struggled very hard to keep [herself] chaste," (*UM* 148) as if he is trying to purify his spokeswoman so that she can reveal the gap between a moral nature with moral inclinations and a system of competitive labor that forces her into immorality.

The women Mayhew interviews repeatedly emphasize the connection between economic and physical necessity and their acts of prostitution. One of them tells of trying to support her mother and herself, but "found that [she] couldn't get food and clothing for [them], so [she] took to live with a young man" (*UM* 148). She continues: "He could make 14s. a week. He told me if I came to live with him he'd take care I shouldn't want, and both mother and me had been very bad off before. He said, too, he'd make me his lawful wife, but I hardly cared so long as I could get food for myself and my mother" (*UM* 148). Finally, she states, as if testifying in a witness box, "If I was never allowed to speak no more, it was the little money I got by my labour that led me to go wrong. Could I have honestly earnt enough to have subsisted upon . . . I should not have gone astray; no, never—As it is I fought against it as long as I could" (*UM* 148). Whether such statements came at Mayhew's prompting or were spontaneous, they reinforce the opposition between an implicitly moral female nature that characterizes the needlewomen and the immoral system of competitive labor inherent in slop needlework. This opposition is reinforced through sheer repetition during Mayhew's famous meeting with needlewomen who had turned to prostitution.[33] Another of Mayhew's interviewees makes virtually the same statement about herself three times during their interview. She also tells of trying to support her young child as well as herself and includes a vivid scene in which she describes staying out begging all night in the snow, rather than resorting again to prostitution, while her child's legs literally freeze to her body. The title Mayhew assigns this story—"A tragic and touching romance"—suggests a bittersweet rendition of the fallen-woman story.[34] The woman is a mixture of madonna and magdalen in her devotion to her child, her attempts to give up prostitution, and her tortured returns to the streets. Mayhew uses the regret shared by all of the women as a bridge between them and the largely middle-class readers of these interviews.

The regret humanizes, individualizes, and psychologizes the women, as suggested by the fictionalizing title "romance." But a countervailing force is also at work in Mayhew's interviews—the generalizing force of the social scientist or investigator. Earlier in his interviews Mayhew writes: "I can assure the reader I am at no little pains in order to arrive at a fair average estimate of the state of those persons to whom I direct my attention. I seek for no extreme cases. If anything is to come of this hereafter, I am well aware that the end can be gained only by laying bare the sufferings of the *class,* and not of any particular individuals belonging thereto" (emphasis in original, *UM* 127). We can presume that Mayhew intends this statement to apply to slop needlewomen who turn to prostitution as well as to the slopworkers in government-contract clothing or cabinetmaking. The significance of such generalization for Mayhew's treatment of prostitution can be seen in several senses. First, the generalization links working-class prostitution to the disintegration of the family-wage version of the working-class family that Mayhew documents so explicitly in other portions of his texts.[35] Second, it introduces an opposition between the working classes and the middle class.

The first woman Mayhew interviews foregrounds this issue as she compares her situation to that of "gentlefolk." In order to emphasize the extremity of her own situation, she invokes the moral standard and conditions of a "lady": "But no one knows the temptations of us poor girls in want. Gentlefolks can never understand it. If I had been born a lady it wouldn't have been very hard to have acted like one. To be poor and to be honest, especially with young girls, is the hardest struggle of all. There isn't one in a thousand that can get the better of it" (*UM* 149). This statement brings us back to the question of working-class morality more generally, and to the relationship between that morality and prostitution. For middle-class Victorians, prostitution was often considered a sign of the degradation of working-class morality in general: the prostitute was a representation of the class. Through his interviews, Mayhew articulates this connection as well, but he does so in order to make an entirely different point. Prostitution, for Mayhew, represents the extremities to which the working classes are pushed under the system of unrestrained competition and all of its manifestations, such as slopwork, the strapping system, and child labor. By separating the evils of prostitution from the individual needlewomen who succumb to it, Mayhew is able to link those evils directly to the system of labor—a system that threatens not just an isolated group of women but a whole class of workers.

If pauperism is the explicit marker of the far end of the spectrum that runs from honorable through dishonorable labor for both the male and the female labor force, then prostitution functions as an implicit marker of the possibility of falling outside the spectrum completely. Nor does the sign of prostitution mark only the female operative. Part of its threatening symbolic power in Mayhew's text comes from its ability to cast its shadow over his accounts of the male worker as well. Though never explicitly sexualized, male workers repeatedly represent their own or others' degradation by images of prostitution or by images that have strong connotations thereof. One of the most powerful of such images comes from a tailor who writes explicitly of the way the slop trade is eroding the honorable trade: "Amongst all the best and oldest houses in the trade at the West-end they are gradually introducing the making of the cheap paletots, Oxonians, Brighton coats, Chesterfields, &c., &c.; and even the first-rate houses are gradually subsiding into the cheap advertising slop tailors. *If the principle goes on at the rate it has been progressing for the last five years, the journeymen tailors must ultimately be reduced to the position of the lowest of the needlewomen*" (emphasis mine, *UM* 189). "The position of the lowest of the needlewomen" had been described by Mayhew one month before in his *Morning Chronicle* letters—and that was the position of prostitution. Whether or not the tailor is consciously drawing upon that image, prostitution is certainly the image evoked for the reader. What makes this passage even more powerful is that this unspoken image is linked not only to the dishonorable trade but, through the image of a progressive downward movement, to the honorable trade as well. Thus, in the very passage where the crucial distinction between honorable and dishonorable is shown to be eroding, Mayhew offers the prostitute to demarcate what is at stake in that erosion.

The most explicit reference to the male worker as prostitute appears in Mayhew's investigation into what he calls the "kidnapping" system of recruiting hands for sweatwork. Mayhew describes this system as "inducing men by false pretences on the part of the *sweaters,* or more commonly, of *sweater's wives,* to work for them at wretched wages" (emphasis in original, *UM* 223). The fact that these men are usually "inexperienced country and Irish hands" only adds to the similarities between this story and that of the young country girl deceived and led astray by a London procuress.[36] Mayhew goes on to tell the story of two Irish hands who were lured away from their hometown by a London sweater's wife. In London they are forced to work in abysmal conditions for virtually no pay, with none of the training in skilled artisan work they had been promised. After three weeks, the two escape. Mayhew continues: "The sweater traced them to where they had got work again, took with him a policeman, and gave them in charge as runaway apprentices. He could not, however, substantiate the charge at the station-house, and the men were set at liberty. Even after that *the sweater's wife was always hanging about the corners of the streets, trying to persuade these men to go back again. She promised one that she would give him a handsome daughter she had for his wife*" (emphasis mine, *UM* 224). I cite this passage at length because of the multiple levels at which it echoes the conventional eighteenth- and nineteenth-century virgin-seduced-to-prostitute story. The escape, followed by pursuit and an accusation of being runaway apprentices, could, with only the slightest modifications, be the story of the young virgin-turned-prostitute escaping from her madam, only to be caught and accused of robbing the house. The sweater's wife hanging around street corners seems prostitute and procuress at once, especially when she offers to prostitute her own daughter in order to reclaim the young laborer. It is in her role as procuress, however, that she presents the more threatening image, because if the sweater's recruiting wife is imagined as a procuress, then the workers she recruits are inexorably placed in the position of prostitute.

By implicitly turning the adult male worker into a prostitute, the competitive system of sweated labor unmans him in the most fundamental way. He is not simply feminized; he is also thoroughly commodified. This transaction strips the man of his masculine independence because his labor is represented as the selling of himself to another. In other words, the sweated laborer not only produces degraded commodities but becomes a commodity himself; as such he is, implicitly, something to be exchanged between men rather than a man himself. This stripping away of masculinity, like the issues of family and self-support, exists on a spectrum or continuum that follows the spectrum of the conditions under which the laborers work. Between the male worker able fully to support his family and the male worker driven to the doors of—if not into—the workhouse are all the laborers who not only rely on their families for additional support but also, even then, exist in conditions that they consider dehumanizing and implicitly (often explicitly) emasculating. The situation of these laborers is expressed through a series of metaphors—used most often by the men themselves but sometimes by Mayhew—linking them to beasts, slaves (often explicitly black slaves), or machines. The first such metaphor occurs when Mayhew turns from the honorable West End portion of the tailors to the East End slop trade: "The honourable part of the trade are really intelligent artisans, while the slopworkers are generally *almost brutified* with their incessant toil, wretched pay, miserable food, and filthy homes" (emphasis mine, *UM* 196). At another point, cheap contract work draws this comparison from one of the laborers: "We are used for all the world like cab or omnibus horses. Directly they've had all the work out of us we are turned off, and I am sure after my day's work is over, *my feelings must be very much the same as one of the London cab horses*" (emphasis mine, *UM* 348). The power of this passage comes from the fact that the worker not only compares his condition and treatment to that of an animal but also asserts that such conditions produce in him the feelings of an animal. Psychologization in this case works not to humanize the worker but to expose his dehumanization. At the same time, the passage suggests emasculation, as the worker compares himself to an entity that is literally someone else's creature.

In an earlier discussion of the dishonorable woodworking trade, psychology is again used to reveal dehumanization when a worker invokes the metaphor of a machine. Mayhew begins by describing an elaborate system of subcontracting and piecework, then explains that "by this process men gradually become *mere machines,* and *lose all the moral and intellectual characteristics* which distinguish the skilled artisan" (emphasis mine, *UM* 340). Mayhew sets up the artisan as a man who possesses a relatively high level of psychological development, marked here by the terms "moral and intellectual characteristics." Likewise, the pairing of "moral" with "intellectual" suggests a specifically masculine psychology. The stripping away of this psychologized subjectivity emasculates and dehumanizes the workers until they become "mere machines," an image that leaves the workers even lower than the maltreated cab horses because machines have no "feelings" whatsoever, not even those of an animal.[37]

Not surprisingly, the most common metaphor for this process of unmanning is that of slavery. This image makes one of its earliest appearances in a description of how low-waged imported foreign laborers are treated. The dishonorable woodworker cited earlier uses the image in terms of child labor—having children, in his trade, is like "breeding slaves" because they work all day and half the night and get no education and because there is no decent or respectable place for them in the trade when they grow up (*UM* 395). But the metaphor also applies to the adult male English workers and again suggests the loss of a masculine interiority. Within the strapping system of the woodworking trades, for example, the method of constant and minute surveillance of the workmen not only drives the men to work harder than black slaves ("No slave works like we do" [*UM* 347]) but also strips the men of any integrity in relation to their own processes of production.[38] The quality, speed, and detail of production are all assessed by the overseer, so the workmen are forced to be always looking over their shoulders—instead of into themselves—for judgments of their labor.

Even more telling is the testimony of a seaman in the British merchant marine service. He states: "It's a shameful thing to see the way we are treated. *We are not treated like men at all;* and what's more, *there's no dependence to be placed on us now.* If a war was to break out with America there's thousands of us would go over to the other country. *We're worse than black slaves;* they are taken care of, and we are not" (emphasis mine, *UM* 301). Although the most immediate connection between the slavery image and the men in this passage is that of being "taken care of," suggesting dependency, the more powerful connection is the sailor's assertion that because they are not treated like men—that is, they are treated worse than slaves—their loyalty to their country cannot be depended upon. In other words, their treatment is so demeaning and emasculating that they cannot be expected to act with manly integrity in a time of national crisis; they will turn traitors, and the guilt for that turning will lie not with themselves but with the system that has treated them as if they had no manly selves at all. This remark is in sharp contrast to the testimony of a Scotsman in the American merchant marine service who asserts: "An English seaman is very little thought of in his own country, but he's well thought of in America. *He's a man* there" (emphasis mine, *UM* 313). The differences he cites between the two services are not only better wages and better food but also, significantly, more respectful treatment. In other words, he gives almost an exact inversion of the English seaman's testimony, with treatment and manliness as the two issues at stake.

Prostitution takes all these metaphors several steps further. First, because the adult male workman is never explicitly compared to a prostitute, and because prostitution *is* exposed as a reality for a number of adult female workers, it retains the potency of a possibility. Mayhew doesn't need to investigate the possibility of actual sexual prostitution among working-class males; in fact, any such specific exploration would disrupt the economy and power of his implicit prostitution metaphor because it is important to his investigative critique that current capitalist labor practices, rather than any actions on the part of the individual worker, position male workers as prostitutes. The possibility that the adult male worker would actually be reduced to prostitution is suggested only in vague terms. However, because of prostitution's status as metaphoric possibility, allusions to it set up another marker, beyond dependent pauperism, on the three overlapping spectrums of masculinity, humanity, and morality along which, according to Mayhew, the London laborers can fall—or, perhaps more accurately in his account, be pushed.

Second, prostitution signifies not only extreme degradation and the loss of a psychological interior, as do the metaphors of beasts, machines, and slaves, but also the commodification of the essential autonomy of the male laborer and the proffering of it for monetary exchange. In Victorian England, the female prostitute is seen to sell that which makes her a woman—her sexual chastity (which for the Victorians meant specifically sex confined to marriage—with its dependency and power asymmetry).[39] The male worker-as-prostitute sells something much less tangible, and something other than simply his labor, but *in selling it,* he also loses something central to his masculinity. This "something," judging from the passages examined earlier, includes most crucially his independence—an independence retained to some degree even by the pauper. For, while the pauper makes him- or herself dependent upon the apparatuses of the state—a state in which he or she can claim a part, and provisions to which he or she can claim a right—the worker-prostitute sells himself and his independence directly to an individual from whom he is otherwise alienated. He thereby makes himself that person's "creature."

I have already argued that Mayhew locates the cause of this descending scale of degradation in unrestrained competition. For example, immediately after the quotation about slavery in the strapping shops, the speaker continues: "The men are everyone striving one against the other. Each is trying to get through the work quicker than his neighbors. Four or five men are set the same job so that they may be all pitted against one another, and then away they go every one striving his hardest for fear that the others should get finished first" (*UM* 347). The strapping system—where the competition among workmen is so structured and so obvious—is actually an unusual case. More frequently, laborers compete among themselves with no knowledge of each other's existence, wages, or conditions except as vague shadows of themselves and their situations.[40] But it is competition among the masters, most of the workers argue, that sets up and drives competition among the workmen. This assertion is made early in Mayhew's interviews by the Spitalfield silk weavers with whom he begins his investigations. Mayhew describes the views of, then quotes from, one of the weavers: "The reduction, he [the weaver] was convinced, arose from the competition in the trade, and *one master cutting under the other.* 'The workmen are obliged to take the low prices, because they have not the means to hold out, and they know that if they don't take the work others will'" (emphasis mine, *UM* 109). This worker does not deny competition among the workmen, but he links it directly to competition among the masters in the trade. The same issue is raised later in a meeting Mayhew holds for the tailors; he poses the ascertaining of their opinions about whether the destructive competition in their trade originated with the trading or the laboring classes as the most significant purpose of the meeting. Mayhew receives a direct and resounding answer to this question, which he asks in terms of the cause of the depreciation of prices in the trade; the workmen at the meeting respond unanimously—"Men of capital underselling each other" (*UM* 203). The very fact that Mayhew positions the question of "whose competition" so centrally to his project suggests that in his earlier interviews with tailors, as well as silk weavers, the workers identified competition among capitalists as an urgent evil. Indeed, Mayhew seems to be in the process of being converted to this point of view. Among woodworkers, and boot- and shoemakers too, the laborers see competition among the capitalists, the middlemen, and the masters as driving the prices—and thus the wages—in the trade ever lower.

One of the workmen Mayhew interviews, however, a woodworker in sawyering, identifies competition itself—regardless of who competes—as the most powerful and also the most destructive force in the trades. The sawyer makes this point in terms of the machinery that is destroying sawyering as a trade for laborers: "Even the machines, some of them, can't hardly raise the price of the coals to get their fire up. When they first set up they had 6d. a foot for cutting veneers, and now they have only 1d. *Machinery's very powerful, sir, but competition is much stronger*" (emphasis mine, *UM* 334–35). As I argued earlier, the most threatening aspect of such competition is, for Mayhew, not simply that it reduces the moral and physical conditions of workers in the dishonorable or competitive trades but also that it erodes the distinction between the honorable and dishonorable portions of each trade. In an attempt at fairness, Mayhew interviews some of the masters in the building trade. He reports that he "found the same opinion entertained by them all as to the ruinous effects of the kind of competition existing in their trade to a master who strives to be just to his customers and fair to his men" (*UM* 350). One of the master builders testifies: "Honesty is now almost impossible among us. . . . It *is* impossible in cheap contract work, for *the competition puts all honourable trade out of the field; high character, and good material, and the best workmanship are of no avail*. Capitalists can command any low-priced work, by letting and subletting and all by the piece. Most of these speculating and contracting people think only how to make money. . . . Their proceedings are an encouragament [*sic*] to every kind of dishonesty. They fail continually, and *they drag good men down with them*" (emphasis mine, *UM* 350).

Even the masters share the sense of a downward pull and an attendant downward slide because of the effects of competition. And though "drag[ging] good men down" in this passage seems to refer to the prospect of bankruptcy, its vague phraseology leaves it open to other interpretations. Tailors and bootmakers echo this sense of the cumulative force of various competitive trade practices, with one bootmaker exclaiming: "I fear that if no check be interposed to the Northampton and slop-system, matters will get worse. The underpaid and inferior workman will drag down the able well-conducted artisan to his level" (*UM* 272).[41]

"Will drag down the able well-conducted artisan to his level": this threat haunts Mayhew's investigations into the dishonorable trade. From the destruction of the family through the dehumanization and emasculation of the workmen to the ultimate evil of prostitution, Mayhew's investigative revelations act as an imaginative magnet, pulling the reader's mind from the moral, intelligent, and psychologized male artisan toward the images of degradation and emasculation that potentially await him. While continuing to blame competition as the central factor in the devastation of the dishonorable trade and the threatened destruction of the honorable trade, later in his letters Mayhew turns to one specific tenet of political economy as a means of focusing and localizing his critique: the law of supply and demand, which holds that wages and prices are determined by a relationship between the supply of labor and the demand for it. As stated earlier, this principle renders the evils that Mayhew describes as the result of overpopulation within the trades—in other words, the "fault" of the workmen themselves. Supply-and-demand theory, likewise, from the perspective of the capitalist, renders the conditions and wages of the workers inevitable—just the natural workings of economic law: no one is to blame (except maybe the workers themselves), and nothing is to be done (except maybe forced emigration).[42]

In response to the amoral inevitability of this theory, Mayhew generates his own set of theories, and he offers intricate calculations to support them. He first attacks the law of supply and demand by showing "statistically" how it does not apply in the case of the cabinetmakers, particularly in the slop cabinet trade: "Notwithstanding the number of cabinet-makers in the metropolis, compared with the rest of the population, decreased no less than 32 *per cent!* between 1831 and 1841, still the wages of the non-society men (whose earnings are regulated solely by competition) have fallen as much as 400 percent [*sic*]—and this while the amount of work done has increased rather than decreased" (emphasis in original, *UM* 363). Using the cabinetmakers as his primary example, Mayhew then lays out the two main tenets of his theory: "Over-work makes under-pay" and "Under-pay makes over-work" (*UM* 384–88). The first of these tenets translates Mayhew's observation that simply by increasing the productiveness of the individual laborer, a trade can become, as it were, overcrowded. The result is the same as if there were a sudden glut of laborers—wages are driven lower and lower, to the point where they constitute "underpay." Once wages begin to be reduced, the individual laborer will work more quickly, for longer hours, and perhaps with less skill and care in order to make up the difference between his earnings and expenditures. Thus, Mayhew arrives at his second tenet—"Under-pay makes over-work."

Mayhew argues that both of these principles complicate the simple law of supply and demand as it was commonly understood by political economists, capitalists, and the general public of his day. He explains that his two complicating tenets are the result of a new category of labor, what he call "interested labor." He first uses this idea to explain the "means to increase the productiveness of labour" that lead to "overwork," which he argues involves "connecting the workman's interest directly with his labour" or "making the amount of his earning depend upon the quantity of work done by him" (*UM* 385). In the next paragraph, Mayhew restates this point by arguing that in piecework or interested labor, "the operative unites in himself the double function of capitalist and labourer, making up his own materials or working on his own property" (*UM* 386). Mayhew repeatedly identifies interested labor as a causal factor in workmen's increasing their hours of labor and producing inferior, or "scamp," work. In fact, he calls such "scamp work" "one of the necessary consequences of all *interested* labour" (emphasis in original, *UM* 387).

These are the immediate evils that stem from interested labor. But the core problem seems to lie within the term "interested labor" itself, particularly as that term is defined in the passage emphasized earlier: "whenever the operative unites in himself the double function of capitalist and labourer." It is as if the collapse of the clear distinction between employer and employed, capitalist and laborer, is at the root of the collapse of the distinction between the honorable and dishonorable trades and all that they represent for Mayhew as well as for the laborers themselves. While this connection may seem counterintuitive (wouldn't it be empowering for the workers to be their own employers, capitalists, and masters?), Mayhew gives an illustration that suggests why the collapse of the laborer/capitalist distinction is, at least in this case, so dangerous. He compares the small manufacturer to the small farmer and argues that the latter labors not for profit but for subsistence. The result is that any increase in his labor contributes directly to his support and comfort. In contrast, "the small master [which is what so many laborers have been forced by the competitive system to become] . . . producing what he cannot eat, must carry his goods to market and exchange them for articles of consumption; hence, *by overtoil, he lowers the market against himself,* that is to say, the more *he* labours the *less* food he ultimately obtains" (first emphasis mine; second and third emphases in original, *UM* 386–87). In other words, the collapse of the distinction between capitalist and laborer is in fact a fissure within the laborer himself. He works *against* himself; he *literally* loses his integrity as a laborer.

This fracture makes him like the fragmented commercial men of Dickens's *Dombey and Son*. More important, however, this situation makes every interested laborer to some degree like the "lowest of the needlewomen"—the prostitute who combines within herself the roles of capitalist, laborer, *and* commodity. This combination of roles results in the fissure between moral female subject and degraded prostitute that Mayhew dwells on in his discussion of the needlewomen. It also helps to explain the power of the prostitution metaphor. Significantly, this is a power that Mayhew defuses in his representation of the actual prostitutes he interviews. He defuses it precisely by splitting off the woman from the prostitute—making the women tragic victims of their circumstances. The need to diffuse this power when prostitution applies to actual women, rather than metaphorically to men, is explained by Lynda Nead in the following terms: "She [the prostitute] is able to represent all the terms of capitalist production; she is the human labour, the object of exchange and the seller at once. She stands as worker, commodity and capitalist and blurs the categories of bourgeois economics in the same way she tests the boundaries of bourgeois morality."[43] I would add to Nead's account the point that the prostitute blurs and tests the boundaries not only of bourgeois economics and bourgeois morality but also, through both, of the moral female subjectivity assigned to her by the ideology of the family wage increasingly adopted by the (male) Victorian working class.

Indeed, the prostitute is the prototypical female laborer, one who does not threaten any male laborer's job but who represents all the female laborers who *are* seen as threatening male employment, and thus working-class masculinity itself. Likewise, the prostitute is the figure of a woman who refuses to be contained within the domestic sphere and "protected" by a man. Thus, she also suggests all the wage-earning women who Taylor says "had become a symptom and symbol of masculine degradation."[44] Mayhew writes of and investigates wage-earning women other than prostitutes, but always with the presumption that they are *forced* to labor in the marketplace, never with the idea that their labor might be voluntary. More significantly, Mayhew's accounts of female labor other than prostitution function to erase that labor by focusing on questions about the male laborer and his ability or inability to maintain his family. Thus, Mayhew naturalizes the public, wage-earning role of the male worker while denaturalizing that role for women; he offers instead a naturalized role within the domestic sphere—a female role on which working-class male subjectivity increasingly depends and in which women's labor is categorically erased as "unproductive."

Mayhew's explicit solution to all of the problems his investigation uncovers goes even further toward establishing gender asymmetry in the workplace and the marketplace. That solution is his support for trade societies. He discusses the benefits of such societies for both workers and masters throughout his letters, ending the series with a paean to the Curriers' Society. But with only one exception—dressmakers—all these trade societies are male. This exception not only occurs in an all-female trade (like prostitution); in Mayhew's account, it is the result of the effort of middle-class philanthropic "ladies" rather than the female workers' self-organization. Thus, when Mayhew invokes the image of the trade society as a large, extended family, he is invoking the image of an all-male family—or at least a family in which all the workers are men, and women and children are dependents. The trade society as a solution to the threats of capitalist competition, then, depends on the erasure of female labor and the occlusion of the wage-earning woman worker. This "solution" is even more significant given Mayhew's characterization of the dishonorable trade, where workers are completely ignorant of each other. Setting up trade societies within these trades, as Mayhew has minutely described them, seems an impossibility—an example of wishful thinking intended to contain the anxieties his letters have exposed. As such, the wishful solution of all-male trade societies reveals even more powerfully the gender dynamics that Mayhew depends on to rescue the male worker.

The image of the trade society is not potent enough to erase the image of the prostitute-needlewoman Mayhew evoked earlier. That image continues its symbolic work as an emphatic marker of the evils of free-market capitalist competition, as do his images of starving laborers and degraded trades. Yet Mayhew's critique of competitive capitalism participates in constructing an ideology of the family wage that served not only to shore up working-class masculinity but also to support the capitalist social structures that facilitated the workings of capitalist economics. The image of the needlewoman-turned-prostitute continues to haunt the reader and to challenge Mayhew's otherwise largely unproblematic erasure of the female worker as well as to indict mid-Victorian competitive capitalism.

chapter six

Rewriting Ricardo/Renewing Smith: The New, Expanded Political Economy of J. S. Mill

John Stuart Mill's *Principles of Political Economy* is in large part an attempt to create a space within economic theory for the concerns that led writers such as Dickens and Mayhew to reject and attack scientific political economy. In this chapter, I examine both the larger structural aspects of Mill's synthetic project and Mill's treatment of specific, central economic issues in order to explore how Mill goes about creating that space and reincorporating ethical concerns into economic theory. After studying how Mill's economic treatise attempts to reintegrate the "human element" of Smithian economics, social philosophy, and romantic poetry, I conclude with a brief discussion of the effects of Mill's attempt to rewrite scientific political economy—both for economic theory and for Mill's project of humanization. The most important effect of Mill's attempt at synthesis lies precisely at the juncture between the "scientific" and "humanitarian" impulses of his project. While Mill successfully constructs a version of political economy that can allow for social amelioration, his vision is hedged in by the Malthusian population principle. The population principle was for Malthus a manifestation of providence and divine will; for Mill it was a naturally given biological fact that, rather than adding meaning to human existence, threatened the human ability to make life meaningful.

Unlike Dickens and Mayhew, Mill critiques scientific political economy from within the tradition of classical political economy. Mill was raised on the political economy of Ricardo and of his own father, James Mill. In his *Autobiography,* John Stuart Mill describes the "complete course of political economy" through which his father took him in 1819:

> Though Ricardo's great work was already in print, no didactic treatise embodying its doctrines, in a manner fit for learners, had yet appeared. My father, therefore, commenced instructing me in the science by a sort of lectures, which he delivered to me in our walks. He expounded each day a portion of

the subject, and I gave him next day a written account of it, which he made me rewrite over and over again. . . . In this manner I went through the whole extent of the science. . . . After this I read Ricardo, giving an account daily of what I read, and discussing, in the best manner I could, the collateral points which offered themselves in our progress.[1]

Mill enumerates other readings and analyses in his economic education, including discussions of Ricardo's pamphlets on money and Smith's *The Wealth of Nations*. "Such a mode of instruction," Mill concludes, "was excellently calculated to form a thinker."[2] Thus, at the age of thirteen, John Stuart Mill began what was to be a lifelong project of thinking about, analyzing, and writing about political economic theory. It is significant that even in 1853–54, when he first drafted the *Autobiography*, he repeatedly and almost emphatically refers to political economy *as* a science.

Mill's approach to scientific political economy, in relation to that of the other writers I have examined, comes closest to the writings of the 1844 Bank Act critics. Like Mill, these critics approached economic questions largely from within the discursive traditions of political economy. Unlike Mill, however, their use of those traditions was largely polemical rather than systematic. Individually and as a group, they drew from a broad range of economic arguments in order to support their polemics; their goal was less to theorize about economic issues per se than to persuade their readers that their opinions were supported by accepted economic doctrine.

Henry Mayhew's *Morning Chronicle* project also exhibits some formal overlap with Mill's writings on political economy. Mayhew claimed to be investigating and revising political economic theory as part of a comprehensive investigation of London labor. In contrast to Mill, however, Mayhew's approach to the scientific aspect of political economy was almost totally inductive; his economic opinions changed through the course of the letters on the basis of what he observed in his investigations. Mill's much more systematic approach to economic theory was much more deductive. Although he, unlike Ricardo, did attempt to incorporate inductive reasoning and observed phenomena into his *Principles of Political Economy*, the essential structure of the book was deductively derived from a few "first principles" of economic theory and social philosophy. Significantly, also, when Mill supported his arguments with "experience," he almost always relied on and quoted the observations of other writers rather than making Mayhew-like investigations and observations of his own. Thus, while Mill and Mayhew wrote about many of the same issues and often used similar terminology, their final written projects bear little formal resemblance to each other.

In terms of the generic forms through which they explore economic questions, Mill's writings on political economy are furthest from those of the novelist Charles Dickens. In these two writers, we find opposing extremes of middle-class Victorian approaches to scientific economic theory—Mill approaching these issues from the tradition of utilitarianism and Ricardian economics and Dickens from an almost purely literary tradition of romance, realism, and satire. At the same time, the literary tradition of which Dickens is a part provides a crucial link. While Mill was raised to be a thoroughly scientific and analytical thinker, his well-known mental crisis and "conversion" to romanticism led him to incorporate some of the ideals of literary romanticism into his philosophy of life and also into his study of economic theory. In the *Autobiography,* Mill explains the alteration of his vision: "I, for the first time, gave its proper place, among the prime necessities of human well-being, to the internal culture of the individual. I ceased to attach almost exclusive importance to the ordering of outward circumstances, and the training of the human being for speculation and for action. . . . The cultivation of feeling became one of the cardinal points in my ethical and philosophical creed."[3] The extension of Mill's sympathies beyond the narrow confines of utilitarianism and eighteenth-century philosophy was fostered and reinforced by his reading of Wordsworth, Coleridge, Carlyle, and nineteenth-century continental literature and philosophy, all of which he saw as a reaction against the eighteenth century.[4] Mill's relationship with Harriet Taylor further supported his movement away from the Benthamism of his father and his own youth. In conjunction with Taylor, Mill extended his new valuation of "internal culture" into his social and economic philosophy. In the *Autobiography,* Mill directly attributes his increasing sympathies toward socialism and the writing of the chapter "On the Probable Future of the Labouring Classes" to Taylor's influence. More generally, he describes her influence on *Principles* in the following terms: "What was abstract and purely scientific [in *Principles of Political Economy*] was generally mine; the properly human element came from her: in all that concerned the application of philosophy to the exigencies of human society and progress, I was her pupil."[5] While many historians and biographers have doubted the accuracy of Mill's account of Harriet Taylor's influence—especially regarding the extent of her influence—the account reveals Mill's high valuation of those parts of his work that go beyond the "abstract and purely scientific" approach to economic theory. Interestingly, Mill's distinction between the "purely scientific" and the "properly human element" of his economic project implicitly reconstructs the contours of the separate-spheres ideology that he rejects in *On the Subjection of Women* and aligns the discursive divide between science and philosophy with the difference between masculine and feminine. Thus, Mill's autobiographical account exposes a gendering of the science/philosophy breakdown that remains largely invisible in the text of *Principles*.

The very organization of Mill's *Principles* reflects his attempt to reconnect the scientific aspects of political economy with human elements of social philosophy. Rather than rejecting scientific political economy in deference to his romantic conversion, Mill attempts to reconstruct the Ricardian legacy of economy theory; he retains in large part Ricardo's abstract theories but uses Adam Smith's *The Wealth of Nations*, rather than Ricardo's *Principles*, as his structural model. He titles his work *Principles of Political Economy* but adds the revealing subtitle, *with Some of Their Applications to Social Philosophy*. In the Preface to the first (1848) edition of *Principles*, Mill announces the integrative goals of his text:

> The design of the book is different from that of any treatise on Political Economy which has been produced in England since the work of Adam Smith.
>
> The most characteristic quality of that work, and the one in which it most differs from some others which have equalled or even surpassed it as mere expositions of the general principles of the subject, is that it invariably associates the principles with their applications. This of itself implies a much wider range of ideas and of topics than are included in Political Economy, considered as a branch of abstract speculation. . . .
>
> It appears to the present writer that a work similar in its object and general conception to that of Adam Smith, but adapted to the more extended knowledge and improved ideas of the present age, is the kind of contribution which Political Economy at present requires.[6]

Mill perceives his return to Smith as a return to the marriage of abstract theory with practical application. Both aspects of this formulation—the marriage *and* the return—are significant. Mill self-consciously formulates his project in terms of an eighteenth-century tradition of writing on social history and theory that, unlike Ricardian economics, did not perceive or study economic phenomena in isolation from other social issues.

For Mill, the reunion of abstract theory with practical application involved a broadening of the very definition of political economy—at least of political economy as formulated by Ricardo, James Mill, Nassau Senior, and J. R. McCulloch. Mill creates an opposition between the narrowness of political economy "considered as a branch of abstract speculation" and the "much wider range of ideas and of topics" that he associates with practical applications. Another passage in the Preface suggests what, for Mill, this Smithian breadth includes: "No attempt, however, has yet been made to exhibit the economical phenomena of society in the relation in which they stand to the best social ideas of the present time, as [Smith] did . . . in reference to the philosophy of the eighteenth century" (*PPE* xxviii). "Practical application," then, involves not simply discussions of "how abstract theory works in the real world" but also the integration of abstract economic theory with other traditions of "social ideas" and contemporary philosophy.

Mill's return to Smith was a structural and methodological return rather than a return to Smithian economic theory per se. Mill refers to his model, *The Wealth of Nations,* as "in many parts obsolete, and in all, imperfect" (*PPE* xxviii). Mill's goal is to combine Smith's "practical mode of treating his subject" with "the *increased knowledge* since acquired of its theory" (emphasis mine, *PPE* xxviii). Similarly, Mill insists that his practical object has not been purchased "by the sacrifice of strict scientific reasoning." Mill concludes the original Preface with the assertion that, "though [the author] desires that his treatise should be more than a mere exposition of the abstract doctrines of Political Economy, he is also desirous that such an exposition should be found in it" (*PPE* xxviii). Each of these statements points to Mill's desire to retain full scientific authority for his treatment of economic theory, even as he extends his investigation beyond abstract economic theory itself. While he returns to Smith as a model for the "applications" of his projects, he retains his Ricardian allegiances in the abstract principles that are the basis for those applications. The question of just how "true" are Mill's allegiances to Ricardian economic theory has been debated by economic historians for years, and I cannot answer it here.[7] Certain aspects of Mill's relationship to Ricardo are, however, generally agreed upon. There is a sense that in most cases Mill retained the traditional aspects of Ricardian economic theories, but that his qualifications, extensions, and applications of those theories more or less changed their essential meaning. For my purposes, the general consensus that Mill was working from a Ricardian framework will suffice to suggest the basic theoretical parameters of Mill's project: Mill retained the labor theory of value, the population principle, and a version of the wages fund theory.

Mill's critique of scientific political economy is a critique not of the theoretical substance of Ricardian economics but rather of the isolation of that substance from the potentially modifying influences of practical application and social theory—the "human element." In fact, the central tension of Mill's *Principles of Political Economy* lies in his desire both to broaden the focus of political economy *and* to retain the authority of "strict scientific reasoning." The nature of this tension is the same schism between "science" and moral or political philosophy that we saw in Ricardo's movement away from Smith and Malthus.

Mill's *Principles* retains the abstractions of Ricardian economics as its scientific basis but attempts to reach beyond those abstractions. Mill's goal is not to connect abstract economic speculations to other sets of abstractions but rather to connect economic abstractions to a more complex conception of human nature and human experience. But the tension between science and social philosophy, and between abstraction and practical application, is not fully resolved by this synthetic structure. Mill's main strategy for retaining scientific authority while creating space for the "human element" is his opposition between the laws of production and those of distribution. I will examine this opposition more closely, but first I want to turn to one of the specific moments at which the difficulty of reconciling these tensions is registered in Mill's text—Mill's discussion of competition, custom, and the regulation of prices and wages.

Mill's discussion of competition falls within the "distribution" section of his treatise—the section in which economic activity is seen to be less materially determined and more a product of adjustable, historically relative human institutions. Mill contends that the influence of competition has been privileged and exaggerated by political economists, and that these same economists have failed to take account of custom as an "other and conflicting principle" in the determination of wages and prices. Mill sees this error as a product of political economists' attempts to render their theories scientific: "This is partly intelligible, if we consider that only through the principle of competition has political economy any pretension to the character of a science. . . . Assume competition to be their exclusive regulator, and principles of broad generality and scientific precision may be laid down, according to which [prices and wages] will be regulated" (*PPE* 242). Mill goes on to justify this exclusivity: "The political economist *justly* deems this his *proper business:* and as an abstract or hypothetical science, political economy cannot be required to do, indeed cannot do, anything more" (emphasis mine, *PPE* 242).

In the next sentence, Mill qualifies this assertion by invoking "the actual course of human affairs." In this sphere of actuality, he argues, custom very often either banishes competition altogether or qualifies and alters its effect. Mill then enumerates a series of examples in which custom is a more significant factor than competition. It would seem that Mill is trying to expand "science" per se to include the "calculation" of variables that, according to Mill's definition of science, are incalculable.

After discussing custom for several pages, Mill concludes: "These observations must be received as a general correction to be applied wherever relevant, whether expressly mentioned or not, to the conclusions contained *in the subsequent portions of this treatise.* Our reasonings must, in general, proceed as if the known and natural effects of competition were actually produced by it. . . . Where competition, though free to exist, does not exist, or where it exists, but has its natural consequences overruled by any other agency, the conclusions will fail more or less of being applicable" (emphasis mine, *PPE* 247). In this passage Mill seems to back away from an attempt to expand the science of political economy itself and seems content instead to call for what is essentially a humbling of the scientific role. Only competition, he concedes, can be scientifically calculated—and his own treatise will proceed *as if* competition has the same influence that "political economists generally" have ascribed to it. At the same time, he self-consciously attempts to hedge his own reasoning and predictions with a significant qualification: where his economic theory of competition meets the human force of custom, his conclusions will "fail . . . of being applicable." By asserting the limitations of abstract reasoning at the same time that he goes forward with such reasoning, Mill exposes the gap between theory and practice, economics as abstract theory and economics as a complex, embedded social discourse. Even though he cannot resolve this tension, Mill goes forward with his synthetic project, using various discursive and analytical strategies to mitigate the tension.

Mill's most successful attempt to reconcile the conflicting forces is his opposition between the laws of production and the laws of distribution. Mill introduces this opposition in his "Preliminary Remarks":

> The production of wealth . . . is evidently not an arbitrary thing. It has its necessary conditions. Of these, some are physical. . . . Combining with these facts of outward nature other truths relating to human nature, [political economy] attempts to trace the secondary or derivative laws, by which the production of wealth is determined. . . .
>
> Unlike the laws of Production, those of Distribution are partly of human institution: since the manner in which wealth is distributed in any given society, depends on the statues or usages therein obtaining. (*PPE* 21)

In this formulation, scientific abstraction is linked to scientific necessity—the necessity of physical and human nature acting in concert according to fixed laws. The human nature Mill mentions in his discussion of the laws of production is the narrow, self-interested, wealth-seeking nature to which he refers in the 1844 essay "On the Definition of Political Economy; and on the Method of Investigation Proper to It" (cited in chapter 1) rather than the "human element" described in the *Autobiography*. In the opening paragraphs of book 2, "Distribution," Mill formulates the necessitudinarian aspect of the laws of production even more strongly: "The laws and conditions of the Production of wealth *partake of the character of physical truths*. There is *nothing optional or arbitrary* in them. Whatever mankind produce, must be produced in the modes and under the conditions, imposed by the constitution of *external things,* and by the own *inherent properties* of their own mental and bodily structure" (emphasis mine, *PPE* 199). Here human nature is left out of the equation altogether, and humanity has been reduced to a "mental and bodily structure." The laws of production do not allow the political economist to legislate, but they do, according to Mill, provide him with the a priori basis for abstract speculation and scientific predictions. In short, they are positive rather than normative.

Just before Mill moves from this backward glance at the laws of production to the laws of distribution, he makes a comment that goes far toward revealing the intentions behind his construction of this opposition. Mill refers to the possibility for future developments within the sphere of production, then adds: "But, howsoever we may succeed in *making for ourselves more space* within the limits set by the constitution of things, we know there must be limits. We cannot alter the ultimate properties either of mind or matter" (emphasis mine, *PPE* 199–200). While the laws of production allow the political economist to aspire to the status of the natural scientist, these same laws severely limit the space of human agency, subjectivity, and relations. All the scientific political economist can do is describe and make predictions based on the givens of physical nature and human psychology.[8]

"It is not so," Mill writes, "with the Distribution of wealth. That is a matter of human institution solely. The things once there, mankind, individually or collectively, can do with them as they like" (*PPE* 200). The laws of distribution, in other words, are structurally almost a complete inverse of the laws of production. They create a much larger space for human agency, on the part of not only the economic subject but also the political economist himself. The economist of the distributive sphere may not yet be able to legislate, but he is able to warn, enjoin, rally, instruct, and generally pave the way for what he perceives to be positive social and economic change. Where the laws of production partake of the natural sciences, the more normative laws of distribution introduce history, veer toward social philosophy, and position the political economist accordingly.

By differentiating between the laws of production and distribution, Mill creates a space both for the abstract and scientific aspects of political economy and for the less scientific and rational, more human and ethical elements with which he is concerned.[9] Abstract science has absolute authority within the sphere of production, but its role within the sphere of distribution is subservient to human institutions. Social scientists can calculate the effects of those institutions, but because institutions are always subject to change, they cannot make the same transhistorical claims for those calculations as for calculations in the physical sciences (*PPE* 200). By treating private property, inheritance, and landed wealth *as* institutions, rather than as inevitable social givens, Mill denaturalizes them. While Mill grants institutions significant power in the shaping of individuals and societies, he also delimits that power, linking it to a particular historical moment and implicitly marking it as artificial and arbitrary.[10] One effect of Mill's denaturalization is that the future is always, for him, potentially a clean slate on which human beings can write whatever institutions they can imagine and create. This effect allows for changes not only in the order of society but also in the individual human agent, to the extent that that agent is a product of human institutions.

Mill's entire discussion of socialism and private property is underwritten by the assumption that the very constitution of human individuals can and will change. For example, while the institution of private property assumes and reinforces self-interest as the primary motivation of the human agent, Mill entertains the possibility that "large bodies of human beings may be trained to feel the public interest as their own" (*PPE* 206). According to Mill, "the present age," rather than human nature, is responsible for the estranged relationship between individual and public interest. With education and a change in community opinion, the apparently fundamental role of self-interest in human activity might be replaced with not-yet-imagined forms of interest and agency. In fact, Mill offers his most unambivalent praise for socialist theorists precisely in their role as visionaries of human potential.

I will return to Mill's discussion of socialism. At this point, I want to examine the role of history and change in Mill's *Principles* more directly. Book 4 of the *Principles* is titled "Influence of the Progress of Society on Production and Distribution." Here, Mill announces, he turns from the "statics" of his subject to the "dynamics." The first five chapters of Book 4 explain the economic mechanisms that eventually and inevitably slow the economic progress of a society and lead to the stationary state. In the last two chapters, "Of the Stationary State" and "On the Probable Future of the Labouring Classes," Mill engages in his most explicit speculations about the possibilities for future change—both in social organization and in the constitution of the individual. Through these speculations, Mill reveals his own moral and social ideals and comes closest to outlining a prescription for the healthy moral development of capitalist societies.

In his discussion of the stationary state, Mill makes one of his most significant breaks with Ricardian economic theory. His biographer Alan Ryan writes succinctly: "What is striking in Mill's account is the way he almost uncritically accepts his predecessors' premises but rejects their gloomy conclusions."[11] Mill accepts the idea that the stationary state is inevitable, but for him that inevitability is positive and full of social possibilities. Rather than a state of economic stagnation and general misery, Mill sees the stationary state as "on the whole, a very considerable improvement on our present condition" (*PPE* 748).

The first benefit of the stationary state would be the expenditure of public moneys on nonproductive philanthropic projects. In an advanced, populous country—that is, one approaching the stationary state of minimal returns upon profits—the government can literally afford to invest its money in "industriously unproductive" projects. Because the economic limit in such countries results not from a shortage of capital and savings but from the exhaustion of fertile land, funds can be diverted into nonproductive projects without damaging the economic well-being of the nation. Such an expenditure of public funds, Mill predicts, would "either be drawn from that portion of the annual savings which would otherwise be sent abroad, or . . . subtracted from the unproductive expenditures of individuals for the next year or two" (*PPE* 741). This kind of government expenditure would in fact "make room" for more money to be saved before the economy reached the point at which money would flow into overseas investments or unproductive consumption. Thus, Mill concludes, "the utmost expense which could be requisite for any of these [philanthropic] purposes, would not in all probability deprive one labourer of employment, or diminish the next year's production by one ell of cloth or one bushel of grain" (*PPE* 741).

With these economic justifications established, Mill creates a space for such government projects as "the industrial regeneration of Ireland" or "a comprehensive measure of . . . public education" (*PPE* 741). The former he includes under the rubric of a "great object of justice," the latter under the label of "philanthropic policy." Mill's revisions in economic theory, then, are very directly linked to his desire to reconnect such theory with ethical values and imperatives. Mill explicitly differentiates this national economic situation from that of a poor, less developed country, where the legislator is still hedged in by economic necessity. This contrast serves to reinforce Mill's claims that different national situations involve very different sets of governmental responsibility. History, again, allows Mill to move beyond the constraints of Ricardian economic theory—in this case to revise aspects of that theory itself as well as to reconnect political economy with social ethics and philosophy.

Mill's discussion of the possibilities of the stationary state are strikingly different from those of Ricardo or James Mill—not only in content but also in tone. The whole tenor of Mill's prose changes from that of the analytical thinker and scientist to one more evocative of Carlyle and Coleridge. In differentiating himself from his Ricardian predecessors, Mill writes: "I confess I am not charmed with the ideal of life held out by those who think that the normal state of human beings is that of struggling to get on; that the trampling, crushing, elbowing, and treading on each other's heels, which form the existing type of social life, are the most desirable lot of human kind, or anything but the disagreeable symptoms of one of the phases of industrial progress" (*PPE* 748). Later Mill adds: "Those who do not accept the present very early stage of human improvement as its ultimate type, may be excused for being comparatively indifferent to the kind of economic progress which excites the congratulations of ordinary politicians; the mere increase of production and accumulation" (*PPE* 749). Together these passages criticize and trivialize the conception of human nature that had been promulgated by the popularizers of scientific political economy, if not by the economic theorists themselves. Those human traits—including the bourgeois virtues of industry and abstinence—celebrated as essential and natural by such writers as Harriet Martineau and J. R. McCulloch are relegated by Mill to "one of the phases of industrial progress" and disparaged as "disagreeable symptoms." The goals of "increase[d] . . . production and accumulation" are minimized with the adjective "mere" and presented as the product of "the present *very early* stage of human improvement"—implicitly in contrast with the more advanced and developed stages toward which humanity should aspire.

Mill spends the remaining pages of the chapter "Of the Stationary State" describing his image of what humanity might look like in those more advanced stages of improvement. First, as a result of increased national prosperity, individual prudence, and wise legislation, Mill imagines that there will be a much better, more even distribution of property. According to Mill, this improvement will allow for "a more well-paid and affluent body of labourers" and also for a "much larger body of persons than at present, not only exempt from the coarser toils, but with sufficient leisure, both physical and mental, from mechanical details, to cultivate freely the graces of life, and afford examples of them to the classes less favourably circumstanced for their growth" (*PPE* 750). Both the laborers and the members of this latter class would be in a much better position than at present to pursue "mental culture"—that Millian watchword of human growth and development. Through such mental culture, in turn, would come "moral and social progress" and improvements in "the Art of Living." In fact, the art of living would, in Mill's stationary state, in large part replace the bourgeois "art of getting on" (*PPE* 751).

In addition to mental culture, Mill calls for population limitation within the stationary state—less for economic than for spiritual well-being. Mill is concerned that overcrowding would limit the spiritual potential of humanity by eliminating the chance for solitude. Sounding almost Wordwsorthian, Mill writes: "It is not good for man to be kept perforce at all times in the presence of his species. . . . Solitude, in the sense of being often alone, is essential to any depth of meditation or of character; and solitude in the presence of natural beauty and grandeur, is the cradle of thoughts and aspirations which are not only good for the individual, but which society could ill do without" (*PPE* 750). Mill's concern with solitude clarifies his commitment to mental culture.

"Mental," for Mill, includes much more than the intellectual, the analytical, or, as he calls them in the *Autobiography,* the active capacities of humankind. Solitude is linked to interiority and the "passive susceptibilities" of an individual—to "*depth* of meditation or of character." In Mill's ideal social state, all members of a culture would have moral, psychological, or spiritual interiors.

Such interiority at the level of the individual would, in turn, allow further development or advancement on the level of the community. "Man" as conceptualized by scientific political economy—"solely as a being who desires to possess wealth"—would be completely subsumed within a more advanced individual human nature. In effect, the scientific approach would no longer be the appropriate way to study human life—either individually or socially—because that life will have become an *art.* When "the Art of Living" replaces the "art of getting on" in the stationary state, the very nature of "art" changes—from lowercase to uppercase, from calculations and activity to the intangibilities of the romantic, developmental self.[12]

Mill discusses a second important facet of his social ideal in the next chapter, "On the Probable Future of the Labouring Classes." In the first paragraph, Mill asserts that general social progress depends fundamentally "on the opinions and habits of the most numerous class, the class of manual labourers" (*PPE* 752). Without development and improvement at this, the "bottom" level of society, Mill implies that *his* social ideal can never be achieved, precisely because a general improvement of all classes *is* his social ideal. While aspects of Coleridge's clerisy appeal to Mill, and traces of intellectual elitism dot his writings, Mill links his advocacy for an educated elite to its role in raising up the economic, social, and mental condition of those below it in the social hierarchy. While Mill does not seem to envision total equality for all social classes, he does repeatedly insist upon an economic lowering of the most financially privileged classes and, more importantly, an economic, social, and moral elevation of the least privileged members of the community. "On the Probable Future of the Laboring Classes" draws a series of pictures of what that elevation might look like.

The overarching theme of Mill's ideal for the laboring classes is "self-dependence." Mill explicitly contrasts this theory with the competing Victorian theory of working-class improvement, "dependence and protection." Mill sees the paternalist theory of dependence and protection as essentially nostalgic, if not reactionary. The problem with this backward-looking vision of protection and generosity on one side, dependence, gratefulness, and loyalty on the other, is that its "virtues and sentiments . . . belong emphatically to a rude and imperfect state of social union" (*PPE* 755). The only thing that gave this social organization validity in the past, Mill argues, were the real needs for protection of certain members of society. Once the original threats are removed, the relationship between protector and protected turns sour: the relationship forces and reinforces the weakness and vulnerability of the "protected" and fosters tyranny in the "protectors." The result, according to Mill, is that "the so-called protectors are now the only persons against whom, in any ordinary circumstances, protection is needed. The brutality and tyranny with which every police report is filled, are those of husbands to wives, or parents to children" (*PPE* 755). This situation is the result of artificial inequities in power that have outgrown their social usefulness, as must all such inequities if society is to progress toward Mill's future ideal.[13]

For Mill, then, the future of the laboring classes must be one of social, political, and economic empowerment rather than dependence and loyalty. Mill sees this future as part of a process that the laboring classes—at least of England and other "advanced countries of Europe"—have already embarked upon. Because the laboring classes have already begun to become self-dependent, they have begun to reject "the patriarchal or paternal system of government." Mill states this point forcefully and repeatedly: "The working classes have taken their interests into their own hands, and are perpetually showing that they think the interests of their employers not identical with their own, but opposite to them" (*PPE* 756). Mill perceives the working-class movements of the 1830s and the 1840s—on the continent and in England—as the irreversible first steps in a necessary and desirable process of social amelioration *and* reorganization. For Mill, the future depends on the continuation of this developmental process, the end point of which is a laboring population made up of independent and rational individuals.

It is precisely Mill's emphasis on the individual that problematizes his relationship to socialism. His sympathies toward socialism seem to have been discussed by every historian who has even briefly considered Mill's economic ideas. These historians have argued about just how sympathetic to socialism Mill was, how much his ideas changed through the course of his life, and Harriet Taylor's impact on his ideas.[14] One of the major foci of the debate has been the revisions Mill made in his discussions of socialism in later editions of the *Principles*—especially in the third edition (1852).[15] Amidst all the debate, one can glean a general consensus about certain important aspects of Mill's discussion of socialism. First, there is a sense that the changes between the second and third editions express an increased sympathy with socialism but that these changes are largely matters of tone rather than substance. Second, historians agree that Mill's sympathy toward socialism is what most sets him apart from his contemporary political economists. Third, economic historians point out that Mill's discussion of socialism was a response to English and French socialist theory rather than to the more revolutionary continental developments associated with the First International. Finally, there is general agreement that Mill had three major sets of reservations about nineteenth-century communist and socialist theory. Since Mill's own text provides ample support for each of these points of consensus, my discussion will be based on my reading of his text rather than secondary accounts. I will look first at Mill's support for and defense of socialist theory and experimentation and then turn to the three major areas in which Mill qualifies his support: competition, the future potential of private property, and individual liberty under socialism.

Most of Mill's explicit discussion of socialism falls within section 3 of his chapter "Of Property" (book 2, chapter 1). This section was added in the 1852 edition of *Principles*. The first point Mill raises in this section concerns individual motivation to work under a system of communal labor and ownership. According to nineteenth-century critics of socialist theory, such social organization would result in each person trying to avoid his or her fair share of labor. While Mill grants this point as a "difficulty" of the communist scheme, he turns the objection back against the critics by showing how little personal interest a factory operative has in his or her work—less, according to Mill, "than a member of a Communist association, since he is not, like him, working for a partnership of which he is himself a member" (*PPE* 204–5). Mill also explores the ways in which the tendency to avoid labor would, in a communist community, be counteracted by the power of opinion; instead of being under the eye of one master, the communist laborer would be under the eyes of the whole community. Thus, for Mill, the dangers of loss of productivity under socialism would be largely, if not completely, mitigated by the incentive of personal interest vis-à-vis membership in a partnership and by the augmented power of public opinion.

The power of public opinion is also the factor that Mill believes would make the communist scheme desirably effective in terms of population control. Mill writes that under communism, "any augmentation of numbers which diminished the comfort or increased the toil of the mass, would then cause (which it does not now) immediate and unmistakable inconvenience to every individual in the association. . . . In such altered circumstances opinion could not fail to reprobate . . . this or any other culpable self-indulgence at the expense of the community" (*PPE* 207). The force of public opinion, that is, would be augmented on the question of population control because the effects of failure to limit population would be at once obvious, and obviously detrimental to all members of the community. In the current situation of private property and wage labor, the natural effects of sexual "intemperance," according to Mill, are often blamed on social inequities—"the avarice of employers, or the unjust privileges of the rich"; with those inequities removed under communism, the true dynamics of population growth would be perceived by the laborers themselves.[16] While population growth has the same effects in either the capitalist or the communist system, the latter would enable the community to perceive more readily the inevitable effects and dynamics of this natural law. Ironically, in other words, through the power of *public* opinion, *personal* interest would again be mobilized to effect what Mill perceives to be the desired result—a responsible and voluntary limitation of population growth.

For Mill, then, communism as imagined by such figures as Robert Owen and M. Louis Blanc had certain major advantages over the system of private property as it was organized in nineteenth-century England and Europe. This was true, however, in relation only to communism's and socialism's ideas about private property, not their criticism of competition. While Mill seems ambivalent about competition in his discussion of the stationary state, he emphatically critiques nineteenth-century communism's extreme demonization of competition. His most explicit criticism occurs at the end of his chapter "Of the Probable Future of the Labouring Classes," where it falls like a scythe across what had seemed to be a logical progression from profit-sharing to cooperation and on to socialism. Invoking "the natural indolence of mankind," Mill argues that competition is a necessary counterforce and stimulus. Mill characterizes humans as having a "tendency to be passive, to be the slaves of habit, to persist indefinitely in a course once chosen" (*PPE* 793). Apparently such passivity is, for Mill, an essential rather than incidental aspect of the human constitution, for he doesn't see humankind as "outgrowing" it. The best that Mill seems to hope for is that competition might become a less prominent aspect of human relations and that, economically, it might be moved from the level of the individual to that of the group (i.e., instead of being "between labourer and labourer," competition would occur "between association and association" [*PPE* 793]). These reformulations allow Mill both to critique the institution of private property and to retain the "stimulating effects" of competition, to embrace cooperation as a social ideal without renouncing competition.

Even while Mill explicitly critiques the institution of private property, he carefully qualifies his critique by differentiating between the institution of private property as practiced in nineteenth-century Europe and a reformed institution of private property as it could be practiced sometime in the future. "To judge of the final destination of the institution of property," Mill writes, "we must suppose everything rectified which causes the institution to work in a manner opposed to that equitable principle, of proportion between remuneration and exertion, on which every vindication of it that will bear the light it is assumed to be grounded" (*PPE* 209). In other words, many, if not all, of the evils of the present social system have less to do with the institution of private property per se than with its unjust and inequitable legislative management. Thus, before private property can be dismissed as a viable form of social organization, society must aspire toward a more just ideal of the institution. Mill points out that socialism and communism as imagined by their advocates are also social ideals rather than realities; thus, it is deceptive to compare "Communism with all its chances, and the present state of society with all its sufferings and injustices" (*PPE* 208). Mill concludes: "We are too ignorant either of what individual agency in its best form, or Socialism in its best form, can accomplish, to be qualified to decide which of the two will be the ultimate form of society" (*PPE* 209). Mill's reservations, in this case, are less about socialism itself than about whether such a drastic change in social organization is necessary to attain the equity to which he aspires.

While Mill's reservation about the need for socialism is, in essence, a question about the future potential of private property, his discussion of spontaneity and freedom under socialism expresses a concern about the future potential of socialism itself. While Mill seems to welcome the effects of an augmented public opinion when discussing motivation to work and population control, he also sees that augmented force as the most serious liability of the socialist system: "The question is, whether there would be any asylum left for *individuality of character;* whether public opinion would not be a tyrannical yoke; whether the absolute dependence of each on all, and surveillance of each by all, would not *grind all down into a tame uniformity of thoughts, feelings, and actions*" (emphasis mine, *PPE* 210–11). The source of this danger, according to Mill, is the "absolute dependence of the individual on the mass" within socialist organizations. Mill sees that dependence as having a negative, repressive power even in its attenuated forms within "the existing state of society" (*PPE* 209). In his social ideal, there would be more room for individuality, "eccentricity," and "diversity of tastes and talents" than in the current social state; and socialism, he fears, would further curtail rather than facilitate such freedom and diversity.

Mill discusses the forms of socialism he considers less extreme than the full communalism and equity of communism. To the extent that these schemes, such as Fourierism, incorporate elements of competition and provisions for individual liberty, Mill supports their social experiments; but to the extent that they partake of the liabilities of their more extreme theoretical cousin, communism, Mill's reservations remain. Mill concludes his discussion of socialism with a double gesture, first reaching toward the future, then turning back to the present:

> It is for experience to determine how far or how soon any one or more of the possible systems of community of property will be fitted to substitute itself for the "organization of industry" based on private ownership of land and

> capital. *In the meantime* we may, without attempting to limit the ultimate capabilities of human nature, affirm, that the *political economist, for a considerable time to come,* will be chiefly concerned with the conditions of existence and progress belonging to a society founded on private property and individual competition; and that the object to be principally aimed at, *in the present stage of human improvement,* is not the subversion of the system of individual property, but the improvement of it, and the full participation of every member of the community in its benefits. (emphasis mine, *PPE* 216–17)

In this statement, Mill explicitly creates a space for socialist theory and experimentation, but he locates that space almost entirely outside the domain of the political economist. While he begins with the apparently pragmatic placement of the political economist "in the meantime," he then extends this temporal location into the indefinite future of "for a considerable time to come"—hence suggesting that the association of the political economist with private property is more than simply pragmatic.

It would be easy simply to conclude from this, as many economic historians have, that Mill's reservations about socialism *ultimately* outweigh his sympathies. This conclusion is accurate as far as it goes, but its generality glosses over important details of Mill's discussion. Mill's sympathies and reservations about socialism reveal significant elements of his social philosophy that go beyond his discussion of socialist theory. One aspect of Mill's attraction to socialism, for example, is captured by the statement that "mankind are capable of a far greater amount of public spirit than the present age is accustomed to suppose possible" (*PPE* 206). Mill sees socialism as aspiring toward a conception of human nature in which self-interest is balanced by a "public spirit"—the individual identifying his or her interest with that of the community. Such a broadened conception of human nature allows the social idealist and philosopher in Mill to imagine a social evolution toward economic and political equity.[17]

The expanded identification of the individual with the group that attracts Mill to socialist theory is also the source of his greatest concern. For Mill, any and all social progress is ultimately registered in terms of the individual. Here Mill's upbringing in eighteenth-century philosophy and his conversion to romanticism converge: these two traditions involve radically different conceptions of the individual, but they are both firmly rooted in this idea. Mill departs from his utilitarian and scientific roots for the most part *not* to qualify the role of the individual but to create space for a more complex and multifaceted individual. One aspect of this Millian ideal is an enlarged capacity for "public spirit," but at least equally important is an enlargement of the individual's capacity for self-reflection, solitude, communion with self and nature, and the other "passive susceptibilities" that Mill associates with individual autonomy and a kind of spiritual depth—what might be characterized as a *romantic* version of bourgeois virtue.

Nor does Mill see such development as remaining at the level of the individual alone; he also sees it feeding back into the individual's social identity and relations. Because of Mill's privileging of the individual in any type of social development, he fears that any great extension of the power of the social will infringe on the cyclical process of individual and social evolution. Once institutionalized at the level of the community, even the most idealized conception of human nature could become frozen, fixed by the power of government and public opinion. Not only would spontaneous and diverse individual development be discouraged by these conditions, but such development, even when it emerged, would fail to feed back into and revitalize the social community. Mill's decision to locate the role of the political economist—and thus, implicitly, his own role—within the institution of private property indicates a deep philosophical allegiance to the individual and a distrust of institutionalized social power.

With the institution of private property as a framework, protecting the rights and autonomy of the individual in theory, if not in current nineteenth-century practice, Mill moves away from socialism to theories of how to reform the existing economic structure to make it more equitable—specifically, so that it would protect the rights of all individuals, not simply those of large property owners. Mill first examines current systems of "peasant proprietorship." Much of his discussion consists of a series of long quotations describing and praising the success of peasant proprietors—mostly on the continent. Mill sets the general tone of the two chapters he devotes to this topic in his introductory paragraph, contrasting the system of peasant proprietorship with that of slavery: "In the regime of peasant properties, as in that of slavery, the whole produce belongs to a single owner, and the distinction of rents, profits, and wages, does not exist. In all other respects, the two states of society are the extreme opposites of each other. The one is the state of greatest oppression and degradation to the labouring class. The other is that in which they are *the most uncontrolled arbiters of their own lot*" (emphasis mine, *PPE* 256). Knowing the high value Mill places on self-dependence—particularly as a means to ameliorate the condition of the laboring classes—it is easy to understand the ethical underpinnings of his polarization of slavery and the system of peasant property ownership. The former is the most extreme form of the paternalism he decries, while the latter provides the economic basis for the individual self-dependence he heralds as the key to the cultural advancement of the laboring classes.

Peasant proprietorship, as it was already practiced through much of Europe, exhibited many of the qualities Mill wished to see more generally diffused throughout the laboring classes. Independence from the wage structure creates a sense of autonomy and self-determination that encourages the peasant proprietor to take responsibility for his own fate and the fate of his children, rather than trusting in paternalist institutions to provide for their present needs and future security. Thus, according to the authorities Mill cites, peasant proprietors are "the most industrious [people] in the world" and are constantly working to augment their small holdings of capital through savings (*PPE* 283, 274–75).

According to Mill, the peasant proprietor's independent situation also has the potential to result in the attainment of two of Mill's most important social goals—a high level of intellectual and moral development and the self-regulation of population growth. In discussing this potentiality, Mill's mode of argumentation shifts from quoting the observations of others to an a priori reasoning of his own. While Mill acknowledges that peasant proprietors receive little formal education, he asserts that their situation involves the constant mental stimulus of "turning to practical use every fragment of knowledge acquired" (*PPE* 286). The resulting "mental habit" renders even the relatively small amount of knowledge such peasants receive through schooling or reading very fruitful, so that it goes much further than such knowledge often does. The independent economic situation of the proprietors also fosters the "moral virtues of prudence, temperance, and self-control" (*PPE* 286). The same circumstances that lead the peasant to be inordinately industrious and concerned to save for the future influence other areas of his or her character. One of the most important of these ancillary areas, for Mill, is sexual temperance. Mill admits that population has increased rapidly among peasant proprietors, but he blames that increase on a low standard of living rather than on the economic organization of proprietorship. Mill contrasts the structure of peasant proprietorship with that of wage labor to determine which has the most potential to encourage such self-regulation. Peasant proprietorship is more effective, Mill concludes, because unlike the wage laborer, "every peasant can satisfy himself from evidence which he can fully appreciate, whether his piece of land can be made to support several families in the same comfort as it supports one" (*PPE* 289).

Mill uses a similar combination of cited authority and independent a priori reasoning in his discussion of profit-sharing and cooperatives in the chapter on the future of the laboring classes. In his discussion of these forms of social organization, Mill retains the broad structure of private property but reimagines that structure so that it can accommodate certain socialist-like economic forms. The key differences between Mill's profit-sharing and cooperatives and the socialist forms from which he shies away are their extent and their relationship to the governmental or political structures of the society:

the social experiments Mill cites in this chapter are relatively small and local, and explicitly economic rather than political. What links them in Mill's thinking is their departure from the system of wage labor, in which productive industry is divided between capitalist and laborer. Both profit-sharing and cooperatives give the laborers a direct economic interest in their labor and more control over the conditions of their labor. In contrast, the traditional system of wage labor pits employer against employed in such a way as to diminish overall productivity and keep laborers in a position of increasingly hostile dependence. Mill predicts that as society continues to develop, "there can be little doubt that the *status* of hired labourers will gradually tend to confine itself to the description of workpeople whose low moral qualities render them unfit for anything more independent: and that the relation of masters and workpeople will be gradually superseded by partnership in one of two forms: in some cases, association of the labourers with the capitalist [i.e., profit-sharing]; in others, and perhaps finally in all, associations of the labourers among themselves [i.e., cooperatives]" (*PPE* 763–64). This passage is from the 1848 edition of *Principles;* the formulation is even stronger in the 1852 edition, where profit-sharing is said to be at most "temporary," and cooperatives are no longer "perhaps" the future but simply the final destination of all wage labor (emphasis in the original, see note 1, *PPE* 764).

Mill cites at length stories of successful profit-sharing and cooperative experiments. He dwells on two areas of improvement in his discussion of these experiments: changes in the habits and morality of the workpeople and increased productivity.[18] For Mill, however, profit-sharing represents only the first stage of improvement in the position and conditions of labor; cooperation is the ultimate goal: "The form of association . . . which if mankind continue to improve, must be expected in the end to predominate, is not that which can exist between a capitalist as chief, and workpeople without a voice in the management, but the association of the labourers themselves on terms of equity, collectively owning the capital with which they carry on their operations, and working under managers elected and removable by themselves" (*PPE* 772–73). With this vision of cooperation, Mill pushes the limits of private property as far as they will go. Capitalists will remain, but they will gradually—without violence or revolution—be forced to cede control over production to the associations of laborers whose efficiency, productiveness, and competitiveness will win a larger and larger share of the market. Mill predicts that owners of capital will increasingly find it to their advantage to lend their capital to such cooperative associations, rather than continuing their own productive operations within the "old system" (*PPE* 791). The laboring population, in turn, will achieve independence and freedom as well as economic advantage. Mill hopefully predicts the results of "the co-operative principle" in terms that clearly establish such a form of organization as his social ideal:

> Eventually . . . we may, through the co-operative principle, see our way to a change in society, which would combine the freedom and independence of the individual, with the moral, intellectual, and economical advantages of aggregate production; and which, without violence or spoliation . . . would realize, at least in the industrial department, the best aspirations of the democratic spirit, by putting an end to the division of society into the industrious and idle, and effacing all social distinctions but those fairly earned by personal services and exertions. (*PPE* 791)

There are competition and individuality in Mill's ideal social order, but these are at once counterbalanced by and channeled through an organization of production that ensures competition on fair terms and individuality justly rewarded. No longer will individual economic and moral development be the sole province of the leisured, or "idle," classes; rather, competition and independence in the economic sphere will garner for the industrious laborer his or her just reward in economic well-being and in the increased possibilities for individual development provided by a better standard of living.

Cooperation represents for Mill the ideal possibilities and limits of the economic system of private property. Other aspects of Mill's ideal social order involve more direct political intervention. Mill is not content to remain solely within the realm of *economic* possibility in the *Principles;* he also ventures outside the sphere of the purely economic in order to advocate measures and changes he believes are necessary for a just, ethical social order. These measures are focused on the individual.

I have already discussed Mill's encouragement of government spending on philanthropic projects in a country approaching the stationary state. Similarly, in book 5, which Mill devotes to the role and influence of the government, he supports "government intervention" in certain areas seen by laissez-faire political economists as the responsibility of the private sector. While economic historians agree that Mill's overall discussion of the government comes down on the side of laissez-faire, they note Mill's explicit exceptions to this principle. In specific cases, Mill even advocates economic assistance to individuals, arguing that "energy and self-dependence are . . . liable to be impaired by the absence of help, as well as by its excess" (*PPE* 967). In cases where an individual's situation is so dire that he or she has no hope of succeeding, wise and limited government intervention can actually stimulate rather than depress the individual's energy and exertions and establish or restore that individual's self-dependence.

The twinned principles of independence and self-dependence also guide Mill's consistent advocacy for the legal and economic equality of women. Mill argues that "women are as capable as men of appreciating and managing their own concerns, and the only hindrance to their doing so arises from the injustice of their present social situation" (*PPE* 959). Mill attacks laws that seek to limit women's independent economic opportunities, such as factory work, and give husbands control over their wives' earnings. Mill recognizes that such laws reflect widespread social attitudes. Thus, his call for their repeal is in its own way interventionist: Mill is demanding that the government set a higher standard of fairness than is generally socially recognized, at the same time equalizing the legal opportunities available to adult men and women. This dual interventionist/anti-interventionist position is suggested by his call for fundamental legal reform in the treatment of women: "It is the great error of reformers and philanthropists in our time to nibble at the consequences of unjust power, instead of *redressing the injustice itself.* If women had *as absolute a control* as men have, over their own persons and their own patrimony or acquisitions, there would be no plea for limiting their hours of labouring for themselves, in order that they might have time to labour for the husband, in what is called, by the advocates of restriction, *his* home" (first emphases mine; last emphasis in original, *PPE* 959). In short, if the law gave women their most basic rights in their own persons and property, it would not have to be constantly intervening on their—or their husbands'—behalf.

Mill's most emphatic statements about the need for government action concern the moral and intellectual development of the community as a whole, especially through education. Mill argues that education is an area in which a consumer often cannot judge the best "commodity" or means of selecting such a commodity. "The uncultivated," he writes, "cannot be competent judges of cultivation. Those who most need to be made wiser, usually desire it least, and if they desired it, would be incapable of finding the way to it by their own lights" (*PPE* 953). Mill stresses the need for a comprehensive system of basic primary education to be provided by the government. Mill's justification of the need for this more specific form of education points to the impulses behind his privileging of government-sponsored educational measures generally. Mill argues that if parents fail to educate their children in certain basic skills and bodies of knowledge, they do a disservice both to the child and to "the members of the community generally."

On one level, this seems to be simply another example of Mill's distrust of parental or familial authority: for Mill, the family is one of the last bastions of tyranny and despotism, and this tyranny comes directly from the power that society grants parents and husbands over their children and wives. Parents' authority to educate—or not educate—their children has been a part of such power. But Mill's formulation suggests other motivations and attitudes. For Mill, children are one of the few groups that require paternalistic protection by the government. Yet Mill's characterization of the "uncultivated" as incapable of selecting the best means for their own cultivation betrays a more general paternalism as well. Mill's justifications for government education suggest that in certain areas and at least temporarily, "self-dependence" is an inadequate social policy.

The policy is inadequate not only for the individuals needing (according to Mill) to be educated but also for the community that needs its members to be educated. Mill's paternalism toward the "uncultivated" goes hand in hand with his sense that, in the sphere of education, the needs of the group are more important than the needs or desires of the individual. Mill is careful to leave some space for the individual in this area, for he demands that the state, while offering and perhaps even mandating education for all, should never monopolize education or require everyone to choose the government's educational institutions. Thus, the individual would always retain a choice between government and private educational institutions, but the more fundamental choice of whether or not to pursue formal education—for oneself or one's children—would apparently not be available. Mill places such a high social and moral value on education that it becomes one of the rare cases in which he is willing to sacrifice the freedom of the individual.

Another instance in which Mill privileges the group over the individual is in the question of the maintenance of a "learned class." Mill argues that because "the cultivation of speculative knowledge" renders services to the community as a whole, rather than to its individual members, it is unlikely that such services will be remunerated by the private sector. If such cultivation of knowledge is to continue and to attract those most fitted to it, then, Mill insists, it must be supported by public funds. While this support only indirectly impedes the freedom of the individual (e.g., in the form of slightly increased taxation), the concept reinforces the exceptionality, for Mill, of education and learning. Mill's emphatic belief in individual freedom and autonomy is subtly but firmly underwritten by a specific definition of the individual; likewise, embedded in Mill's belief in the improvability of human nature is a significant caveat. Mill firmly believes that individual human nature is malleable, but he just as firmly, if less overtly, believes that this malleability must be actively and self-consciously cultivated in order to produce wisely self-dependent, public-spirited, and moralized individuals.

Mill's belief in the possibilities of such cultivation and his commitment to the process of individual cultivation are the factors that take him furthest from the scientific political economy of Ricardo; Senior; and Mill's father, James Mill. The focus of that cultivation *on* the individual, however, and

Mill's commitment to the individual in general link him to Ricardian economics and to the individualist strain within eighteenth-century moral philosophy that is the common root of both Ricardo's and J. S. Mill's economic theories. Because so many of Mill's ideals focus on the individual, he is constantly drawn to the need to protect the individual against external threats when he moves from abstract theory to application. In many cases Mill identifies and defines such threats differently than other nineteenth-century political economists, but the fundamental theoretical bias behind such protection is the same: both Mill and the Ricardian economists locate and naturalize the individual as the basic element in any social or economic system. Such systems can function properly—and, for Mill, advance or evolve—only if the individual is allowed to act freely within that system. For Ricardo and other scientific political economists, the individual needs to be protected from the constraints of monopolies, government regulation, excessive taxation, and so forth; for Mill, the individual also needs to be protected from "enslaving" want and poverty, ignorance, the excessive power of community opinion, and overcrowding.

While Mill's differentiation between the inevitable laws of production and more arbitrary laws of distribution to some extent denaturalizes the individualist mandate, that mandate returns in a very different, but almost equally powerful, form in the guise of moral and ethical injunction. For many critics of scientific political economy—critics whom Mill specifically had in mind when writing *Principles*—the structural shift from natural inevitability to moral injunction addressed many of their basic concerns. Yet the individualist content of Mill's vision continued to determine his vision of social and economic change. One telling evidence of the effect of Mill's individualism is his withdrawal from the brink, as it were, of socialism and the reasons he gives for that withdrawal. Another significant effect of Mill's individualism is his almost obsessive Malthusian concern with population control. Mill repeatedly emphasizes the need to limit population growth: he praises communism and the system of peasant proprietors because of their potential to control population growth; he argues that the empowerment of women will curtail population growth; and his ideals for individual moral development in the stationary state are predicated upon the stabilization of population. To some extent, Mill's concern with population growth can simply be read as a Malthusian holdover, or as the site where the inevitable laws of production impede the more flexible laws of distribution. But if we add to these readings of Mill's concern the question of why population becomes the critical point in the transition between the "old" and the "new" (or Millian) political economy—or between the laws of production and distribution—then the issue of population takes on broader significance.

Population, for Mill, is critical because the autonomy of the individual is always threatened by the natural force of population growth; the social aggregate is always threatened by the prospect of becoming an indiscriminate social *mass*. Mill's insistent advocacy of population limitation is his way of trying to ensure enough social and natural space so that the boundaries of the individuals that make up the aggregate do not blur. In fact, Mill's ideal society is one in which those boundaries are much stronger than he perceived them to be in mid-nineteenth-century England. The individual may become more "public-spirited," but such spirit must emerge from within the individual will rather than being forced upon the individual by the group. Similarly, competition can operate as a positive social force and stimulus for the individual only if there are not too many people competing for too few resources—only if individual activity can ensure enough resources that the agent can develop and retain a largely privatized interiority through education, contemplative solitude, and leisure.

Population control is an essential, rather than incidental, aspect of Mill's social and economic vision. Ironically, the centrality of the issue to Mill's vision makes his *Principles,* in certain ways, more a return to Malthus than a return to Smith. The difference is that for Malthus the population principle is a manifestation of divine will and providence—that is, the population principle is a natural, biological fact of human existence, but such "facts" are themselves manifestations of divine intention. The growth of population is, for Malthus, a divinely ordained goad to human self-improvement. As such, the population principle is continuous with the theological framework that for Malthus constitutes "the meaning of human existence." In contrast, Mill's version of human meaning is centered on the private and autonomous individual. Individual human agents must make life meaningful for themselves *and* their societies. By threatening the interiority of the individual, the population principle is much more fundamentally problematic in Mill's schema than in Malthus's. Despite the grand space-clearing gesture of separating the laws of production from those of distribution, Mill's individualism, combined with his scientific naturalization of certain economic laws, locks him into a space delimited by the ratio of population to resources. Even more damaging to Mill's vision is the fact that space—the space of human meaning—is not only delimited by the biological force of population but always threatened by it.

Mill's "conservatism," as exemplified by his distrust of socialism and his retention of the Malthusian population principle, is a fundamental result of his attempt to preserve political economy as a science while reconnecting that science with the "human element" of social philosophy, ethics, and romanticism. Mill's *Principles of Political Economy* represents one of the last attempts made from within the scientific tradition of economic theory to integrate scientific analyses with nonscientific social philosophy and theory without privileging one of these elements over the other. Viewed as a function of that attempt, Mill's obsession with the question of population control is striking less as an anachronistic blind spot in an otherwise progressive project than as a particularly telling trace of the ambitiousness and exceptionality of that attempt. Mill's individualistic philosophy presented him with some significant theoretical problems and led him to some untenable solutions, but it also served as the bridge between two discursive traditions that, after Mill, became increasingly unbridgeable.

Perhaps the crucial weakness in Mill's vision is the ideal of individual identity as autonomous, rather than intersubjective, as Smith had imagined it in *The Theory of Moral Sentiments*. Mill's return to Smith, in other words, was limited to a reading of Smith's *The Wealth of Nations* from which the psychologized morality of the earlier text had been largely erased. For Smith, an intersubjective model of the individual subject was crucial to both his conception of economic development and his ethical reservations about that model. Mill's very different set of reservations about social and economic development makes visible the difference between the nineteenth century's conceptualization of the individual—whether romantic or economic/utilitarian—and Smith's eighteenth-century moral philosophy. Instead of being interdependent and mutually constituted, Mill's individual moral and economic subjects are imagined as privatized and autonomous. Dependence and social interaction, rather than constituting the individual subject, are seen as a constant threat to it.

Just as Mill was unable to think of the individual in the intersubjective terms of Smith's moral philosophy, so he was unable to make the analytical and imaginative leap performed by his contemporary Karl Marx. Marx, more than the English and French socialists upon whom Mill drew, identified the "individual" as a reified, historically specific effect of capitalist economics. If Mill had been able to make this conceptual leap, he might have perceived socialism as the answer rather than as a threat to the moral and ethical foundations of his system. Such an answer, however, would have involved a reframing of the economic and ethical questions posed by his texts as questions of *politics* as well as economics and ethics. The failure of Mill's synthetic attempt to create an ethical economic science, then, needs to be read in terms of his inability to articulate an ethical vision outside the discursive and ideological categories not only of classical political economy but also of classical liberalism.

In my final chapter, I trace the legacy of Mill's failure in two very different "economic" critiques of his project: those of John Ruskin in *Unto This Last* and William Stanley Jevons in *Theory of Political Economy*. While connections have legitimately been made between their criticisms of Mill's *Principles*, Ruskin's and Jevons's economic writings are most significant in their divergences. Ruskin takes Mill's "human element" and, instead of positioning it as secondary and subordinate to scientific economic "laws," makes it the center of his definition of economic value and of what he sees as a true economic "science." The result is a text is now canonized within *English*, rather than economics, departments. In contrast, Jevons's project is an attempt to render political economy more narrowly and authoritatively scientific. While rejecting Ricardo's (and thus also Mill's) value theory, Jevons's *Theory* can be seen as a formal return to and refinement of Ricardo's mathematically structured economic discourse. The distinction Mill draws between the natural and invariable "scientific" laws of production and the historically malleable principles of distribution is rendered insignificant by Jevons's redirection of economic theory from production to consumption, from the labor theory of value to the marginal utility theory of value. With Jevons, scientific political economy becomes explicitly mathematical: a science of quantities and calculations rather than a science of social values.

chapter seven

Morals and Mathematics: Critical Revisions of Scientific Economic Theory in the 1860s and 1870s

By 1860, J. S. Mill's *Principles of Political Economy* had been canonized as *the* dominant and authoritative text of nineteenth-century British political economy. It was not only the most widely read book of scientific economics in Britain as a whole; it was also taught in universities throughout Britain as the primary textbook for the study of economic theory. Because of the text's dominant discursive position, it also became the central target for attacks on classical economic theory. For twentieth- and twenty-first-century readers, the most famous and enduring of these attacks is Karl Marx's *Capital,* in which Mill becomes Marx's whipping boy, accused of sloppy thinking as well as ideological blindness.[1] For British readers in the 1860s and 1870s, however, the more famous and familiar attacks on Mill's *Principles* came from nonsocialist writers who positioned their critiques well within the confines of the capitalist economic structure. John Ruskin and William Stanley Jevons both criticized Mill not for his collusion in developing a procapitalist economic theory and ideology but rather for what they saw as his mistaken theory of value and the erroneous methodological apparatus through which he defined and approached economic issues.

There, however, the similarities between the critical and revisionary economic writings of Ruskin and Jevons end. The differences between their economic writings are fundamental and extensive, including differences in definitions, scope, discursive form, and methodology as well as readership, reception, and institutional location. These differences, in turn, tell a striking story about what was involved in the successful establishment of "economics" as a science and as an autonomous academic discipline in the final decades of the nineteenth century. Likewise, the differences between the revisionary economic projects of Ruskin and Jevons suggest the increasing discursive, ideological, and institutional reification of the distinction Raymond Williams has identified as emerging between "society" and "culture" during the nineteenth century, a distinction that naturalized the disaggregation of human experience into two separate domains of knowledge, one scientific and amoral and the other aesthetic and moral.[2] "Culture" becomes the ideological container of the nonrationalizable, including not only the artistic and aesthetic but also the moral and ethical. As part of this epistemological and ideological process, Ruskin's critique of Mill's *Principles* has become the province of departments of English and economic rhetoricians, while Jevons's revisionary text claims a canonical role in histories of contemporary economic thought.

This difference in the disciplinary and historiographic status of Ruskin's and Jevons's economic writings is inextricably bound up with the discursive specificities of their texts. In placing Ruskin's *Unto This Last* alongside Jevons's *Theory of Political Economy*, what is most striking is the discursive distance between the texts, an almost unbridgeable formal gap between the articulation of concerns examined together in Mill's *Principles*. In his seminal history of capitalist economic thought, *The Worldly Philosophers,* Robert Heilbroner locates the gap in late-Victorian economic theory between the institutionalized equilibrium theory of Alfred Marshall and what he calls the "underworld economics" of Karl Marx, Henry George, and J. A. Hobson. Their underworld status and lack of influence on the shape of professionalized economic knowledge, Heilbroner notes, were as much a product of their refusal to accept the initial terms of canonical economic theory as of their unpopular conclusions (these two factors, of course, were not unconnected, as we will see in Ruskin's work). Heilbroner ends his chapter on the disjunction within Victorian economics with a pathetic (in the high Greek classical sense) appeal to the intellectual and historical opportunities missed by the economic establishment through its unwillingness to listen to the "underworld" outsiders.[3] My examination of the growing discursive gap between Ruskin, the "outsider" critic of classical political economics, and Jevons, the "insider" critic, carries with it the same sense of lost possibility, though in this case focused more on the loss of formal possibilities and alternatives rather than the loss of a specific theoretical insight.[4]

In emphasizing the gap between the writings of Ruskin and Jevons, my reading of this discursive moment differs fundamentally from that of another recent "literary" examination of the marginalist revolution, even as it is aligned with it in many ways. In *Insatiability of Human Wants,* a capacious and insightful work of cultural history, Regenia Gagnier focuses upon the similarities between discursive shifts in economic and aesthetic models in the late nineteenth century.[5] Gagnier's insights into these convergences and their twentieth-century effects and manifestations are persuasive and compelling, both politically and intellectually. By emphasizing a gap where she locates a convergence, my argument does not take issue with hers but rather identifies a different epistemological and ideological problem: the two-cultures divide that emerged in the nineteenth century and that still organizes most of the authoritative knowledge produced by the twenty-first-century academy. While Gagnier identifies and explores significant parallels between the late-nineteenth-century models of economic and aesthetic consumption, to do so she must read against the grain of the very disciplinary divides that Victorian economic theorists such as Jevons worked to instantiate. Whereas this approach provides valuable insight into the artificiality of such divides, it does not forestall the closer examination of those divides themselves. While historical work such as Gagnier's reenvisions the nineteenth and twentieth centuries by self-consciously working across disciplinary divides, other historians—equally aware of the artificiality of those divides—continue to chart their emergence and effects. The work of Mary Poovey and Immanuel Wallerstein, working from different disciplines and ideological perspectives, has been particularly influential in the humanities and social sciences.[6]

What *all* these historical projects share, including the work of Gagnier and Heilbroner as well as Poovey and Wallerstein, is the combined sense of the crucial role that nineteenth-century discourses and institutions played in the disciplining of social knowledges *and* of the conceptual, imaginative losses that this process entailed. Some Marxist historiographers, such as Wallerstein, seem to have a sense of how such epistemological and political losses might be redressed. For the most part, however, cultural and epistemological historians of nineteenth-century academic disciplinarity are left with the task of marking and excavating the historical and discursive ground into which an unimagined range of alternative knowledges were subsumed. It is in this spirit that I begin by examining Ruskin's alternative economics before turning to Jevons's work. In *Unto This Last,* Ruskin decries the social, political, and conceptual losses he sees classical political economy as having already entailed and begins to outline his alternative model of economic *knowledge* as well as economic *activity.* When this text is read next to that of Ruskin's canonical contemporary, W. S. Jevons, and in light of its marginal status in histories of academic or professional economic thought, it becomes a significant index of some of the possible—if not necessarily desirable—alternative knowledges about the economy that were lost in the course of the nineteenth century.

In *Unto This Last,* a series of four essays originally published in the *Cornhill Magazine* in 1860, Ruskin criticizes Mill's labor theory of value—and economic value theory in general—for being too narrowly defined, for excluding too many factors as "noneconomic" or irrelevant. Ruskin's critique of political economy's notions of value is part of a larger critique of the whole "scientific" approach to the study of economic issues. In particular, Ruskin sees political economy's scientific approach to economic and social issues as excluding important moral and ethical considerations that he believes should be central to any "economic" analysis. In sharp contrast, Jevons's criticism of Mill's text and of the labor theory of value is part of an argument that calls for a *more* scientific approach to economic theory in general and to value theory in particular. While Ruskin focuses on and elaborates political economy's *moral* and *ethical* aspects, Jevons concentrates on and reconstructs its *scientific* aspects. For Jevons, as for Ricardo fifty-four years earlier, the scientific authority of economic theory depends upon—indeed is predicated upon—a narrowing of the boundaries of the science, particularly the excision of the social, moral, and ethical concerns of popular critics.

This chapter examines Ruskin's *Unto This Last* and Jevons's *Theory of Political Economy* (1871) in terms of these questions of ethics, morality, analytical method, and scientific scope.[7] In particular, I show how each writer's construction and deployment of specific discursive forms facilitated his revisionary economic project, including the connections, inclusions, and exclusions upon which such projects depend. This analysis, in turn, exposes the extent to which the fate of moral and ethical concerns in economic theory was bound up with the formal demands and possibilities of a discursive mode that has since become *the* authoritative method and form of scientific economic thought. As historians of economic discourse have noted, the classical political economy of Ricardo and Mill, in retrospect, looks inclusive, even holistic, compared to the neoclassical economics founded in part by Jevons and the marginalist revolution.[8] Given this observation, it is no wonder that the moral and ethical economics of John Ruskin fall almost completely off the historiographical grid of significant nineteenth-century economic thought. Infinitely more "inclusive" and "holistic" than Ricardo, Mill, or Jevons, Ruskin is also rendered infinitely less significant for—if not irrelevant to—the development of scientific economic thought.

In its radical rejection of the form, as well as the content, of scientific economics, Ruskin's critical project comes closest to that of Dickens, among the popular critics I have examined. In fact, in a long footnote to the first essay in *Unto This Last*, "The Roots of Honor," Ruskin praises the critical and moral vision of economics that Dickens develops in *Hard Times*.[9] Ruskin's social critique and analysis of the effects of economic science are also heavily indebted to the earlier writings of Thomas Carlyle, especially "Signs of the Times," *Past and Present*, and *The Latter-Day Pamphlets*.[10] Like Dickens and Carlyle, Ruskin identifies the narrowly defined scientific approach of classical political economy as central to its failure to adequately theorize the domain of "the economic." Ruskin announces and explains his rejection of the dominant scientific form of political economy in the first of the four essays that make up *Unto This Last*.[11] Going straight to the heart of the matter, he begins by stating: "Among the delusions which at different periods have possessed themselves of the minds of large masses of the human race, perhaps the most curious—certainly the least credible—is the modern *soi-disant* science of political economy, based on the idea that an advantageous code of social action may be determined irrespectively of the influence of social affections" (*UTL* 167). The problem, Ruskin argues, is not that political economists deny the presence of the "social affections" but that they see them as "accidental and disturbing elements in human nature" (*UTL* 167). Self-interest, in contrast, is reified by political economists as a "constant," and thus as the appropriate basis for a determination of natural economic law. For Ruskin, the abstract and deductive scientific method theorized by Mill cannot produce accurate knowledge about social and economic behavior because it is predicated upon the excision of precisely those forces that Ruskin sees as most fundamental to such behavior.

Ruskin reinforces and illustrates this point in the following paragraph, in which he compares political economy first to a science of gymnastics that assumes men have no skeletons and then to one that assumes that men are all skeleton:

> Observe, I neither impugn nor doubt the conclusion of the science if its terms are accepted. I am simply uninterested in them, as I should be in those of a science of gymnastics which assumed that men had no skeletons. It might be shown, on that supposition, that it would be advantageous to roll the students up into pellets, flatten them into cakes, or stretch them into cables; and that when these results were effected, the re-insertion of the skeleton would be attended with various inconveniences to their constitution. The reasoning might be admirable, the conclusions true, and the science deficient only in applicability. Modern political economy stands on a precisely similar basis. Assuming, not that the human being has no skeleton, but that it is all skeleton, it founds an ossifiant theory of progress on this negation of a soul; and having shown the utmost that may be made of bones, and constructed a number of interesting geometrical figures with death's-head and humeri, successfully proves the inconvenience of the reappearance of a soul among these corpuscular structures. I do not deny the truth of this theory: I simply deny its applicability to the present phase of the world. (*UTL* 168)

I cite this passage at length because it starkly demonstrates both the style and the logic of Ruskin's rejection of scientific economic theory. And while Ruskin asserts that he finds the science simply irrelevant rather than subject to condemnation, the tone of his opening statement, combined with the remaining sweep of his argument, makes clear his sense that the scientific mode of inquiry is immoral and unethical as well as "inapplicable." Indeed, this condemnation is embedded in the glib and subtle violence of the gymnastics metaphor, in which human students are deformed and deanimated into "pellets," "cakes," and "cables." Like this imaginary science of gymnastics, the current science of political economy deforms and deanimates its student subjects into nonhuman objects of violent social, rather than physiological, experimentation. Even Ruskin's use of such an elaborate, extended metaphor marks his rejection of the scientific methodology of classical political economy. As the economic historian and rhetorician Willie Henderson has noted, "Ruskin is conducting a methodological debate in literary rather than scientific language."[12]

In addition to his "literary" style and his studied refusal to accept the scope, distinctions, and exclusions on which the scientific authority of classical political economy depends, Ruskin also attacks the scientific method more directly. Rather, Ruskin doesn't attack the method itself so much as its deployment in the domain of human social and economic life. In "The Roots of Honor," where he argues for the crucial role of the affections in human social and economic action, Ruskin insists not only that this "motive force" renders "every one of the ordinary political economist's calculations nugatory" (*UTL* 171) but also that it is not a force that *can* be calculated by the scientific apparatus of the economic theorist: "Even if he desired to introduce this new element into his estimates, he has no power of dealing with it; for the affections only became a true motive power when they *ignore every other motive and condition of political economy*" (emphasis mine, *UTL* 171). The human affections, that is, are a kind of force that refuses calculations; they can function to fuel human labor and effort only when they are uncontaminated by the self-interested and profit-seeking motives that the political economist posits as the ground of his science.[13]

Throughout *Unto This Last,* Ruskin links his critique of classical political economy and its scientific methodology to this alternative model of economic inquiry, in part through the construction of oppositions between what he sees as true versus false versions of economic science. Thus, early in his essays, he constructs an opposition between political economy, which he defines as "the production, preservation, and distribution ... of useful or pleasurable things," and mercantile economy, defined as "the accumulation, in the hands of individuals, of legal or moral claim upon ... the labor of others" (*UTL* 181). Later Ruskin makes a distinction between the currently reigning "bastard science" of political economy and a "real science" that would "teach ... nations to desire and labor for things to lead to life" (*UTL* 209).

By exposing the falsifications and failures of "mercantile economy," "the bastard science," and "nescience," Ruskin seeks to clear a discursive space for his alternative model of political economy, a model that is not built around individual self-interest and does not figure human society in quantifiable, mechanistic terms.[14] Such a political economy would constitute itself not as an abstract, positive science but rather as a normative, social, and ethical project. It would still, however, Ruskin insists, *be* political economy. It would still, in other words, be an authoritative form of knowledge about economic behavior and relations. In fact, for Ruskin it is precisely because of its new form that it would be a much more accurate and authoritative form of knowledge than that currently celebrated as "scientific economics."[15] In the following discussion, I will focus particularly upon the ways in which Ruskin's alternative economic model is embedded in the particular rhetorical strategies he deploys, namely his redefinition, recontextualization, and refiguration of scientific economic theory's economic terms and problems. Through these specific discursive strategies, Ruskin seeks simultaneously to invalidate "scientific" economic theory; to construct his alternative economic model; and to demonstrate this model's fundamental grounding in human affection, morality, and ethics.[16]

One of Ruskin's most powerful and consistent discursive strategies is to redefine and defamiliarize key terms of economic analysis.[17] In "The Veins of Wealth," Ruskin begins the process of redefining wealth itself, perhaps the central term of political economy. Ruskin's first move is to explicitly introduce into the concepts of riches and wealth the concept of power. In this striking move, Ruskin strips political economy's object of analysis—wealth—of any claim to being outside the domain of the political and ethical. He writes: "What is really desired, under the name of riches, is, essentially, power over men; in its simplest sense, the power of obtaining for our own advantage the labour of servant, tradesman, and artist; in a wider sense, authority of directing large masses of the nation to various ends" (*UTL* 182). Ruskin goes on to explain that this power depends on the relative lack of such power—or poverty—of others and upon the proportional rarity of others who possess the same such power. As a result, Ruskin claims that what is really meant by the "art of becoming 'rich'" includes not only the art of accumulating money but also the "art" of "contriving that our neighbors shall have less" (*UTL* 182).

The moral—as well as ethical and political—embeddedness of economic issues for Ruskin becomes even clearer in the definitions developed in the final essay of *Unto This Last,* "Ad Valorem." The first and most important of the terms Ruskin reworks here is "value." First introducing and challenging the scientifically authoritative definitions of the term developed by Mill and Ricardo, Ruskin then moves temporarily away from these political economic authorities to the authority of Latin etymology. Chiding well-educated merchants for rejecting their classical educations, Ruskin writes: "*Valor,* from *valere,* to be well or strong . . . ;—strong, *in* life (if a man), or valiant; strong *for* life (if a thing), or valuable. To be 'valuable,' therefore, is to 'avail toward life.' A truly valuable or availing thing is that which leads to life with its whole strength" (emphasis in original, *UTL* 208–9).[18] By taking the word "value" outside its traditional economic contexts of "value in exchange" and placing it into the context of its own etymology, its own long history in classical thought, Ruskin displaces a quantitatively figured scientific abstraction with a qualitative idealist *and* material standard.[19] "Life," here, is at once a rather abstract ideal of vitality and a very material invocation of human bodies. At the same time that he redefines this key term, Ruskin also effectively recontextualizes the whole problem of "value," removing it from the narrow boundaries and premises of nineteenth-century economic theory into the moral and ethical domains associated with classical philosophy.

When Ruskin returns to his redefinition of the term "wealth," now linking it to his newly defined conception of "value," he not only reinvokes his earlier redefinition but also returns temporarily to that authority of economic theory, J. S. Mill. Ruskin begins by citing and glossing Mill:

> "To be wealthy," says Mr. Mill, "is to have a large stock of useful articles."
> I accept this definition. Only let us perfectly understand it. . . .
> We have . . . to ascertain in the above definition, first, what is the meaning of "having," or the nature of Possession. Then what is the meaning of "useful," or the nature of Utility. (*UTL* 209–10).

Ruskin goes on to redefine possession and use in specifically moral terms, particularly in terms of the moral capacity of any given individual to possess, rather than to be possessed by, things of value and the individual's moral capacity to use that which he or she possesses in a positive, or "valiant," manner. Having redefined possession and utility, Ruskin has also exploded the material, economistic definition of value that he supposedly accepted. Now wealth, rather than being a primarily quantitative measure (i.e., "a large stock") of unproblematically defined qualitative value (i.e., "useful"), is instead a complex moral entity that encompasses qualitative characteristics of both possessor and use. Moral judgment, instead of being written out of the definition of wealth, is placed at its core and directed toward both "economic" entity and actor. Wealth is, Ruskin proclaims, "THE POSSESSION OF THE VALUABLE BY THE VALIANT" (*UTL* 211).

Through such redefinitions, Ruskin works to recontextualize the terms of economic science within the moral, ethical, social, and political vocabularies through which they had been theorized by classical thought, eighteenth-century moral philosophy, and the Christian religious tradition, and from which Ricardo, in particular, had worked to disentangle them.[20] The strategy of recontextualizing political economy's terms and concerns within a moral and social universe is one that Ruskin deploys throughout his text, even when he is not explicitly engaged in the redefinition of terms. Many of the most powerful of his recontextualizations, in fact, use images rather than language per se to resist the orthodoxies of economic theory. Often these images force upon the readers connections that scientific economic theory has denied are relevant to the kinds of knowledge it produces and the social relations it naturalizes. Even if the reader ultimately rejects the analytical validity of these connections, the force and logic of the images is such that they continue hauntingly to unsettle the economic abstractions to which they have been attached.

One of the most powerful of these connections is made in Ruskin's argument that not only consumption but also the mode of consuming should be given greater attention in political economy, particularly in the determination of whether the consumption of an item is a true sign of wealth, whether it avails toward life. The question of the ethical and moral value of consumption, in turn, also makes visible another set of the moral and ethical stakes involved in production. Ruskin writes,

> But if our consumption is to be in anywise unselfish, not only our mode of consuming the articles we require interest him [the laborer who produces them], but also the *kind* of article we require with a view to consumption. As thus . . . : it matters, so far as the labourer's immediate profit is concerned, not an iron filing whether I employ him in growing a peach, or forging a bombshell; but my probable mode of consumption of those articles matters seriously. Admit that it is to be in both cases "unselfish" [i.e., not for personal consumption], and the difference, to him, is finally, whether when his child is ill, I walk into his cottage and give it the peach, or drop the shell down his chimney, and blow his roof off. (*UTL* 221)

The image of the a bomb dropped on a poor laborer's cottage works on a number of levels. Most powerfully, it collapses economic science's carefully constructed distances. It collapses the distance between consumption and production, and thus also between consumer and producer. Instead of being linked to one another through a set of economic laws (i.e., Say's law) and processes (exchange), the producer and consumer fuse together into an immediate social encounter with potentially devastating effects on the former. In addition, the image of a leisured consumer strolling up to a poor man's cottage also insists upon the power differential involved in such economic exchange. This differential is, Ruskin insists, almost as significant for the empowered consumer as it is for the relatively disempowered producer, for it is the moral responsibility of the economically powerful to use their power for the benefit of the nation rather than merely for their own gratification.

The image also, through the use of first-person pronouns, collapses the distance between author and reader and between reader and text. Thus, knowledge, rather than being objective and "out there," independent of the subject of knowledge (both producer and consumer of knowledge), is rendered subjective, having specific social effects that are dependent upon the agency of the person who wields that knowledge. As Willie Henderson has argued, the reader, the possessor of Ruskin's new economic knowledge, is consistently associated in Ruskin's text with the economically powerful, in this illustration the leisured consumer who either delivers a peach or drops a bomb.[21]

The final level on which the bomb image works involves more a recontextualization than a connection. Perhaps more accurately, it involves the reconstruction of such a massive and repressed connection that it amounts to a dramatic recontextualization: that is, the connection of the abstract, analytic world of scientific economic theory to the pathetic, affective world of familial relations. It is not simply the adult producer upon whom the bomb is inflicted but also, more importantly, his sick child. In constructing this miniature narrative scenario, Ruskin insists upon the inextricable role of "the social affections" in economic analysis, just as he does in his opening essay. Here, though, Ruskin's insistence is embedded in his use and choice of illustrative narrative rather than argued explicitly through other rhetorical strategies. This illustrative narrative can also use such familial affections to figure the moral significance of economic questions as well as to insist on the connections between the economic and affective realms. The reader's (sentimental) emotional attachment to the image of the sick child, however temporary and tenuous, becomes part of the discourse in which the moral stakes of the consumer's economic choice are registered.

The image of the bomb and the sick child is just one of the many textual moments in which Ruskin uses familial images, examples, and analogies to recontextualize "economic" concerns within the moral, ethical, and social domains. Repeatedly, for example, he asks the reader to imagine the relationship between employer and employee as that of a father and son.[22] Likewise, at one point he uses "rearing children" as the example of the most positive, that is, life-producing, form of labor (and opposes it to murder). And, in order to illustrate that oppositional interests do not necessarily lead to antagonistic relations, Ruskin evokes the image of a starving mother and her children with only one crust among them. All these familial and domestic images construct a very clear model of precisely what kind of moral and social universe Ruskin is constructing along with his alternative model of economic knowledge. It is paternalistic and hierarchical as well as collective and intersubjective. The "individual" is figured in terms of connection and moral responsibility rather than autonomy or freedom. It is a universe in which analysis presumes and builds upon, rather than displacing, affect and moral sensibility. Human passions and connections, rather than rational self-interest, are at the center of this universe.

Obviously, this is not the kind of moral and ethical universe toward which Mill is attempting to push economic discourse. Nor is it that of Adam Smith, though there is more overlap with his work. The "virtues" of Ruskin's vision are neither bourgeois nor aristocratic; they are domestic. Like Dickens and Mayhew, Ruskin sees domesticity as a potential haven of moral virtue amid the immoral social and economic forces of competitive capitalism. More than either of these other writers, however, Ruskin attempts to reconstruct economic knowledge *around* and ground it *upon* the feminized virtues of domesticity. That is, rather than constructing female figures as carriers of this virtue who can function as complements or antidotes to the immoralities of the commercial sphere, Ruskin works to domesticate the science—and the functioning— of the sphere itself. In so doing, Ruskin's economic writings not only make connections between but actually work to disrupt the increasingly powerful discursive oppositions between rationalized society and nonrational culture and between the public/market and the private/domestic spheres of human activity. Throughout *Unto This Last,* Ruskin repeatedly demonstrates how each side of these two dominant oppositions is imbricated in and dependent upon the other.

Ultimately, however, Ruskin's text works primarily not to deconstruct the entire oppositional apparatus but rather to reconfigure it and to privilege one set of oppositional terms over the other. For example, Ruskin doesn't reject the category of scientific knowledge, with its accompanying methodology of mechanistic laws, abstract reasoning, and quantitative calculation. Instead, as I mentioned earlier, Ruskin rejects the relevance of scientific methodology to the concerns of human social and economic life. While scientific methodology can still be useful within the natural, material sciences of biology, astronomy, chemistry and physics, it is worse than counterproductive when applied to the domains of human existence. Calling instead for a different sort of methodology in the investigation of these concerns, Ruskin effectively collapses the society-versus-culture opposition but retains what C. P. Snow would later call the "two-cultures" divide. For Ruskin, both culture *and society* belong to the nonrationalizable, nonquantitative side of this discursive and institutional opposition. Thus, the methodology for understanding society (and economics as a part of that) as well as culture should work to perceive, make visible, and explain the significance of all kinds of connections—figurative and emotional as well as logical ones. Logical connections are not invalid for Ruskin but must be subordinated to the larger epistemological frameworks of imagination and affect.

Ruskin's deconstruction of the public/market-versus-private/domestic opposition is more radical than his engagement with the "two cultures" divide. By placing affect at the center of all social activity, Ruskin effectively feminizes and domesticates both oppositional terms. While it is clear from *Sesames and Lilies* that Ruskin is not working to deconstruct the oppositional structure of gender itself, his economic writing shows that he is at least reconfiguring certain aspects of the dominant interpretation of that structure. In *Unto This Last*, emotionality and morality are as firmly attached to male social actors as they are to female social actors. The bomb-and-sick-child image, for example, is constructed around a father rather than a mother. Thus, the male social actor in Ruskin's text is, in terms of the dominant Victorian discourse of gender, feminized, taking on attributes that the separate-spheres ideology assigns only to women. This deconstruction of the separate-spheres oppositions is crucial for Ruskin's reconfiguration of the emergent two-cultures binary. It is because Ruskin's text reveals the "masculine" social as domesticated and feminized that a rationalist scientific methodology is no longer relevant to it.

Masculinity does remain an important term in *Unto This Last*, but it is at odds with, rather than derived from, the demands of the capitalist commercial sphere.[23] In fact, one way to understand Ruskin's deconstructive project is in terms of not simply a feminization of the public social sphere but also, simultaneously, a certain remasculinization of the private domestic sphere. Such an understanding is reinforced by Ruskin's invocation of a classical model of *oikonomia*, "house law," or the economy of the household, where the household's patriarchal character is assumed (*UTL* 161). For the classical author Xenophon, the household is the basis for the patriarch's social authority, not as a complementary sphere that morally grounds this authority but as part of a continuous practice of masculine moral and social command, including self-command.[24] Ruskin's appeal to the pre-enlightenment model of masculinity, domesticity, and economic agency is significant because this model enables him to evade the binaries of enlightenment rationalist thought in order to construct a complex and, by nineteenth-century standards, contradictory discourse of a sentimental, but also ideally masculine, "science" of economic activity.

Ruskin's domestic and aesthetic model of political economy assumes its full significance not only in relation to the classical texts of Ricardo and Mill, to which his text was a response, but also in relation to the very different critique of classical economics that emerged not long after his: W. Stanley Jevons's. Jevons first outlined his marginalist economics in a paper presented to the British Association for the Advancement of Science, Section 5, in 1862. While this paper went largely unnoticed, Jevons's book-length study, *Theory of Political Economy*, published in 1871, quite rapidly gained the status of a major and authoritative economics treatise, helping to disrupt the orthodoxy and dominant status of Mill's *Principles*.[25] In contrast, the publication of Ruskin's *Unto This Last* in the *Cornhill* was suspended by the publisher with the fourth essay because of adverse and vocal public response.[26] When Ruskin republished the four essays in book form as *Unto This Last* in 1862, the book sold only eight hundred copies in eleven years. This was not the only difference between the fates of the two economic projects. While Ruskin's text was read by some academically based and professional economists, his largest audiences were, first, the hostile middle-class public that led to the suspension of the magazine publication and, later, various working-class organizers and labor politicians who found in his text a theoretical rationale for their pro-labor positions.[27] Ruskin scholars have been able to trace lines in theoretical continuity, and even influence, between Ruskin's economic vision and that of later professional economic models, but these lines are necessarily disconnected from the formal elements of Ruskin's economic discourse. In fact, those formal elements were at times bemoaned by his defenders, even when the text began to gain a new popularity. Furthermore, Alan Lee has argued persuasively that when the text began to be more widely read in the final decades of the century, it was read less for its economy theory than for its ethics, its call for justice.[28]

    In contrast to the tortuous publication history of *Unto This Last* and Ruskin's other economic writings, Jevons's *Theory* was widely discussed in both the popular and the academic press and gained increasing authority within the university curriculum. By the late 1870s, Jevons was preparing a second edition for publication. In fact, Jevons's text laid much of the theoretical and methodological groundwork for the marginalist economics that developed into a new orthodoxy for an increasingly professionalized body of academic economics. Along with Carl Menger and Leon Walrus, historians of economic thought identify Jevons as one of the founders of the "marginalist revolution" that was the precursor to neoclassical economics. Like Ruskin, Jevons criticizes both classical economic value theory and the method of classical political economy. Also like Ruskin, Jevons argues for the importance of consumption and the consumer in any economic model, against classical theory's sole focus on production. But beyond these two general points, the similarities between the two economic projects cease. For while Ruskin wants to *add* considerations of consumption into an economic model that also continues to address issues of production and distribution, Jevons's model of economic consumption functions to analytically displace, and even erase, the categories of production and distribution, subsuming them *within* the logic of rational consumer choice. Similarly, while Ruskin criticizes classical value theory and method for being too *narrow* in their scope, Jevons criticizes them for being too *broad*—not adequately rationalized and not sufficiently scientific.

Jevons, as Margaret Schabas argues, is the founder of not only the *marginalist revolution* in economic science but also the *mathematical revolution*.[29] In fact, Jevons's writing demonstrates the interdependence of the two "revolutions," the first redefining the source of value as consumer desire rather than labor power, the second constructing mathematical models to quantify, calculate, and rationalize the effects of that desire. Thus, while Mill attempts to revise the analytical narrowness and exclusiveness imposed by the mathematical logic of Ricardo's prose and Ruskin explicitly identifies and excoriates that narrow exclusivity, Jevons develops a methodology that embraces and extends the rationalized, mathematical form of economic science. This form, in turn, at once facilitated and *necessitated* a further circumscription of the "scientific" scope of political economy.

In both the Preface and the introductory chapter of the first edition, Jevons proclaims that because economics deals with quantities, "it *must* be a mathematical science" (emphasis mine, *TPE* vii).[30] Constructing a distinction between logical and mathematical sciences, he argues that "if there be any science which determines merely whether a thing be or be not . . . it must be a purely logical science, but if the thing may be greater or less, or the event may happen sooner or later, nearer or farther, then quantitative notions enter, and the science must be mathematical in nature, by whatever name you call it" (*TPE* 8). The essence of what distinguishes the logical sciences from the mathematical sciences is, for Jevons, the role of quantities and quantification. This points to what is probably the most fundamental difference between his and Ruskin's reconstruction of the science of political economy. For Ruskin the science has relied too much on quantification and must be revised to account for the significant qualitative considerations that are essential to his model of human action and relations. For Jevons, the science has failed to adequately address the quantitative aspects of economic behavior and processes by refusing to develop and deploy the mathematical tools of quantitative reasoning. By reconstructing the entire science around the notion of quantitative difference and quantitative relations, Jevons dramatically refocuses economic inquiry away from the complex moral, ethical, and social concerns taken up, however differently, by Mill and Ruskin. Reiterating Ricardo, Jevons insists that economic science is about what is rather than what ought to be.[31] But more than Ricardo, Jevons reimagines the "what is" in terms that can be figured only in mathematical language.

Essential to this reimagination is his radical redefinition of value in terms of utility—the marginal utility to a consumer—rather than in terms of labor. Unlike labor value, which classical economics figured in terms of determinate material human needs and the determinate material limits of agricultural production, the value of utility is a contingent and immaterial "circumstance." Furthermore, that value is not an objectively determined but a subjectively relative "circumstance," dependent in the movements of the individual mind. Drawing directly upon Jeremy Bentham's utilitarian model of a pleasure/pain calculus, Jevons locates the creation of economic values in the individual desire to seek pleasure and avoid pain.

While value is subjectively determined for Jevons, it also manifests itself in the objectively observable phenomenon of prices. Perhaps more accurately, because Jevons needs to be able to identify some determinate measure or quantity of value, he argues that prices, interest rates, and wages are a direct phenomenal manifestation of subjective valuation, of utility value. Thus, he writes, "far be it from me to say that we shall ever have the means of measuring directly the feelings of the human heart. A unit of pleasure or of pain is difficult even to conceive; but it is the amount of these feelings which is continually prompting us to buying and selling, borrowing and lending, laboring and resting, producing and consuming; and it is from the *quantitative effects* of feelings that we must estimate their *comparative amounts*" (emphasis mine, *TPE* 13). Jevons's desire to reconstruct mathematics as an economic science also leads to the crucial distinction he draws between total and marginal utility. For Jevons, it is not total utility but "marginal" utility that determines the "ratio of exchange" that is, for him, the quantitative measure of value. Thus, he explains that "the theory turns upon those critical points where pleasures are nearly, if not quite, equal. I never attempt to estimate the whole pleasure gained by purchasing a commodity; the theory merely expresses that, when a man has purchased enough, he derives equal pleasure from possessing a small quantity more or from the money price of it" (*TPE* 20). The critical points are those of "marginal utility," the "final degree of utility" that tips the scale between purchase or abstinence. It is the commodity's marginal utility to the consumer that will determine the price he or she will or won't pay for an item, money's marginal utility to the borrower and lender that will determine its interest rate, and a wage's marginal utility to a laborer that will determine whether he continues or ceases to labor. In each case, the subjective valuation of an economic agent will be reflected in a quantitative form that can be mathematically graphed, charted, and calculated, all of which Jevons does throughout *Theory*.[32]

Before further exploring Jevons's reconstruction of political economy, we must examine the conception of the human that lies at the center of this new economic theory: the individual psychology of economic man. Early in *Theory of Political Economy*, Jevons announces the absolute centrality of a specific version of human psychology to his economic model. Thus, he writes, "a few of the simplest principles or axioms concerning the nature of the human mind must be taken as its first starting point, just as the vast theories of mechanical science are founded upon a few simple laws of motion. That every person will choose the greater apparent good; that human wants are more or less quickly satiated; that prolonged labor becomes more and more painful, are a few simple inductions on which we can ground . . . a complete deductive mathematical theory" (*TPE* 24). One of the first things to note about this passage is Jevons's analogy between a psychologized economics and the mechanistic science of physics. Where Ruskin uses such analogies primarily to argue for the inapplicability of such mechanistic models, Jevons self-consciously constructs his human science upon their basis. Whereas earlier economic theorists and popularizers had been trained in moral philosophy or received a more general liberal education, Jevons initially came to economic theory through the route of a university training in the natural sciences and only later returned to the university to study moral philosophy and political economy. His initial university training was in chemistry, and throughout his academic and professional career he continued to draw upon the natural sciences as heuristic models of economic behavior and authoritative models of economic science.[33] Thus, for Jevons the mechanistic metaphor carries an intellectual commitment to reconstructing economic theory—and with it human psychology—along such lines.

Jevons lists three features of human psychology or human nature as "axioms" or "inductions" on which his mechanistic economic model is built. Two derive directly from Bentham's utilitarian philosophy and psychology: "Every person will choose the greater apparent good" and "Prolonged labor becomes more and more painful" (*TPE* 24). Jevons also derives from Bentham's model the notion that the "good" described here is a self-interested and subjective good—Jevons's person seeks his own good rather than that of other people. Thus, later, in developing his theory of exchange, Jevons writes: "Every individual must be considered as exchanging *from a pure regard to his own requirements* or *private interests*" (emphasis mine, *TPE* 85–86). Jevons's conflation of self-interest with "good" is, of course, not a new one. Ever since Ricardo's *Principles of Political Economy and Taxation*, nineteenth-century scientific political economy had depended upon this conflation. What is new is Jevons's connection of this definition to a redefinition of labor solely in terms of disutility or pain (rather than as a source of productive value) and his new emphasis on the satiation of human wants, his second axiom. Taken together, these three axioms establish a psychological and economic model in which the human mind is the critical crossing point of desire for specific pleasures, satiation with specific pleasures, and desire to avoid prolonged labor. The human mind feels all these things, but, of equal importance for Jevons, the mind also *measures* all these things. All human economic action, for Jevons, is a direct manifestation of the mind's comparative measurement of its own feelings. The economist himself does not need to measure an individual's subjective feelings; the individual does that him- or herself and expresses that measurement through his or her quantifiable economic choices. Because the economist can only "estimate [the] . . . comparative amounts" of feelings through their quantitative effects, he can also account for those feelings only *in terms of* their quantitative effects. That is, any feeling that is not registered quantitatively does not register at all in the account of the marginalist theorist. Thus, while Jevons puts human psychology at the center of his economic model, he also subordinates that psychology to the mathematical apparatus of the model.

One of the reasons that psychology and feelings can be discussed only in terms of their quantitative effects, according to Jevons, is that the human mind has no capacity for the sympathetic identification or intersubjective comparisons of value.[34] Thus, Jevons can write that "the reader will find, again, that there is never, in a single instance, an attempt made to compare the amount of feeling in one mind with that in another. I see no means by which such a comparison can ever be accomplished. . . . Every mind is thus inscrutable to every other mind, and *no common denomination of feeling is possible*. Even if we could compare the feelings of different minds, we should not need to do so; for one mind only affects another indirectly" (emphasis mine, *TPE* 21). This psychological model has three sets of implications for economic science. First, as mentioned earlier, it creates a situation in which the economist can justify limiting his discussion of feelings to their quantitative effects and manifestations. Second, it creates a human social world in which the individual agent *must* act solely from self-interest, since he or she cannot accurately perceive any other agent's interest. Third and finally, it constructs a social world in which individuals are imagined as interacting with one another only *through* quantitative, financial transactions. Economic science does not deny that other forms of transaction occur (though they too would have to be externally mediated), but it does render them analytically invisible and insignificant.

Jevons conducts a similar type of analytical erasure when he discusses the possibility of "higher motives" than those of self-interested pleasures and bodily wants. Here again he does not deny the existence of higher motives, but he argues that a science of economics can and should proceed on the presumption of the lower: "The feelings of which a man is capable are of various grades. He is always subject to mere physical pleasure or pain, necessarily arising from his bodily wants and susceptibilities. He is capable also of mental and moral feelings of several degrees of elevation. A higher motive may rightly overbalance all considerations belonging even to the next lower range of feelings; but so long as the higher motive does not intervene, it is surely both desirable and right that the lower motives should be balanced against each other" (*TPE* 29–30). In fact, Jevons goes on to argue, it is precisely "the lowest rank of feelings" that is the proper concern of political economy. The powerful irony of this reductive focus is that once economic science has developed a rational calculus of this lowest rank of feelings, it has also tended to generalize its findings and methods to other domains of feelings and motivation, creating in effect a colonizing model of autonomous, calculating, and self-interested human nature. This colonization is facilitated, in turn, by the reductiveness of the initial analytical gesture. Once "higher motives" become invisible within a scientifically authoritative model of human behavior and human social relations, there is little epistemological ground for resistance to the generalization of the "lower" calculus that such motives would, Jevons grants, disturb.

While Jevons's economic model is supposedly derived from human psychology, it is a psychology from which there have been significant erasures. It is a psychology that is manifest only in economic choices and relates to others primarily through economic transactions. Furthermore, it is a psychology founded upon the analytical suppression of all but the "lower motives" of "bodily wants and susceptibilities." These are precisely the kinds of erasures effected earlier by Ricardo and, to a lesser extent, Mill and decried by Ruskin in *Unto This Last*. The logical demands of Jevons's mathematical method, however, facilitate, naturalize, and even necessitate such foreclosures to a much greater extent than the earlier discursive methods of classical economics. Only variables that can be figured quantitatively and whose effects can be generalized through mathematical formulae can be accounted for in Jevons's economics. Conversely, once such formulae are set up as the authoritative mode of treating economic issues, only quantitatively rendered considerations seem relevant to their description and determination.

Nonquantifiable terms such as Ruskin's "social affections" and "soul" may be granted a certain kind of subjective reality, but they are outside the domain of the scientifically knowable and relevant.

Jevons's mathematical method also has another significant effect on his psychological model. The individual mind that is said to be the foundation of the entire economic system, it turns out, is not really an "individual" mind at all. Rather, it is a singular term derived from an aggregate or average. Jevons explains:

I must here point out that, though the theory presumes to investigate the condition of a mind, and bases upon this investigation the whole of Political Economy, practically it is an aggregate of individuals which will be treated. The general form of the laws of Economy is the same in the case of individuals and nations; and, in reality, it is a law operating in the case of multitudes of individuals which gives rise to the aggregate represented in the transactions of a nation. Practically, however, it is quite impossible to detect the operation of general laws of this kind in the actions of one or a few individuals The motives and conditions are so numerous and complicated, that the resulting actions have the appearance of caprice, and are beyond the analysis and prediction of science. (*TPE* 21–22)

There is an interesting movement back and forth between theory and practice here. The *theory* of political economy is based upon the psychology of the individual, autonomous mind. The *practice* of that theory, however, can be manifested only in a large aggregate. Thus, any evidentiary support of the theory of the individual must be based upon the analysis of the nation as a whole, or some large aggregate. Once an economic law has been demonstrated on the level of an aggregate, it cannot be used to explain the behavior of any individual within that aggregate "unless," Jevons specifies, "all those individuals be of the same character and position as regards wealth and habits" (*TPE* 22). The very uniformity informing the individual psychology on which Jevons's theory depends, that is, is a uniformity constructed by the mathematical operations of the theory itself. The psychological and social variables of "character and position" are presumed to be neutralized by the law of averages and thus, again, rendered analytically insignificant.

The net effect of such analytical erasures and simplifications is quite evidently the further reification of scientific political economy's model of "economic man," precisely the model parodied by Ruskin's metaphor of a gymnastic science built around the assumption that men have no skeletons. Jevons's economic man is even more abstract and generalized than Ricardo's or Mill's. For the two earlier classical economists, an individual's character and behavior is derived from his position within the economic system, whether landlord, capitalist, or laborer. Jevons's model of individual psychology is generalized to all agents in the economic system at the same time that it is the basis of that system. Furthermore, because the economic system is derived from a universalized model of human psychology, there is no opportunity for a change in economic relations to effect a change in human character, along the line imagined in the later chapters of Mill's *Principles of Political Economy*. The economic model is completely closed and, in effect, tautological.[35]

As should be evident at this point, Jevons's redefinition of value, combined with his mathematical methodology and model of human psychology, together function to reshape the form of economic science itself. These three revisions of classical economic theory enable Jevons to construct political economy as what he calls, in the Preface to the second edition of *Theory of Political Economy*, "the mechanics of self-interest and utility."[36] They also allowed him to isolate and narrow the domain of economic theory much further than his classical predecessors, especially Mill. Such disaggregation of "the economic," combined with analytical and discursive strategies that universalized economic theory, played an important role in the further professionalization of economic knowledge. For some historians, in fact, marginalism is seen as virtually effecting that professionalization. Donald Winch summarizes this position in his essay, "Marginalism and the Boundaries of Economic Science":

> For such historians as Knight, Schumpeter, and Stigler, the introduction of the marginal principle . . . marks a kind of coming of age, when "economic theory was transformed from an art, in many respects literary, to a science of growing rigour." Associated with an advance on the analytical front were certain methodological gains. Economists, it is claimed, acquired a stricter sense of what was logically, rather than politically or morally, relevant to explanations of economic reality. The categories of economic analysis were made more distinct from those sanctioned by philosophical, political, and ethical debate. Prescientific vestiges and survivals were purged; economists became more self-conscious about maintaining the distinction between improvements in the analytical tools and more effective solutions to social problems. In this way, therefore, marginalism both reflected and contributed to the process of professionalization . . . of economics as an organized discipline which took place after 1870.[37]

Although Winch distances himself from this position—especially from its celebratory tone—in several respects during the course of his essay, his argument overall supports the linkage between the marginalist and mathematical revisions of W. S. Jevons and the process of the professionalization of economic science in Britain. I cite this passage at length because it touches upon so many aspects of Jevons's revisionary project and identifies how those aspects fit into a narrative of professionalization. In particular, the passage points to the disaggregation of "economic" from moral, political, and ethical concerns and the disentanglement of theory from practice as key discursive developments in the process of professionalization. In other words, the passage identifies precisely the discursive strategies initially deployed in the construction of economic knowledge in the work of David Ricardo. The difference between Ricardo and Jevons is, from this perspective, primarily one of degree, with Jevons developing methodological and analytical tools that enabled him to take these processes further.

There is, however, another important difference between these two nineteenth-century attempts to render the study of political economy "scientific": the difference of institutional context. By the 1870s, when Jevons wrote, political economy was much more firmly established within the universities. Jevons himself, of course, had received formal university training and taken a degree in political economy. Furthermore, he did much of his writing while holding academic positions at Owens College, Manchester, and University College, London. While his university positions never enabled him to establish the kind of oral tradition that Alfred Marshall established at Cambridge, his texts, theories, and methods did find a significant university audience among students and professional colleagues.[38] In addition, though there was as yet no specialized journal of economic science, *Theory of Political Economy* was reviewed by other professors, advanced students, and informal scholars of political economy in the *Manchester Guardian*, the *Athenaeum*, the *British Quarterly Review*, the *Westminster Review*, the *North American Review*, the *Fortnightly Review*, the *Academy*, and the *Saturday Review*. As suggested by this list, the audience for Jevons's economic theory was popular as well as academic. But that popular audience seems to have accepted the academic and professional discourse rather than finding it alien and unreadable (as Ricardo's audience found his prose).

In any case, the success of Jevons's text was not dependent primarily upon that readership. Many, if not all, aspects of his theory found support from academic economists throughout Britain, including Thomas Edward Cliffe Leslie, John Kells Ingram, Henry Sidgwick, H. Foxwell, and Neville Keynes. Even the staunchest critic of Jevons's theory, John Cairnes, granted the theory a certain kind of legitimacy and authority, both by publicly reviewing it and by echoing some of its claims. In fact, Margaret Schabas argues that by the final decades of the nineteenth century, the discipline of economics was firmly enough established to tolerate a diversity of theoretical and methodological practices.[39] Thus, Jevons's *Theory of Political Economy* did not need to dominate over all opposing views in order to establish its institutional authority. It needed only to remain in print and to continue to find an academic audience and academic advocates in order to exercise its influence over the emerging discipline. Nor was Jevons's text alone in calling for the marginal utility theory of value and the use of mathematical tools and symbols. As the discipline of economics became internationalized, the marginal theory of value was reinforced by Carl Menger in Austria and Leon Walras in France. Within England, the mathematical treatment of economic theory was given support by Alfred Marshall (even though Marshall's attitude toward Jevons's own work was decidedly cool) as well as Foxwell and Keynes.

Thus, while the professionalization of economics was by no means complete in the closing decades of the nineteenth century, it was much more firmly established than in the initial and middle decades. Its place within the university, in particular, was much more secure and independent, particularly from religion, than in the 1820s and 1830s. This change enabled Jevons's revisionary model of economic science to define its own terms and methods and to delineate its own scope with much more success than Ricardo's earlier revisionary discourse. In other words, the institutional context of increasing professionalization and the discursive strategies of Jevons's text worked together to effect the kind of disaggregation and autonomy of "the economic" and of "economic knowledge" that Ricardo had attempted to bring about more than fifty years earlier.

Jevons's successful discursive and analytic reification of a distinct domain of economic behavior, activity, and relations was particularly important in disabling critiques of the science that were framed in terms of moral and ethical considerations. On the one hand, by rewriting economic theory in the language of mathematics, Jevons created a barrier of specialization and expertise that most non-university-trained economic thinkers could not cross.[40] The language of mathematics also carried associations of neutrality and objectivity that helped to insulate economic writings from the appearance of political and subjective biases. On the other hand, the marginal utility theory of value developed by Jevons also goes further than Ricardo's labor theory of value in constructing economic agency in terms of self-interested, autonomous, even isolated individuals. Marginal utility theory places this image of the economic agent at the center of its theoretical model, making it, as it were, the engine and naturalized origin of the capitalist economic system. Then the theory self-consciously strips that agent of the capacity for intersubjectivity. While Ricardo's prose style stripped the reader of the capacity for sympathetic identification through its use of abstraction and hypothetical scenarios, Jevons's theory goes further by making psychological isolation a fundamental analytical feature. Jevons's creation and reification of "economic man" is also more effective than Ricardo's because it is able to fold into itself certain of the irrational as well as rational aspects of human subjectivity. Thus, while Jevons's economic man cannot sympathize, he can have irrational desires without disrupting the rational functioning of the system as a whole. In fact, the system actually depends, in part, on the ultimate insatiability of these irrational desires.[41]

Marginal utility theory also has other important theoretical differences from classical political economy that facilitate the disaggregation of "the economic," especially from moral and ethical claims. By basing the economic system on individual psychology rather than on a tripartite class structure, Jevons's theory analytically erased the major power differences and inequities of the nineteenth-century class system. Because labor, as disutility, is analytically equivalent to commodities rather than productive of them, the laborer and capitalist are said to enter the economic domain on an equal footing. The laborer has no privileged relation to value, as he does in Ruskin's writing as well as in classical and Marxist theory. Nor is he disadvantaged by his need to sell his labor to survive. Laborer and capitalist are both neutral, equivalent economic "persons" within marginal theory. Jevons writes: "Every person whose wish for a certain thing exceeds his wish for other things [including leisure or rest], acquires what he wants, provided he can make a sufficient sacrifice in other respects. No one is ever required to give what he desires more for what he desires less, so that perfect freedom of exchange must be to the advantage of all" (*TPE* 134). Within this economic scenario, or "law," the coercion of physical necessity—of abject poverty, hunger, economic disenfranchisement, and wage dependency—is completely erased.

The final way in which marginal theory functions to reify "the economic" and separate it from the domains of morality and ethics, as well as politics and the social, involves the creation of a static, rather than dynamic, model of the economic system. Classical economic theory evolved from and was bound to a stage theory of social and political as well as economic development. The developmental aspects of this theory were attenuated, but not excised from, Ricardo's *Principles of Political Economy and Taxation*. Ricardo largely confined his discussion of development and "progress" to economic considerations, such as economic growth and profit margins. His popularizers, however, teased out and deployed the providential logic embedded in the economic narrative, claiming for economic growth the extra-economic benefits of social, political, and moral well-being, on both individual and national levels. Later, John Stuart Mill reinterpreted the narrative of economic growth *and stagnation* (i.e., the stationary state) in terms of possibilities for individual intellectual and moral development via greater economic equity and stability, and the greater leisure such economic developments could grant to all. Mill even saw this economic narrative as possibly moving beyond capitalism altogether, creating an alternative economic system of collectivism or socialism. Jevons's static model of the economic system, in contrast, naturalizes and universalizes capitalist social arrangements and the capitalist psychology of economic man. Jevons self-consciously rejects Mill's qualitative and moral privileging of some forms of pleasure over others. Pleasures are morally equal within the marginalist model, distinguished only quantitatively, rather than qualitatively. At the same time, with the engine of the system transferred from the physically grounded activity of production to the psychologically fueled activity of consumption, there is no basis for narrative progression whatsoever. Capitalism, including economic growth, is outside time, or rather, it is its own time, isolated from histories of political and social transformation. Such growth will lead neither to Mill's ideal of a more morally and ethically enlightened socioeconomic world nor to McCulloch's and Martineau's image of a morally and politically superior nation-state of Britain.

By placing economics outside a developmental narrative, marginal utility theory helps to further disaggregate the domain of the economic as a discrete and distinct domain of scientific investigation and knowledge. At least, it does so *analytically* and *methodologically.* Narratives of economic growth and "development" will still be (and still are) imbricated with and deployed for political, social, moral, and ethical ends. Economic claims will still be imbued with moral and ethical meaning. But economic theory itself will increasingly construct its authority in the abstract, isolated, and "objective" discourse of mathematics and in the specialized institutional domains of the academic departments of economics, scientific societies, and professional journals. As Jevons's work clearly demonstrates, the authority of these specialized discourses and domains depends on the *erasure* of all such connections between the economic and these "other" realms of human experience. Economic theory does not develop a model of "bourgeois virtue," as Deirdre McCloskey has argued, because the boundaries of economic theory have been constructed largely to *isolate* the economic from the moral and ethical considerations associated with "virtue."[42] In the nineteenth century, those boundaries were still being contested—both discursively and institutionally—but by the end of the century, those boundaries were largely in place. They were, and are, still contested. However, they were increasingly contested from the decidedly disadvantaged and nonauthoritative position of the outsider, the populist critic, the nonexpert.

To some extent, of course, this was also the position from which Dickens, Mayhew, and Ruskin criticized the boundaries and claims of economic science. But, as I have shown, the position of the populist writer was significantly more authorized and empowered in mid-nineteenth-century England, before the study of economic issues had been professionalized. By the 1860s, however, when Ruskin published *Unto This Last,* the popular critic of scientific economic theory was being marginalized by his refusal to accept the conventions and boundaries—as well as claims—of that theory. Even though Ruskin tried much more fully and self-consciously than Dickens or

Mayhew to develop an *alternative* model of political economy, his critique of the dominant discourse found a much smaller, more hostile, and more dismissive audience. The structure of economic science as a profession seems to have already begun to dictate the terms in which claims to economic knowledge could be granted any discursive authority. This same structure, in contrast, enabled Jevons to launch a very successful critique of the dominant classical model of economic theory from *within* the professional discourses and institutions of economic science. It also helped to ensure that authoritative knowledge about the economy would be increasingly indifferent to the moral and ethical effects produced by the political and social deployment of that knowledge, and increasingly immune to criticisms of its claim made by nonexpert witnesses to those effects.

There have been exceptions to this trend in institutionalized economic science, the emergence and passing dominance of welfare economics in the mid-twentieth century being the most notable. In fact, the very existence of welfare economics as a professionalized discourse would seem to render the nineteenth-century narrative of economic discourse that I have traced largely irrelevant. There are many reasons to argue, however, that this is not the case. Ultimately such arguments are beyond the scope of this study, but I can note several circumstances to suggest the continuing importance of this narrative for twenty-first-century economic theory. Perhaps the most significant is the number of dominant "internalist" histories of economic thought, such as those cited by Winch, that connect the increasing authority and scientific validity of economic theory to its isolation of economic from moral and ethical concerns. Another notable factor is that welfare economics, while addressing concerns of social welfare and development, continues to draw upon many of the mathematical tools and marginalist premises developed by late-nineteenth-century economic theorists such as Jevons. Welfare economics, that is, makes its arguments and interventions into "the social" not through moral and ethical appeals that are largely nonrationalizable but rather through rationalized theoretical revisions, supplemented by quantifications and calculations. Finally, it must be remembered that the discourse of welfare economics has lost much of its authoritative status within the discipline of economics over the course of the past twenty to thirty years. During this time, economic theory has reconstructed itself along the lines of deductive logic and mathematics embraced by Jevons in the 1870s, self-consciously rejecting the claims, definitions, and concerns of welfare economics. Thus, while Jevons's *Theory of Political Economy* may not have laid the ground for the entire discursive and methodological history of twentieth- and twenty-first-century economics, it has certainly done so for the contemporary liberal-neoclassical and econometric incarnations of the discipline.

Ruskin, in contrast, has been canonized by departments of English. His critique of nineteenth-century economic discourse has been relegated to the unsystematic, unscientific, and nonrationalizable domain of "culture."[43] While his work is probably much more widely read today than Jevons's, he and his economics have even less cultural authority than they did in the 1860s. Perhaps more accurately, his writings—along with those of other nineteenth-century critics of political economy—have *only* "cultural" authority, while the capitalist economic engine has joined together with the institutional and discursive structures of the university to create a situation in which only rationalized, scientific knowledges can carry any "real" social or political weight. Ultimately, the uneven *developments* of nineteenth-century economic discourse have led to radically uneven *distributions* of social, political, and cultural power, even within the elite domains of the twenty-first-century Western academy. These unequal distributions of power, in turn, have profound effects on the epistemological possibilities for—as well as authority of—the kinds of knowledges produced by the disciplined academy today.

Toward the end of his essay, "Should We Unthink the Nineteenth Century?" Immanuel Wallerstein writes:

> If economy, polity, and culture are not discrete arenas . . . then the whole organizational structure of history cum social science has no intellectual justification whatsoever. If in addition we cast doubt on Newtonian linearity . . . , it is no longer self-evident that scientific activity looks toward the statement of elegant sparse laws. It may inversely look toward the elaboration of complex, dense interpretive schema, in which case our methodologies must inevitably be quite different, and in which case we may have to reopen the assumption that there are "two cultures"—science and art.[44]

In trying to reimagine scientific knowledge—particularly "social scientific" knowledge—after the deconstruction of the nineteenth-century assumptions upon which so much of our twentieth- and twenty-first-century knowledges and institutions have been built, Wallerstein invokes a model and methodology more reminiscent of and indebted to a Ruskin essay or a George Eliot novel than a Jevons equation.

It is not that Wallerstein, Gagnier, Poovey, or I believe that "culture," particularly Victorian culture, holds the answers to the political, economic, and epistemological problems created by the disaggregation of the "economic" from the political, moral, ethical, and aesthetic domains. Rather, we and other scholars are reclaiming some of the discursive and formal features that have been relegated to the supposedly apolitical and unscientific domain of culture in our twenty-first-century attempts to think beyond the nineteenth-century legacy inherited by the West. One of the things involved in this reclamation is an exploration of forms of knowledge and agency that have been gendered "feminine" or "domestic" for at least the past two hundred years. Further, as postcolonial and world-systems scholars have argued, this process of reimagining authoritative forms of knowledge also involves reconceptualizing our Western definitions and models of "culture," "civilization," and knowledge.

There is much vital work being done in these areas in the humanities and "softer" social sciences—anthropology and political theory. There is also some such "rethinking" going on within the "harder" social sciences such as economics, political science, and sociology. However, to earn for these new models of knowledge the cultural authority lost in the nineteenth century, we "cultural" critics and historians need to change the very structure of the academy, including not only its internal organization but also its relationship to the broader populations of "mass culture." Doing this, it seems increasingly clear, will involve the restructuring not merely of knowledge but also of "society" and the "economic" itself.

notes

Notes to Introduction

1. Among such traditional histories of economic thought, I include Marian Bowley, *Studies in the History of Economic Theory before 1870* (London: Macmillan, 1973); Phyllis Deane, *The Evolution of Economic Ideas* (Cambridge: Cambridge University Press, 1978); Samuel Hollander, *The Economics of David Ricardo* (Toronto: Heinemann, 1979); Joseph Schumpeter's *History of Economic Analysis* (London: George Allen and Unwin, 1954); and Piero Straffa, *Production of Commodities by Means of Commodities: Prelude to a Critique of Economic Theory* (Cambridge: Cambridge University Press, 1960).

2. See, for example, Scott Gordon's *History and Philosophy of Social Science* (New York: Routledge, 1991) and Richard Olson's *The Emergence of the Social Sciences 1642–1792* (New York: Twayne Publishers, 1993) and *Science Deified, Science Defied* (Berkeley: University of California Press, 1990).

3. I am linking morality, ethics, and virtue together as one discourse because they are so intermeshed in the late eighteenth and early nineteenth centuries. Through the course of my analysis, however, I will be using each word in more specific ways, giving each a distinct significance and historical location. I use the word "morality" as the nineteenth-century counterpart to the aspects of the word "virtue" in eighteenth-century moral philosophy that connect judgments of one's intersubjective and social relations to normative evaluations of one's personal and individual spiritual or psychological status. That is, I use the terms to point to the ways that external social relations and actions were seen, in the nineteenth century, as reflecting internal "morality." Morality developed this significance in part through the increasing cultural significance of evangelical discourse, even among nonevangelicals. "Ethics," in contrast, hearkens back more to the classical roots of "virtue" and concerns more public and other-oriented social actions and relations. Ethics concerns the way in which one judges and moderates one's social behavior not out of concern for one's own moral well-being but rather out of concern for the good of others.

4. See chapter 1.

5. By "materiality of language," I allude to the poststructuralist argument that language is constitutive of reality rather than merely reflective of it. Foucault develops this concept with particular significance for the history of science and ideas. See my discussion of Foucault and Poovey in the following paragraphs.

6. The classic discussion of the emergence of the modern concept of culture is Raymond Williams's *Culture and Society: 1780–1950* (New York: Columbia University Press,

1958, 1983). More recently, see John Guillory, *Cultural Capital: The Problem of Literary Canon Formation* (Chicago: University of Chicago Press, 1993). See also Mary Poovey, "Aesthetics and Political Economy in the Eighteenth Century," in George Levine, ed., *Aesthetics and Ideology* (New Brunswick, N.J.: Rutgers University Press, 1994), 79–105.

7. For a discussion of some of the contradictions and developments in Foucault's own model of historical analysis, see Herbert L. Dreyfus and Paul Rabinow, *Michel Foucault: Beyond Structuralism and Hermeneutics,* 2d ed. (Chicago: University of Chicago Press, 1983), 79–125.

8. Emphasis in the original. Michel Foucault, *The Archaeology of Knowledge and the Discourse on Language,* trans. A. M. Sheridan Smith (New York: Pantheon Books, 1972), 47–48.

9. This is a point at which my emphasis differs somewhat from Foucault's, for I address not only the emergence and formation of certain discourses but also the question of their *legibility* to and for a reading audience. In other words, I do not assume that just because a discourse can be written at a certain historical moment, it can also be widely readable and comprehensible at that moment. The socially and historically constructed reading audiences for texts play a role in the development of a discursive formation.

10. Michel Foucault, "Politics and the Study of Discourse," in Graham Burchell, Colin Gordon, and Peter Miller, eds., *The Foucault Effect: Studies in Governmentality* (Chicago: University of Chicago Press, 1991), 58.

11. I refer to a general critique of Foucault's work that argues that "power" becomes just such a totalizing force within Foucault's own historical writings.

12. Louis Althusser, "Ideology and the Ideological State Apparatus," in *Lenin and Philosophy and Other Essays,* trans. Ben Brewster (New York: Monthly Review Press, 1971), 127–86; Louis Althusser and Etienne Balibar, *Reading Capital,* trans. Ben Brewster (London: New Left Books, 1970), esp. 199–308. For Jameson's discussion of mediation, see Fredric Jameson, *The Political Unconscious* (Ithaca, N.Y.: Cornell University Press, 1981), 39–44.

13. Raymond Williams, *Marxism and Literature* (Oxford: Oxford University Press, 1977), 121–27.

14. Mary Poovey, *A History of the Modern Fact: Problems of Knowledge in the Sciences of Wealth and Society* (Chicago: University of Chicago Press, 1998), 7.

15. In "Politics and the Study of Discourse," Foucault defines these criteria for the identification of a "discursive formation": "What individualizes a discourse such as political economy or general grammar is not the unity of its object, nor its formal structure; nor the coherence of its conceptual architecture, nor its fundamental philosophical choices; it is rather the existence of a set of rules of formation for *all* its objects . . . , *all* its operations . . . , *all* its concepts . . . , *all* its theoretical options. . . . There is an individualized discursive formation whenever it is possible to define such a set of rules" (54). I have revised this definition in order to recognize that discursive formations, like social formations, have emergent, dominant, and residual moments and modes. In a discursive formation's emergent and residual forms, it will not be as coherent and internally consistent as Foucault's criteria imply.

16. See Ellen Messer-Davidow, David R. Shumway, and David J. Sylvan, eds., *Knowledges: Historical and Critical Studies in Disciplinarity* (Charlottesville: University Press of Virginia, 1993). Timothy Lenior's essay in this volume ("Discipline of Nature/Nature of Disciplines," 74) describes a discursive formation simply as "a historically conditioned system of regularity for the coexistence of statements."

17. Immanuel Wallerstein, "Should We Unthink the Nineteenth Century?" in Francisco O. Ramirez, ed., *Rethinking the Nineteenth Century* (New York: Greenwood Press, 1988), 186.

18. See note 2. See also Albert O. Hirschman, *The Passions and the Interests: Political Arguments for Capitalism before Its Prime* (Princeton, N.J.: Princeton University Press, 1977); Robert Heilbroner, *Behind the Veil of Economics* (New York: W. W. Norton, 1988); Gary Langer, *The Coming of Age of Political Economy, 1815–1825* (New York: Greenwood Press, 1987); Menachem Fisch, *William Whewell, Philosopher of Science* (Oxford: Clarendon Press, 1991); and Richard R. Yeo, "Scientific Method and the Rhetoric of Science in Britain, 1830–1917," in John Schuster and Richard R. Yeo, eds., *The Politics and Rhetoric of Scientific Method* (Dordrecht and Boston: D. Reidel, 1986).

19. See Eric Heavner, *Food, Sex and God: The Christian Social Theory of T. R. Malthus*, Ph.D. diss., Johns Hopkins University, 1993; Donald Winch, *Riches and Poverty: An Intellectual History of Political Economy in Britain, 1750–1834* (Cambridge: Cambridge University Press, 1996); Boyd Hilton, *The Age of Atonement: The Influence of Evangelicalism on Social and Economic Thought, 1795–1865* (Oxford: Clarendon, 1988); A. C. Waterman, *Revolution, Economics, and Religion: Christian Political Economy, 1798–1833* (Cambridge: Cambridge University Press, 1991); and Alon Kadish, "An Introduction to the Variety of Arguments for Free Trade," in Alon Kadish, ed., *The Corn Laws: The Formation of Popular Economics in Britain*, vol. 1 (London: William Pickering, 1996).

20. Two other recent books by literary scholars also resituate the discourse of political economy in relation to literary texts in particular: James Thompson's *Models of Value: Eighteenth-Century Political Economy and the Novel* (Durham, N.C.: Duke University Press, 1996) and David Kaufmann's *The Business of Common Life: Novels and Classical Economics between Revolution and Reform* (Baltimore, Md.: Johns Hopkins University Press, 1995). While Thompson and Kaufmann use contemporary theoretical frameworks to construct a relationship between canonical texts of political economy and equally canonical novels, my Foucauldian approach focuses on specific historical texts that existed in a more immediate discursive relationship to the texts of political economy and the novel that they cite as complementary (Thompson) or competing (Kaufmann). See also Mary Poovey's book *A History of the Modern Fact* and her article "Aesthetics and Political Economy in the Eighteenth Century."

Notes to Chapter 1

1. Walter Bagehot, "The First Edinburgh Reviewers," originally published in the *National Review*, October 1855; reprinted in *Collected Works of Walter Bagehot*, vol. 1, ed. N. St. John–Stevas (Cambridge, Mass.: Harvard University Press, 1965), 311.

2. As I discuss later in this chapter, Malthus's political economy was not actually secular, though many of his Romantic critics read it as such. Malthus's providential economics actually did find some support within the traditional English universities, whereas Ricardo's economic model was more contested.

3. See, for example, Robert Heilbroner, *Behind the Veil of Economics* (New York: W. W. Norton, 1988); Hirschman, *The Passions and the Interests*; William Letwin, *The Origins of Scientific Economics* (London: Methuen, 1963); and Olson, *Science Deified, Science Defied*.

4. For histories that identify Ricardo as central to the process of rendering political economy "scientific," see Winch, *Riches and Poverty*; Marc Blaug, *Ricardian Economics* (New Haven, Conn.: Yale University Press, 1958); S. G. Checkland, "The Propagation of

Ricardian Economics in England," *Economica* (February 1949): 40–52; Frank Fetter, "The Rise and Decline of Ricardian Economics," *History of Political Economy* 1 (1969): 67–84; Karl Polanyi, *The Great Transformation* (Boston: Beacon Press, 1944); and Gertrude Himmelfarb, *The Idea of Poverty* (New York: Knopf, 1984). See also Ellen Frankel Paul, *Moral Revolution and Economic Science* (Westport, Conn.: Greenwood Press, 1979); Gary Langer, *The Coming of Age of Political Economy* (New York: Greenwood Press, 1987); and T. W. Hutchinson, *On Revolutions and Progress in Economic Knowledge* (Cambridge: Cambridge University Press, 1978).

5. See Poovey, *A History of the Modern Fact*, 264–306, and my discussion later in the chapter for a fuller explanation of my use of the phrase "providential logic."

6. David Ricardo, *The Principles of Political Economy and Taxation* (London: Dent and Sons, 1973), 75. Further references are cited parenthetically in the text.

7. See Richard Yeo, *Defining Science: William Whewell, Natural Knowledge, and Public Debate in Early Victorian Britain* (Cambridge: Cambridge University Press, 1993), and S. G. Checkland, "The Advent of Academic Economics in England," *The Manchester School of Economic and Social Theory before 1870* (1951): 43–70.

8. See Poovey, *A History of the Modern Fact*, 3, 297–326.

9. Duncan Forbes argues that the tradition these writers created involved a social philosophy based on or deduced from the two "natural laws" of the progress of society and the heterogeneity of ends. Calling this philosophy "scientific whiggism," Forbes identifies its stress on scientific method within the study of society as the basis of the social and economic theories of J. R. McCulloch, James Mill, and John Stuart Mill. See Duncan Forbes, "'Scientific' Whiggism: Adam Smith and John Millar," *Cambridge Journal* 7 (1953–54): 645–70. For a thorough discussion of this tradition in relation to inductive and deductive forms of thought, see Poovey, *A History of the Modern Fact*, 214ff.

10. Stephen Gudeman, "Ricardo's Representations," *Economics as Culture: Models and Metaphors of Livelihood* (London: Routledge and Kegan Paul, 1986), 52.

11. Ibid., 69.

12. David Simpson, *Romanticism, Nationalism, and the Revolt against Theory* (Chicago: University of Chicago Press, 1993).

13. The most comprehensive of these rereadings of *The Theory of Moral Sentiments* and *The Wealth of Nations* and the relationship between them is Athol Fitzgibbons's *Adam Smith's System of Liberty, Wealth, and Virtue: The Moral and Political Foundations of* The Wealth of Nations (Oxford: Clarendon, 1995). Other important rereadings upon which I have drawn include Leonard Billet, "The Just Economy: The Moral Basis of the *Wealth of Nations*," *Review of Social Economy* 34 (1976): 295–315, and Richard F. Teichegraeber III, *"Free Trade" and Moral Philosophy: Rethinking the Sources of Adam Smith's* Wealth of Nations (Durham, N.C.: Duke University Press, 1986). See also Jan Peil, *Adam Smith and Economic Science: A Methodological Reinterpretation* (Cheltenham, U.K., and Northhampton, Mass.: Edward Elgar, 1999), and Jeffrey T. Young, *Economics as a Moral Science: The Political Economy of Adam Smith* (Cheltenham, U.K., and Lyme, N.Y.: Edward Elgar, 1997).

14. See J. G. A. Pocock, *The Machiavellian Moment: Florentine Political Thought and the Atlantic Republican Tradition* (Princeton, N.J.: Princeton University Press, 1975), and "The Mobility of Property and the Rise of Eighteenth-Century Sociology," in *Virtue, Commerce, History: Essays on Political Thought and History, Chiefly in the Eighteenth Century* (Cambridge: Cambridge University Press, 1985), 103–24.

15. For discussions of eighteenth-century formulations of bourgeois virtue, especially

in relation to Smith, see Fitzgibbons, *Adam Smith's System of Liberty, Wealth, and Virtue,* 16,193; Teichegraeber, *"Free Trade" and Moral Philosophy,* 13; Hirshman, *The Passions and the Interests,* 42, 129; Peter Mintowitz, *Profits, Priests, and Prices: Adam Smith's Emancipation of Economics from Politics and Religion* (Stanford, Calif.: Stanford University Press, 1993), 79; Thomas Miller, "Adam Smith and the Rhetoric of a Commercial Society," in *The Formation of College English* (Pittsburgh: University of Pittsburgh Press, 1997), 182, 187, 189–90; and Dana Harrington, "Gender, Commerce and the Transformation of Virtue in Eighteenth-Century Britain," *RSQ: Rhetoric Society Quarterly* 31, no. 3 (2001): 33–52.

16. See especially Billet, "The Just Economy"; see also Teichegraeber, *"Free Trade" and Moral Philosophy,* 155–56, and Mintowitz, *Profits, Priests, and Prices,* 33.

17. See Billet, "The Just Economy," 299, 306–7.

18. Fitzgibbons, *Adam Smith's System of Liberty, Wealth, and Virtue,* 181; Teichegraeber, *"Free Trade" and Moral Philosophy,* 309.

19. Fitzgibbons, *Adam Smith's System of Liberty, Wealth, and Virtue,* 145–48; Young, *Economics as a Moral Science,* 53; Billet, "The Just Economy," 302.

20. Billet, "The Just Economy," 302.

21. Adam Smith, *The Theory of Moral Sentiments,* ed. D. D. Raphael and A. L. Macfie (Indianapolis: Liberty Fund, 1984), 86. Further references are cited parenthetically in the text.

22. Billet, "The Just Economy," 309.

23. Ibid., 298; Teichegraeber, *"Free Trade" and Moral Philosophy,* 27, 135; Miller, "Adam Smith and the Rhetoric of a Commercial Society," 189–90.

24. Teichegraeber, *"Free Trade" and Moral Philosophy,* 27, 135; Miller, "Adam Smith and the Rhetoric of a Commercial Society," 189–90, 202.

25. For a fuller discussion of this paradox, see Peil, *Adam Smith and Economic Science,* 61, 86.

26. See Razeen Sally, *Classical Liberalism and the International Economic Order: Studies in Theory and Intellectual History* (London and New York: Routledge, 1998), for a discussion of this and other differences between Smith's liberalism and what Sally calls the "neoclassical" liberalism of Ricardo and his nineteenth- and twentieth-century followers See also Peil, *Adam Smith and Economic Science,* 40–41, 82, 87.

27. Drawing upon Bakhtinian literary theory, Vivienne Brown calls this intersubjective aspect of Smith's moral-psychological model "dialogic"; see Vivienne Brown, *Adam Smith's Discourse: Canonicity, Commerce, and Conscience* (London and New York: Routledge, 1994).

28. See Peil, *Adam Smith and Economic Science,* 83.

29. Kathryn Sutherland, "Adam Smith's Master Narrative: Women and the *Wealth of Nations,*" in *Adam Smith's* Wealth of Nations*: New Interdisciplinary Essays,* ed. Stephen Copley and Kathryn Sutherland (Manchester and New York: University of Manchester Press and St. Martin's Press, 1995), 97–121.

30. For a discussion of the gendering of virtue in eighteenth-century moral discourse, see Harrington, "Gender, Commerce and the Transformation of Virtue." As Harrington points out, many of Smith's contemporaries explicitly associated virtue with the private, domestic sphere and saw women as the guarantors of the new, individualist bourgeois virtue, thus further setting up the disaggregating move Ricardo and other nineteenth-century theorists were to make. Harrington points out that even some passages of *Theory of Moral Sentiments* make the association between domesticity and virtue.

31. In contrast, Ricardo credits Malthus and an unnamed "Fellow of the University College, Oxford" with almost simultaneously presenting to the world the "true doctrine of rent," which he identifies as crucial to an understanding of the problem he has defined.

32. G. D. H. Cole, *A History of Socialist Thought*, Vol. 1: *Socialist Thought: The Forerunners, 1789–1850* (London: Macmillan, 1977); Max Beer, *A History of British Socialism* (London, 1929); Noel Thompson, *The People's Science* (Cambridge: Cambridge University Press, 1984); and Gregory Claeys, *Machinery, Money, and the Millenium: From Moral Economy to Socialism, 1815–1860* (Princeton, N.J.: Princeton University Press, 1987).

33. This is precisely the kind of "master narrative" that Kathryn Sutherland (see note 29) reads Smith as constructing in the *Wealth of Nations*. The difference is that Ricardo's version of this master narrative is much more reductive than Smith's.

34. See Letwin, *The Origins of Scientific Economics;* Hirschman, *The Passions and the Interests;* Heilbroner, *Behind the Veil of Economics;* and Olson, *Science Deified*.

35. Adam Smith, *An Inquiry into the Nature and Causes of the Wealth of Nations*, ed. Edwin Canaan (Chicago: University of Chicago Press, 1976) 7. Further references are cited parenthetically in the text.

36. This process of disaggregation began long before Ricardo's *Principles*. See Letwin, *The Origins of Scientific Economics;* Olson, *Science Deified;* and Poovey, *A History of the Modern Fact*. As I argue later, Ricardo's text just takes the process further and provides a discursive form that helps to effect it.

37. McCulloch republished his *Encyclopedia Britannica* article as *Outlines of Political Economy, with Some Inquiries Respecting Their Application*, ed. John McVickar (New York: Augustus M. Kelly, 1966), 7.

38. Quoted in Donald Winch, "Higher Maxims: Happiness versus Wealth in Malthus and Ricardo," in Stefan Collini, Donald Winch, and John Burrow, eds., *That Noble Science of Politics* (Cambridge: Cambridge University Press, 1983), 80.

39. Olson, *Science Deified*, 146. See also Louis Dumont, *From Mandeville to Marx* (Chicago: University of Chicago Press, 1977, 1983), 36.

40. John Stuart Mill, "On the Definition of Political Economy; and on the Method of Investigation Proper to It," *Collected Works IV: Essays on Economics and Society, 1824–1845*, ed. J. M. Robson (London: University of Toronto Press, Routledge and Kegan Paul, 1967), 321.

41. J. R. McCulloch, *A Discourse on the Rise, Progress, Peculiar Objects and Importance of Political Economy* (Edinburgh: Constable, 1825), 74. Further references are cited parenthetically in the text..

42. J. R. McCulloch, "Ricardo's *Political Economy,*" *Edinburgh Review* 40 (March 1824): 64.

43. Checkland, "Propagation," 51. Terry Peach's recent revisionary reading of Ricardo argues against the consensus that Ricardo was a systematic thinker by meticulously pointing out the theoretical and logical inconsistencies in Ricardo's *Principles*. However, even while Peach critiques the logical consistency of Ricardo's theoretical writings, he acknowledges that Ricardo self-consciously strove to create an internally coherent theoretical system. See Terry Peach, *Interpreting Ricardo* (Cambridge: Cambridge University Press, 1993), 136, 225.

44. Quoted in Winch, "Higher Maxims," 79.

45. For other descriptions and discussions of Ricardo's distinct analytical method, see Fetter, "Rise and Decline"; Peach, *Interpreting Ricardo*; Hutchinson, *On Revolutions and Progress;* and Schumpeter, *History of Economic Analysis*.

46. James MacKintosh, *Ethical Philosophy*, quoted in *Oxford English Dictionary*, 2d ed. (New York: Oxford University Press, 1989), 1068.

47. In fact, Malthus was often attacked for the kind of theoretical reductionism that Ricardo, rather than Malthus, propounded. When his Romantic contemporaries condemned Malthusianism, they were usually criticizing an amalgamated entity of "political economy" having more to do with the writings of other economists than with the writings of Malthus. Furthermore, when Coleridge and Southey did correctly identify features of Malthus's own writing, they almost exclusively referred to the first edition of his *Essay on the Principle of Population* rather than on his substantially revised and expanded later editions. See Winch, *Riches and Poverty*, 289–93, 336–37, 343, and Poovey, *A History of the Modern Fact*, 295–96.

48. For the Noetics at Oxford in the 1820s through the mid-1830s, this religious framework was largely compatible with many aspects of Ricardian economic thought, but by the late 1830s, the logical, rationalist tradition of the Noetics was replaced by that of the Tractarians, for whom Ricardian theory was anathema. For an extended discussion of the religious contexts of academic economics in early Victorian England, see Checkland, "Advent."

49. See Checkland, "Propagation," 41, 47–51. See also Winch, *Riches and Poverty*, 247, 355.

50. Biancamaria Fontana and Gary Langer, among others, explicitly argue that more people became aware of Ricardian economic theory through McCulloch's writing than through Ricardo's own texts. See Biancamaria Fontana, *Rethinking the Politics of Commercial Society: The Edinburgh Review 1802–1832* (Cambridge: Cambridge University Press, 1985), 17, and Langer, *Coming of Age*, 67.

51. Gudeman, "Ricardo's Representations," 69.

52. Mitchell Dean makes this crucial distinction between foundational and derivative moral statements in his Foucauldian history, *The Constitution of Poverty: Toward a Genealogy of Liberal Governance* (London: Routledge, 1991). He explains the distinction thus: "The first place is one in which morality is construed in a 'foundationalist' manner . . . , i.e. as an order of statements which claims the privilege of being able to evaluate, and even derive and organize, other types of statements. The second is one in which moral statements are held to be derivative of other, more fundamental orders of consideration, e.g. in the case of political economy, the natural laws regulating production, exchange, and distribution" (111).

53. A notable contemporary exception to this general trend is the work of Amartya Sen. See in particular his collection of essays *On Ethics and Economics* (Oxford: Basil Blackwell, 1987).

Notes to Chapter 2

1. See for example the collection of essays edited by Terry Shinn and Richard Whitley, *Expository Science: Forms and Functions of Popularisation* (Dordrecht: D. Reidel Publishing Co., 1985); Ludmilla Jordanova, "The Popularization of Medicine: Tissot on Onanism," *Textual Practice* 1 (1987): 68–79; and Richard Yeo, "Science and Intellectual Authority in Mid-Nineteenth-Century Britain: Robert Chambers and *Vestiges of the Natural History of Creation*," *Victorian Studies* 28 (Autumn 1984): 1–31.

2. Richard Whitley, "Knowledge Producers and Knowledge Acquirers: Popularisation as a Relation Between Scientific Fields and Their Publics," in Shinn and Whitley, eds., *Expository Science: Forms and Functions of Popularisation*, 3–28 (Dordrecht, Holland and Boston: 1985).

3. Ibid., 7.

4. Such relative proximity, Whitley argues, not only facilitates the communication of knowledge from experts to publics but also increases the feedback from publics to expert "producers."

5. Richard Altick, *The English Common Reader* (Chicago: University of Chicago Press, 1957), 260–293, and Alan Rauch, *Useful Knowledge* (Durham, N.C.: Duke University Press, 2001), 22–59.

6. See Altick, *English Common Reader,* 281.

7. Rauch, *Useful Knowledge,* 37; Altick, *English Common Reader,* 280.

8. Rauch, *Useful Knowledge,* 28–29.

9. Altick, *English Common Reader,* 276–77.

10. Ibid., 274.

11. Altick writes: "The truth was that the Useful Knowledge Society expected the common reader, whose formal education likely had ended at twelve or fourteen, if not much earlier, to relish a home university course. Not only were the topics of the books too difficult for all but the most ambitious or brilliant students; the manner of treating them was undeviatingly dull" (ibid., 270–71).

12. See Whitley, "Knowledge Producers," 22. See also Judith Newton, "Engendering History for the Middle Class: Sex and Political Economy in the *Edinburgh Review,*" in *Rewriting the Victorians,* ed. Linda Shires (New York: Routledge and Kegan Paul, 1992), 1–17, and Checkland, "Advent," 43–70.

13. Whitley, "Knowledge Producers," 15.

14. Checkland, "Propagation," 47, and Blaug, *Ricardian Economics,* 130, 138.

15. Adam Smith, "The Principles Which Lead and Direct Philosophical Enquiries; Illustrated by the History of Astronomy," *Collected Works,* vol. 3, eds. R. H. Campbell and A. S. Skinner (Oxford and New York: Clarendon Press and Oxford University Press, 1976), 105.

16. For more in-depth discussions of Smith's "History of Astronomy," see Olson, *Science Deified,* and Poovey, *A History of the Modern Fact.*

17. See also Poovey, *A History of the Modern Fact.*

18. See Forbes, "'Scientific' Whiggism," 645–48, and H. M. Hopfl, "From Savage to Scotsman: Conjectural History in the Scottish Enlightenment," *Journal of British Studies* 17 (1978): 24–40.

19. Dugald Stewart, "Account of the Life and Writings of Adam Smith, LL.D.," in Adam Smith, *Collected Works,* vol. 3, 292.

20. Ibid.

21. Hopfl, "From Savage to Scotman," 23.

22. See especially Forbes, "'Scientific' Whiggism," 643–53.

23. Biancamaria Fontana makes a similar argument about the connection between the duty to learn political economy and the tradition of conjectural history in *Rethinking the Politics of Commercial Society,* 7.

24. J. R. McCulloch, "The Rise and Fall of Profits," *Edinburgh Review* 40 (1824): 20. Further references are cited parenthetically in the text.

25. J. R. McCulloch, "The Abolition of the Corn Laws," *Edinburgh Review* 44 (Sept.ember1826): 358. Further references are cited parenthetically in the text.

26. J. R. McCulloch, "Poor Laws," *Edinburgh Review* 57 (May 1828): 303. Hereafter citations will be provided parenthetically in the text.

27. J. R. McCulloch, "Causes and Cures of Disturbances and Pauperism," *Edinburgh*

Review 53 (March 1831): 47. Further citations are cited parenthetically in the text.
  28. Pauperism 56.

Notes to Chapter 3

  1. Mrs. [Jane] Marcet, *Conversations on Political Economy* (London: Longman, Hurst, Ress, Orme, and Brown, 1816), 18.
  2. Preface, iv. The Preface was published with volume 1, *Life in the Wilds*. My references to Martineau's novellas are to an 1834 bound reprint: Harriet Martineau, *Illustrations of Political Economy* (London: Charles Fox, 1834). Further references to the Preface and the individual novellas will be provided parenthetically in the text. The original publication dates of the novellas that I cite, and the abbreviations I use, are *The Hill and the Valley* (*HV*); *Demerera* (*DM*); and *Weal and Woe in Garveloch* (*WW*), 1832; and *A Manchester Strike* (*MS*), 1833; *Berkeley the Banker I and II* (*BB1, BB2*) and *Cinnamon and Pearls* (*CP*), 1833; and *The Moral of Many Fables* (*MMF*), 1834.
  3. The literary critic Catherine Gallagher also notes this connection in her discussion of one of Martineau's most famous novellas, *A Manchester Strike*. See Catherine Gallagher, *The Industrial Reformation of English Fiction, 1832–1867* (Chicago: University of Chicago Press, 1985), 52. For a more general discussion of the relationship between providential and realist narrative, see Thomas Vargish, *The Providential Aesthetic in Victorian Fiction* (Charlottesville: University Press of Virginia, 1985).
  4. Knowledge, morality, and providence go hand in hand for Martineau, but her use of each of these terms is highly specific. She conceives of a providential order in terms of a natural economic order rather than a divine order, unlike evangelical Christians or even most natural theologians (though she is much closer to the latter). Thus, she is Ricardian, rather than Malthusian, in her fundamental attitudes toward the economic principles she espouses.
  5. For example, George Poulett Scope wrote in the *Quarterly Review:* "Poor innocent! She has been puzzling over Mr. Malthus's arithmetical and geometrical ratio, for knowledge which she should have obtained by a simple question or two of her mamma"; and, later in the same review: "a *female Malthusian.* A *woman* who thinks childbearing a *crime against society!* An *unmarried woman* who declaims against *marriage!!* A *young woman* who depreciates charity and provision for the *poor!!!*" (emphasis in the original). [George Poulett Scope], "Miss Martineau's Monthly Novels," *Quarterly Review* 49 (April 1833): 141, 151. A favorable reviewer in *The Spectator* wrote: "Here are scenes for the picturesque pen of Miss Martineau: they are painted with a power and quiet self-possession not exceeded in any of her former works," and "perhaps no other female ever occupied the same proud position of a national instructress, on the topics of the country's most essential interests." "Miss Martineau's Little Novels," *The Spectator* (July 7, 1832): 639.
  6. Simpson, *Romanticism*, 40–63.
  7. See Thompson, *The People's Science*.
  8. [William Empson], "Mrs. Marcet—Miss Martineau," *Edinburgh Review* 57 (April 1833): 9.
  9. My use of the terms "sentiment" and "sentimental" stems from two traditions—one British and one American. My reading of the eighteenth-century British tradition is indebted to G. J. Barker-Benfield, *The Culture of Sensibility* (Chicago: University of Chicago Press, 1992); Claudia L. Johnson, *Equivocal Beings: Politics, Gender, and Sentimentality in the 1790s* (Chicago: University of Chicago Press, 1995); and Catherine Gallagher's

reading of *Mary Barton* in *The Industrial Reformation of English Fiction*. My reading of the predominantly nineteenth-century American tradition of sentimentalism is informed by Shirley Samuels, "Introduction," *The Culture of Sentiment: Race, Gender, and Sentimentality in Nineteenth-Century America* (Oxford: Oxford University Press, 1992); Gillian Brown, *Domestic Individualism: Imagining Self in Nineteenth-Century America* (Berkeley: University of California Press, 1990); and Jane Tompkins, "'Pray, therefore, without ceasing': From Tracts to Texts," *Genre* 16 (Winter 1983): 423–36.

10. Brown, *Domestic Individualism*, 39–60.

11. Although Martineau attempts to mitigate this effect in many of her narratives by offering the promise of hope for the characters' future generations, her consolation fails to ameliorate the frustration generated by her stories. The "in the long run" resolutions offered by the narrator cannot channel and contain the emotional response generated by the reader's sympathetic identification with the characters. Precisely because the reader is drawn into the narrative through identification with the characters, resolutions that promise satisfaction only to the abstraction of future generations fail to harness the reader's imaginative sympathies.

12. Samuel Richard's *Pamela* springs to mind as one major prototype of such a sentimental heroine.

13. Thus, Hester thinks: "Her many long days of disappointment, and nights of weary watching were forgotten, and all sense of pain and injury were lost in her present emotion of grateful pleasure" (*BB2* 9).

14. Perhaps even more damning to Martineau's didactic message is the fact that Henry Craig argues in support of Cavendish's bank at the beginning of the story, and that he makes that argument along the lines of "correct" political economic principles.

15. In an early conversation between Paul and Mr. Wallace, Paul actually warns Mr. Wallace against providing his wife with so many luxuries since he sees her opulent lifestyle as an ill preparation for any potential reverse of fortunes (the kind of reverse he is always fearing and preparing for himself).

Notes to Chapter 4

1. Charles Dickens, *Dombey and Son,* ed. Alan Horsman (Oxford: Oxford University Press, 1982), 77. Further references to this edition are cited parenthetically in the text.

2. For a reading of the novel as an exploration of this feminine influence, and of male anxieties about its potency and range, see Judith Newton, "Making—and Remaking—History: Another Look at 'Patriarchy,'" in Shari Benstock, ed., *Feminist Issues in Literary Scholarship* (Bloomington: Indiana University Press, 1987); see also Julian Moynihan's critique of Dickens's use of feminine influence as "an over-simplified idea of human community" in "Dealings with the Firm of Dombey and Son: Firmness versus Wetness," in John Gross and Gabriel Pearson, eds., *Dickens and the Twentieth Century* (Toronto: University of Toronto Press, 1962), 121–31. For a discussion of the Victorian separate-spheres ideology more generally, see Mary Poovey, *Uneven Developments: The Ideological Work of Gender in Mid-Victorian England* (Chicago: University of Chicago Press, 1988), esp. chapter 1, 1–23.

3. Fred Kaplan, *Sacred Tears: Sentimentality in Victorian Literature* (Princeton, N.J.: Princeton University Press, 1987), 6.

4. S. G. Checkland, *The Rise of Industrial Society in England, 1815–1885* (London: Longman, 1964), 192.

5. These fourteen million pounds, called the Fiduciary Issue, were "covered" or represented by government securities. The Act also legislated the note issue of all other English banks, forbidding their issue "to exceed their average issue of the twelve weeks preceding 17 April 1844" (ibid., 200).

6. Checkland describes the debate as follows: "The [Banking School] said, in effect, 'Trust the Bankers.' Demand convertibility of the note issue, but beyond that leave discretion to those in charge of banking policy. . . . Do not impair the scope and flexibility of the Bank's actions by an insistence upon rigid rules. The Currency School, on the other hand, denied that the bankers should be left so free of control. They said, in effect, that the issue of notes by the Bank of England should be backed pound for pound, by gold reserves. Paper currency would thus be convertible at all times, with the result, so it was argued, that liquidity crises could not occur. . . . The essential need was for a 'regulation based upon principle'" (ibid., 198).

7. The Act was based on Ricardo's Quantity Theory of Money, which saw a connection between money supply and prices—and through prices, a connection between money supply and imports, exports, and foreign exchanges; in short, Ricardo's theory identified money supply as the determining factor for a large portion of the economy as a whole.

8. Quoted in *The Present State of the Currency Practically Considered: Proving the Justice and Necessity of Immediately and Effectually Revising the Currency Measures of 1819 and 1844* (London: G. Briggs, 1847), 9.

9. Quoted in [William Newmarch], "The Financial Pressure," *Quarterly Review* 81 (June 1847): 230–73.

10. These writers saw Britain's progressive economy as based on credit (bills of exchange, the ledger, moneys of account, etc.) rather than gold or legal tender representing gold. This credit base meant both that most of the commercial transactions of the country were carried out by these means and that only such credit moneys enabled the kind and extent of the enterprises that made Britain "the first commercial country" of the world. The Act's critics felt that it failed to provide (or allow) sufficient credit moneys for the growing demands of England as a progressive commercial nation.

11. One critic of the Act writes: "A scarcity of money was apprehended from the combined action of the drain of gold and the currency bill, and *the apprehension it created before the nominal amount of the circulation had undergone any diminution;* all parties determining to meet the danger by holding fast what they had got (emphasis mine). [Thomas Charles Banfield], "The Bank Charter Act: Currency Principles," *Westminster Review* 47 (July 1847): 424.

12. Thomas Charles Banfield, "Coin and Currency: The Bank Charter Act," *British and Foreign Quarterly Review* 17, no. 33 (1844): 29–31.

13. Ibid., 37.

14. See Boyd Hilton, "Chalmers as Political Economist," in A. C. Cheyne, ed., *The Practical and the Pious: Essays on Thomas Chalmers (1780–1847)* (Edinburgh: St. Andrews Press, 1985), 147.

15. In the article cited in note 2, Judith Newton conflates these two roles and thus generates a reading of the novel in which Florence and her feminized moral influence are perceived as a threat, through Dombey, to the Dickens-identified narrator (and to Dickens himself). For Newton, Dickens as well as Dombey is reacting with anxiety to the claims made by and for Victorian women for increased feminine influence through and beyond the domestic sphere. By placing Dombey in the context of political economy, however, Dickens can establish him as a representative of a specific kind of Victorian man rather

than of all Victorian men. The narrator, then, can be aligned with an alternative version of Victorian manhood for which Florence's influence is essential rather than pernicious. In "Wholesale, Retail and for Exportation: Empire and the Family Business in *Dombey and Son*" (*Victorian Studies* 33 [1990]: 603–20), another critic, Suvendrini Perera, uses Newton's framework and critique of Florence but sees the threatening elements of her character as generated by Dombey's "refusal to accommodate Florence within the economy of the family business," which in turn "denies her a role in the domestic economy." The danger of Florence, then, is the danger of "forbidden sexuality" and "domestic rebellion." One of the first and most influential critical readings of Florence as threat was Julian Moynihan's article "Dealings with the Firm of Dombey and Son" (cited in note 2). Moynihan, like Newton, reads Florence as a general threat, but, interestingly, he does not see her as a threat to Dickens or his narrator. Rather, Florence appears to be a threat to Moynihan himself, or at least to his understanding of an appropriate solution to the problems of industrial society. Moynihan reads Dombey's change of heart as an infantilizing second childhood and the whole novel as a movement "from complexity towards a weltering simplicity" (127).

16. Even these characters' names indicate their alliance with false surfaces, for the narrator rarely refers to either by her "real" name, Mrs. Skewton or Mrs. Marwood. Rather, he refers to the former as "Cleopatra," the name given to her youthful portrait whose image she daily attempts to reconstruct with makeup and artifice, and he calls the latter "Good Mrs. Brown," the name she falsely adopts in her deceptive abduction of Florence.

17. My discussion of the problematic of sameness and difference in the construction of Victorian social identity under capitalism is heavily indebted to Mary Poovey's essay "Reading History in Literature: Speculation and Virtue in *Our Mutual Friend*," in Janet Smarr, ed., *Historical Criticism and the Challenge of Theory* (Urbana: University of Illinois Press, 1993). See also Eve Sedgwick, *Between Men: English Literature and Male Homosocial Desire* (New York: Columbia University Press, 1985).

18. George Fisk, "The Moral Influence of the Commercial Spirit of the Day," in *Lectures Delivered before the Y.M.C.A.* or *The Exeter Hall Lecture Series* 3 (1848): 302–3.

Notes to Chapter 5

1. Quoted in Anne Humphreys, *Travels into the Poor Man's Country: The Work of Henry Mayhew* (Firle, Sussex, and Athens: Caliban Books and University of Georgia Press, 1977), 37.

2. See the chapter "The Metropolitan Correspondent" in ibid., 31–64 and the chapter "Mayhew's Rich World of Poverty" in Regenia Gagnier, *Subjectivities: A History of Self-Representation in Britain, 1832–1920* (New York and Oxford: Oxford University Press, 1991), 62–93. As is evident, my work on Mayhew's *Morning Chronicle* letters is deeply indebted to these two critical accounts. However, while both critics discuss the effects of Mayhew's letters in terms of the representation of working-class subjectivity as part of his criticism of economic doctrine, neither addresses the gender differential of Mayhew's treatment.

3. Henry Mayhew, *The Unknown Mayhew: Selections from the* Morning Chronicle, *1849–1850*, eds. E. P. Thompson and Eileen Yeo (London: Merlin Press, 1971), and Henry Mayhew, *London Labour and the London Poor*, 4 volumes, originally published 1861–62, reprint ed. John Rosenberg (New York: Dover, 1968).

4. In the introduction to volume 4, Mayhew reclassifies workers and nonworkers

within the economic system. His critique here revises John Stuart Mill's classification system by placing capitalists among the "auxiliaries" to the productive process rather than identifying them as performing any productive role themselves. Even as he makes this reclassification, Mayhew backs away from its obvious implications, writing: "Whether the gains of some of these auxiliary classes are as disproportionately large, as the others are disproportionately small, this is not the place to enquire. My present duty is merely to record the fact of the existence of such classes, and to assign them their proper place in the social fabric, as it is presently constituted." Mayew, *London Labour*, vol. 4, p. 9.

The tone of disavowal in this passage presents a striking contrast with the more explicit assertation of critique in the *Morning Chronicle* letters and *Low Wages, Their Causes, Consequences and Remedies* (excerpted in *The Unknown Mayhew*).

5. Gagnier, "Mayhew's Rich World of Poverty," 84.

6. See ibid., 84–93, and Humphreys, *Travels into the Poor Man's Country*, 65–110.

7. E. P. Thompson, "Mayhew and the *Morning Chronicle*," in *The Unknown Mayhew*, 42.

8. Humphreys, *Travels into the Poor Man's Country*, 65–69.

9. With the exception of Humphreys and Gagnier, there are the two major strands of Mayhew criticism. Part of the difference between these critical traditions is an effect of the difference in Mayhew's own agenda in his two major investigative projects. Those writers focusing on *London Labour and the London Poor* build their interpretations around an explicit or implicit concept of social deviancy, playing off Mayhew's own construction of London street workers as virtually another race or drawing on his investigations of "those who won't work," such as thieves and prostitutes. Although in each case critics such as Catherine Gallagher and Christopher Herbert link their interpretations of Mayhew's investigations to a critical analysis of Victorian culture as a whole, they always define the actors in Mayhew's narratives in opposition to the normative standards of Victorian culture—particularly middle-class Victorian culture. See, for example, Catherine Gallagher, "The Body versus the Social Body in the Works of Thomas Malthus and Henry Mayhew," in Catherine Gallagher and Thomas Laqueur, eds., *The Making of the Modern Body: Sexuality and Society in the Nineteenth Century* (Berkeley: University of California Press, 1987), and Christopher Herbert, *Culture and Anomie: Ethnographic Imagination in the Nineteenth Century* (Chicago: University of Chicago Press, 1991).

In contrast to the focus on social deviancy, when cultural historians such as E. P. Thompson and Eileen Yeo have focused on the letters to the *Morning Chronicle,* they read Mayhew's text as directly concerned with more mainstream Victorian issues. E. P. Thompson, for example, sees the series as aimed at "social reconciliation" between the middle and working classes. Eileen Yeo sees the letters as part of the birth of social science, participating in the same trend that precipitated parliamentary investigations of English factories and mines. These arguments for the cultural centrality of Mayhew's *Morning Chronicle* letters, however, tend to produce unproblematic readings of the text that elide its internal contradictions; focusing on what Mayhew has accomplished in the letters as a whole, Thompson and Yeo read for the coherent alignments that enable them to position Mayhew's project as central, and thus as historically significant. E. P. Thompson, "Mayhew and the *Morning Chronicle*," in *The Unknown Mayhew* (9–55); Eileen Yeo, "Mayhew as a Social Investigator," in *The Unknown Mayhew* (56–109).

10. The best and most comprehensive discussion of working-class masculinity available is Sonya Rose's theoretically informed historical account in *Limited Livelihoods: Gender and Class in Nineteenth-Century England* (Berkeley: University of California Press,

1991). My discussion relies heavily on the arguments Rose develops about the relationship between working-class masculinity and the working-class family, respectability, domesticity, female labor, conditions of labor, and the "family wage," particularly chapters 2 and 6 of her book.

11. For a similar reading of the central role of working-class domesticity in a middle-class social investigation text, see the chapter "Domesticity and Class Formation: Chadwick's 1842 Sanitary Report" in Mary Poovey, *Making a Social Body: British Cultural Formation 1830–1864* (Chicago: University of Chicago Press, 1995), 115–31. Poovey's analysis of the earlier text gives her the opportunity to read Chadwick's report as a response to Chartism as well as to the more general issues of poverty and sanitation.

12. In the honorable portions of the trade, payment was determined by agreements between trade associations and masters, while in the dishonorable trade, competition was the sole determinant of the worker's wage. Soon after ending the *Morning Chronicle* survey, Mayhew explicitly interpreted this difference as a difference between good and bad wages. See Mayhew, *Low Wages*, excerpted in *The Unknown Mayhew*.

13. Ricardo, *Principles of Political Economy*, 52–53. For a more extended analysis of this passage, see my discussion of Ricardo's prose in chapter 1.

14. Oswald St. Clair, *A Key to Ricardo* (London: Routledge and Kegan Paul, 1957), 108. See also Bowley, *Studies in the History of Economic Theory*; Bowley writes: "Malthus and Ricardo between them made it clear that fundamentally the progress of the working classes depended on themselves, on their prudence in propagation" (207).

15. St. Clair, *A Key to Ricardo*, 83–86, 106–8.

16. Bowley, *Studies in the History of Economic Theory*, 158–59.

17. See Himmelfarb, *The Idea of Poverty*, chapter 6, "The New Poor Law: Pauper versus Poor," especially 158–63. Himmelfarb writes that for the Poor Law Commission, "it was . . . a matter of definition and distinction—of separating the able-bodied from the laboring poor" (161). This distinction was crucial because only those who couldn't work due to physical incapability (i.e., the *non*-able-bodied) could receive poor relief without moral stigma. It was the able-bodied pauper who caused the most concern for the commission. For example, Himmelfarb quotes the commission as finding that "'in every district . . . the condition of this class [the independent labourer] is found to be strikingly disinguishable from that of the pauper, and superior to it, though the independent labourers are commonly maintained upon less money'" (163).

18. Humphreys, *Travels into the Poor Man's Country*, 33.

19. Mayhew, *The Unknown Mayhew*, 102. Further references to this edition are cited parenthetically in the text.

20. Mayhew's terms "honest" and "dishonest" need to be kept distinct from the terms that describe workers' trades—"honorable" and "dishonorable." Mayhew categorizes as "dishonest" those who are unwilling to work, whether in portions of the trade regulated by custom or those regulated by competition. Conversely, one can be "honestly" poor and still work within a dishonorable trade; in fact, it is precisely that category of worker that most garners Mayhew's interest and outrage.

21. See Rose, *Limited Livelihoods*, 140–41.

22. On middle-class masculinity and independence, see Norman Vance, *The Sinews of the Spirit: The Ideal of Christian Manliness in Victorian Literature and Social Thought* (Cambridge: Cambridge University Press, 1985), 10, and Leonore Davidoff and Catherine Hall, *Family Fortunes: Men and Women of the English Middle Class, 1780–1850* (Chicago: University of Chicago Press, 1987), 269.

23. Another way to understand this distinction is that the "honorable" trades required and supported skilled labor, while the "dishonorable" trades eroded categories and conditions of that labor. For discussions of the links between skilled labor and working-class masculinity, see Rose, *Limited Livelihoods,* 22–29, 142–44; Ava Baron, "Contested Terrain Revisited: Technology and Gender Definitions of Work in the Printing Industry, 1850–1920," in Barbara Dryhulski Wright et al., eds., *Women, Work, and Technology* (Ann Arbor: University of Michigan Press, 1987), 58–83; Cynthia Coburn, *Brothers: Male Dominance and Technological Change* (Concord, Mass.: Pluto Press, 1983); and Cynthia Coburn, *Machinery of Dominance: Women, Men, and Technological Know-How* (Dover, N.H.: Pluto Press, 1985).

24. The ideal and ideology of the family wage developed within working-class culture through the course of the nineteenth century, particularly the second half. The rhetoric of the family wage was used in working-class movements for the Factory Acts and in Chartism. How much this rhetoric was aimed specifically at a hegemonic bourgeois audience and how much it constituted and/or was adopted as an actual or organic ideal for the working classes themselves in the 1850s is a question that is beyond the scope of this study. The question is further problematized in Mayhew's text because of the relationship between bourgeois interviewer and working-class interviewee. For historical accounts of and debates about the ideology of the family wage, see Rose, *Limited Livelihoods,* especially chapters 3 and 6; Heidi Hartmann, "Capitalism, Patriarchy, and Job Segregation by Sex," *Signs* 1 (1976): 137–69; Jane Humphries, "Class Struggle and the Persistence of the Working-Class Family," *Cambridge Journal of Economics* 1 (1977): 241–58; Hilary Land, "The Family Wage," *Feminist Review* 6: (1980): 55–76; and Michele Barrett and Mary McIntosh, "The 'Family Wage': Some Problems for Socialists and Feminists," *Capital and Class* 11 (1980): 51–72.

25. Note that Mayhew constructs this paternalist reprensentation of trade societies rather than a more radical image of a working-class organization constituted to advocate for political and economic rights, or even for the power of collective bargaining.

26. This sentiment is echoed by a boot- and shoemaker, who says: "A man's own children will soon be the means of driving him from the market altogether, or compelling him to come down to their rate of wages"(*UM* 240).

27. Barbara Taylor, *Eve and the New Jerusalem: Socialism and Feminism in the Nineteenth Century* (New York: Pantheon, 1983), 94, 110.

28. Ibid., 111.

29. Lynda Nead, *Myths of Sexuality: Representations of Women in Victorian Britain* (Oxford: Basil Blackwell, 1988), 106, 114. See also Judith R. Walkowitz, *Prostitution and Victorian Society: Women, Class, and the State* (Cambridge: Cambridge University Press, 1980), 11–48, and Frank Mort, *Dangerous Sexualities: Medico-Moral Politics in England since 1830* (London: Routledge and Kegan Paul, 1987), 37–41, 47–53.

30. Nead, *Myths of Sexuality,* 116–120.

31. Ibid., 102–3, 117–18.

32. Ibid., 94–95.

33. Their individual testimonies are shorter than the two formal interviews, but virtually all include similar statements. Thus, one of the first speakers at the meeting says: "For the sake of my lodgings and a bit of bread I've been obligated to do what I am very sorry to do, and look upon with disgust" (*UM* 168). Following her, seven other speakers are recorded as expressing almost identical sentiments.

34. Lynda Nead devotes a whole chapter of her book to the "Prostitute as Victim." The genre of romance tragedy is often adopted to portray the prostitute as a passive victim of

social forces—a portrayal that domesticates and contains her threatening linkages with social chaos. This generic portrayal is also frequently used in literary and artistic representations of the prostitute.

35. The speakers themselves make this connection explicit. One tells of being turned out of doors by her father because he couldn't support her. Another woman compares her own state and the state of those like her to those who have mothers and fathers to help support them: "I am satisfied there is not one young girl that works at slop work that is virtuous, and there are some thousands in the trade. *They may do very well if they have got mothers and fathers to find them a home and food,* and to let them have what they earn for clothes; *then they may be virtuous,* but not without" (emphasis mine, *UM* 148). Thus, the speaker implies that if the male-dominated working-class family were intact and self-supporting—even if that self-support included the labor of the children—there would be no prostitution among needlewomen.

36. One of the needlewomen interviewed by Mayhew tells a version of just such a story: "My landlord turned me out, and I had nowhere to go, till I was taken to a brothel by a person that I met, but I don't know who it was. I remained in that condition till such time as I fell in the family way" (*UM* 171).

37. Gagnier also notes Mayhew's representation of the workers' dehumanization but, again, does not acknowledge that the very standard of "the human" that is deployed is an implicitly masculine one.

38. The importance of this relation between the male worker and his process of production is established in relation to middle-class masculinity by Davidoff and Hall, *Family Fortunes,* 229, 269, 410.

39. Nead, *Myths of Sexuality,* 91.

40. See for example, Mayhew's discussion of piecework among the tailors on p. 186 and of cabinetmakers working for garret masters and slaughterhouses on p. 382.

41. Mayhew also devotes a section to the degradation of the honorable trade as a conclusion to his investigation of the cabinetmakers. The section is titled, "The Effect of Slop Business upon the Honorable Trade" (*UM* 398–99).

42. McCulloch and Martineau, for example, both blame workers and their excess numbers for their low wages, and McCulloch advocates forced emigration as a solution to the "overpopulation" of the laboring class. See my discussions of McCulloch and Martineau in chapters 2 and 3.

43. Nead, *Myths of Sexuality,* 99.

44. Taylor, *Eve and the New Jerusalem,* 111.

Notes to Chapter 6

1. John Stuart Mill, *Autobiography,* ed. Jack Stillinger (Boston: Houghton Mifflin Co., 1969), 18.

2. Ibid.

3. Ibid., 86.

4. Ibid., 97.

5. Ibid., 149.

6. John Stuart Mill, *Principles of Political Economy, with Some of Their Applications to Social Philosophy,* ed. Sir William Ashley (London: Augustus M. Kelly Publishers, 1987), xxvii–xxviii. Further references to this edition are cited parenthetically in the text.

7. Mark Blaug is the economic historian most critical of Mill's use of Ricardian eco-

nomic theory. According to Blaug, Mill's adaptations of Ricardian principles result in "an emasculated version of Ricardo's system" (*Ricardian Economics,* 167). Alan Ryan and Pedro Schwartz see Mill's adaptations of Ricardian theory as at times betraying the fundamental premises of that theory, but they also emphasize Mill's allegiances to Ricardo. In contrast to Blaug, Samuel Hollander argues that Mill remained essentially loyal to Ricardo. Hollander acknowledges that Mill placed Ricardo's theory "in a new setting" but does not see that new setting as altering the fundamental Ricardian tenets of Mill's political economy. See Alan Ryan, *J. S. Mill* (London: Routledge and Kegan Paul, 1974); Pedro Schwartz, *The New Political Economy of J. S. Mill* (Durham, N.C.: Duke University Press, 1972); and Samuel Hollander, *The Economics of John Stuart Mill,* vol. 2: *Political Economy* (Toronto: University of Toronto Press, 1985).

8. Not all of human psychology is "given"; many aspects can be changed. Certain aspects of human psychological makeup, however, fall within Mill's category of the laws of production and thus, according to him, are unalterable.

9. Mill's opposition between the laws of production and distribution has been read as a philosophical space-clearing gesture by other Mill scholars and economic historians. See, for example, Blaug, *Ricardian Economics,* 166, and Ryan, *J. S. Mill,* 163ff.

10. See Regenia Gagnier's discussion of Mill in *The Insatiability of Human Wants* (Chicago: University of Chicago Press, 2000), 27–35.

11. Ryan, *J. S. Mill,* 180.

12. On the developmental self as a romantic construct, see Clifford Siskin, *The Historicity of Romantic Discourse* (New York: Oxford University Press, 1988), 152–74.

13. The inequities that Mill imagines surviving into the advanced, ideal social order are those of individual talent and morality, rather than differentiations based on birth, gender, and so forth—differentiations that Mill sees as arbitrary and artificial.

14. See, for example, Blaug, *Ricardian Economics,* 191ff; Ryan, *J. S. Mill,* 184–89; Schwartz, *New Political Economy,* 156–210; Hollander, *The Economics of John Stuart Mill,* 790–99; and John M. Robson, *The Improvement of Mankind: The Social and Political Philosophy of John Stuart Mill* (Toronto: University of Toronto Press, 1968), 248–50.

15. See especially Hollander, *The Economics of John Stuart Mill,* 790–91, and Schwartz, *New Political Economy,* 175ff.

16. Mill writes earlier in the *Principles* that "the niggardliness of nature, not the injustice of society, is the cause of the penalty attached to overpopulation" (*PPE* 191).

17. Mill's model of progress is shaped more in terms of "evolution" than the "providence" invoked by McCulloch and Martineau. There is less sense of inevitability and guidance in the evolutionary model.

18. M. Leclaire's profit-sharing experiment in France is the first such experiment that Mill discusses at length. Mill describes the structure of the experiment: "M. Leclaire . . . employs on an average two hundred workmen, whom he pays in the usual manner, by fixed wages or salaries. He assigns to himself, besides interest for his capital, a fixed allowance for his labour and responsibility as manager. At the end of the year, the surplus profits are divided among the body, himself included, in the proportion of their salaries" (*PPE* 768). In other words, Leclaire retained full control of his own private capital but no longer claimed sole possession of the profits. Hence, the interest of every workman was linked directly to the profitability of the industry. The result of Leclaire's experiment, according to Leclaire himself and independent investigators, was increased overall productivity, higher earnings for the workmen, and an improvement in the moral habits of the laborers at work and beyond the workplace.

Notes to Chapter 7

1. See Karl Marx, *Capital*, vol. 1, trans. Ben Fowkes (London: Penguin Books, 1976), esp. 652–54.

2. For contemporary critiques of this opposition from a very different perspective than that of Ruskin, see John W. Meyer, "Society without Culture: A Nineteenth-Century Legacy," and Wallerstein, "Should We Unthink the Nineteenth Century?" both in Ramirez, ed., *Rethinking the Nineteenth Century*.

3. Heilbroner writes: "The complacence of the official world was not merely a rueful commentary on the times; it was an intellectual tragedy of the first order. For had the academicians paid attention to the underworld ... the great catastrophe of the twentieth century might not have burst upon a world utterly unprepared for radical social change." Robert Heilbroner, *The Worldly Philosophers*, 5th ed. (New York: Simon and Schuster, 1953, 1980), 209.

4. For Heilbroner the lost theoretical insight was the "underworld" assertion that radical social change is a fundamental aspect of human history rather than a factor that could be "externalized" in a socioeconomic world that has achieved it ideal equilibrium. See ibid., 168–209.

5. Gagnier, *Insatiability of Human Wants*.

6. For Mary Poovey's work on the disaggregation and disciplining of knowledge, see especially her *Making a Social Body* and her essay "Aesthetics and Politics in the Eighteenth Century." For Immanuel Wallerstein's more theoretical "world-systems" discussions of the emergence of the social sciences, see his essays "Should We Unthink the Nineteenth Century?"; "A World-System Perspective on the Social Sciences," in Immanuel Wallerstein, *The Capitalist World-Economy* (Cambridge: Cambridge University Press, 1979); "The Development of the Concept of Development," in Immanuel Wallerstein, *The Politics of the World-Economy* (Cambridge: Cambridge University Press, 1984); and "Eurocentrism and Its Avatars: The Dilemmas of Social Science," *New Left Review* 226 (1997). See also his book *Historical Capitalism, with Capitalist Civilization* (London: Verso, 1995).

7. I distinguish between "ethics" and "morality" throughout this chapter. The terms certainly overlap; both indicate value-laden codes of conduct and behavior. "Ethics," however, is the more complex and other-oriented term, concerned with relations between self and other but also with social relations that supersede this relation, such as the institutionally structured relationships of capitalist economics. "Morality," in contrast, is focused more on self-regulating codes of behavior and action. In the nineteenth century, in particular, morality is imbricated with the Christian evangelical focus on the individual as site of spiritual and religious values. With morality, the concern is often on how one's actions and social relations reflect one's personal spiritual status rather than on the welfare of the social body more generally.

8. See, for example, Donald Winch, "Marginalism and the Boundaries of Economic Science," in R. D. Collison Black, A. W. Coats, and Craufurd D. W. Goodwin, eds., *The Marginal Revolution in Economics* (Durham, N.C.: Duke University Press, 1973), 75. See also the cultural historian Regenia Gagnier's discussion of the differences between classical economics and marginalism in *Insatiability of Human Wants*, especially chapter 1, 19–60.

9. John Ruskin, *Unto This Last and Other Writings*, ed. Clive Wilmer (London: Penguin Books, 1985, 1997), 171. Further references to this edition are cited parenthetically in the text.

10. For Carlyle's influence on Ruskin's economic writings, see Alan Lee, "Ruskin and

Political Economy: *Unto This Last,*" in Robert Hewison, ed., *New Approaches to Ruskin* (London: Routledge and Kegan Paul, 1981), 75. See also James Sherburne, *The Ambiguities of Abundance* (Cambridge, Mass.: Harvard University Press, 1972).

11. Ruskin's rejection of the scientific form—and of the boundaries inherent in that form—is cited by most of the twentieth-century critics who have examined his economic writing. See Willie Henderson, *John Ruskin's Political Economy* (London and New York: Routledge, 2000), 33, 43–48, 121, 128; John Fain, *Ruskin and the Economists* (Nashville, Tenn.: Vanderbilt University Press, 1956), 36; Jeffrey Spear, *Dreams of English Eden: Ruskin and His Tradition in Social Criticism* (New York: Columbia University Press, 1984), 137–67; Lee, "Ruskin and Political Economy"; and Sherburne, *Ambiguities,* 97–101, 124.

12. Henderson, *Ruskin's Political Economy,* 46. See also Spear, *Dreams of English Eden,* 148.

13. Ruskin also insists on the need for a new method for economic "analysis" through his description of the dynamics of exchange: "I have hitherto carefully restricted myself, in speaking of exchange, to the use of the term 'advantage'; but that term includes two ideas: the advantage, namely, of getting what we *need,* and that of getting what we *wish for.* Three-fourths of the demands existing in the world are romantic; founded on visions, idealisms, hopes, and affections; and the regulation of the purse is, in its essence, regulation of the imagination and the heart. Hence, the right discussion of the nature of price is a very high metaphysical and psychical problem; sometimes to be solved only in a passionate manner" (*UTL* 214–15).

14. Sherburne calls this model "organic" and places it in a linear tradition with Coleridge and Carlyle (*Ambiguities,* 1–26, 94–124).

15. Other critics and historians of economic thought have discussed Ruskin's alternative political economy at length. For citations of their work, see notes 10 and 11.

16. Ruskin further developed his project of reconstructing political economy in essays published in *Fraser's Magazine* in 1863 and republished in book form as *Munera Pulvis* (1872); reprinted in *The Works of John Ruskin,* vol. 17, eds. E. T. Cook and Alexander Wedderburn (London: George Allen, 1905), 119–298.

17. This is particularly the project of the second and fourth essays, but Ruskin uses it throughout the text. In the first essay, for example, Ruskin redefines the meaning of the term "merchant." Instead of being one who buys and sells in order to reap a profit, for Ruskin the merchant is one of the "five great intellectual professions, relating to daily necessities of life," that function in virtually every civilized society (*UTL* 177). Already Ruskin has significantly shifted the context in which the term "merchant" is normally understood, defining the merchant primarily in terms of his service to society rather than his pursuit of his own interest and profit. Once "merchant" is identified as one of the five great professions that service civilized nations, Ruskin pushes the definition further as he claims that "the duty of all these men is, on due occasion, to *die* for it [i.e. the nation]" (*UTL* 177). Ruskin has already set the stage for this move by listing the soldier as the first of the great service professions. Now he can introduce what he sees as the stakes involved in the merchant's performance of his social role: it would be better for the merchant to die or suffer poverty and distress himself than for him to "fail in any engagement, or consent to any deterioration, adulteration, or unjust and exorbitant price of that which he provides" (*UTL* 178). By redefining commerce as a service profession and then identifying the duty of that profession with the provision of quality products at a fair price (at the cost even of death), Ruskin strips political economy and capitalist economics more generally of their prototype of economic man, the engine and facilitator of the entire economic system.

In his place, Ruskin constructs a social actor whose primary characteristics are honesty, integrity, and discernment—one who can perceive the true value of things (metaphysical as well as economic value) and who would rather suffer loss himself than purchase or sell at other than this "true" value.

18. This definition then becomes the immediate basis for an assertion about what would constitute a "real science of political economy," that is, "that [science] which teaches nations to desire and labour for the things that lead to life" (*UTL* 209).

19. Jeffrey Spear discusses Ruskin's use of etymologies as part of his larger rhetorical strategy in *UTL*. See Spear, *Dreams of English Eden*, 150–51.

20. Spear notes that Ruskin was carefully schooled in Smith's *The Theory of Moral Sentiments* from a young age: obviously a very different parental education than that received by J. S. Mill.

21. See Henderson's excellent rhetorical analysis of Ruskin's construction of the role of the reader in *Unto This Last* in Henderson, *Ruskin's Political Economy*, 45, 54, 58, 62–63.

22. See, for example, Ruskin's arguments about employment, hiring, and employer responsibility (*UTL* 179, 223).

23. Ruskin includes an extended discussion on the mutually destructive interactions between (true) manly character and purely monetary, material value (*UTL* 211–12).

24. For an extended discussion of Ruskin's appropriation and use of this classical model of economics, see Henderson's chapter "Xenophon, Ruskin, and Economic Management," in *Ruskin's Political Economy*, 64–85. My reading is also indebted to Michel Foucault's discussion of Xenophon's text in *The Use of Pleasure: The History of Sexuality*, vol. 2, trans. Robert Hurley (New York: Vintage, 1990; Random House, 1985), esp. 152–65.

25. The dominance of Mill's orthodoxy was also challenged by the new historical school of economics. See Margaret Schabas, *A World Ruled by Number: William Stanley Jevons and the Rise of Mathematical Economics* (Princeton, N.J.: Princeton University Press, 1990), 112, and Alon Kadish, *Historians, Economists, and Economic History* (London: Routledge, 1989).

26. For a discussions of the popular and critical response to *Unto This Last*, see Clive Wilmer, "Introduction," *Unto This Last*, 28.

27. See Henderson, *Ruskin's Political Economy*, 2, and Lee, "Ruskin and Political Economy," 83–84.

28. Lee, "Ruskin and Political Economy," 83–84.

29. See Schabas, *A World Ruled by Number*. See also R. D. Collison Black, "W. S. Jevons and the Foundation of Modern Economics," in R. D. Collison Black, A. W. Coats, and Craufurd D. W. Goodwin, eds., *The Marginal Revolution in Economics* (Durham, N.C.: Duke University Press, 1973), 107, 111–12. Black argues that the mathematical aspects of Jevons's project were probably more important for the development of modern economic theory than his marginalist theory.

30. William Stanley Jevons, *Theory of Political Economy*, 1st ed. (London: Macmillan and Co., 1871), vii. Further references to this edition are cited parenthetically in the text.

31. Jevons's exact statement is: "In the science of Economy we treat men not as they ought to be, but as they are" (*TPE* 45).

32. Margaret Schabas provides the strongest account of how Jevons's marginal utility theory of value and his mathematical method worked together and reinforced one another: "What is remarkable about Jevons's work was his ability to shed the classical analytic apparatus and to incorporate ever greater abstraction and generality. And for these steps the heuristic value of mathematics was uppermost. The calculus guided him toward the mar-

ginal analysis of prices and costs. . . . His use of geometry, particularly in the analysis of labor, his recognition of the dimensions of the variables of his theory, and the discussion of limiting cases and exceptions to the equations all stemmed from a mathematical approach. . . . And by casting the key economic variables, including labor, in terms of utility, he envisioned an economy of unprecedented plasticity. Jevons was the one who released economics from its material constraints and shifted the focus to the deliberations of the mind. The economist would henceforth look to psychology rather than to physics for his fundamental principles" (*A World Ruled by Number*, 1). Despite Schabas's celebratory tone, her assessment of Jevons's "accomplishment" is astute and persuasive. The tone itself suggests the extent to which Jevons's revision of classical political economy's value theory and method were crucial for the formation of twentieth-century economic models and of the modern discipline of economics itself. In particular, the image of "an economy of unprecedented plasticity" points to the simultaneous untethering of capitalist economic structures (marketplace and corporation) and economic science from the embodied human concerns and environmental constraints theorized by Mill, Ruskin, and even, though to a lesser extent, Ricardo.

33. For a discussion of Jevons's commitment to the model of the natural sciences, see R. D. Collison Black, "Jevons's Contribution to the Teaching of Political Economy in Manchester and London" in Alon Kadish and Keith Tribe, eds., *The Market for Political Economy* (London: Routledge, 1993), 162–83, esp. 164–66. See also Black, "W. S. Jevons and the Foundation," 103.

34. Thus, while Jevons is more interested in human psychology than were other nineteenth-century economic theorists, that interest does not lead him back to the psychological model developed by Smith in *The Theory of Moral Sentiments*. While for Smith intersubjectivity is the primary foundation of human psychology, for Jevons such psychology is imagined as completely autonomous and isolated.

35. A less prominent effect of Jevons's mathematical and psychological model of human psychology is the way it functions to contain the irrational within a rational structure. Whereas Ricardo's economic model presumes a rational economic actor, Jevons's model can accommodate within itself all sorts of irrational passions and desires while still maintaining its rational, mathematical structure. At one point Jevons writes: "Anything which an individual is found to desire and to labour for must be assumed to possess for him utility" (*TPE* 45). No matter how irrational a desire might seem to an outside observer, viewed from the perspective of the economist such a desire "must be assumed" to have a utilitarian logic. Neither the economist nor anyone else can "assume" otherwise, since there is no basis for the intersubjective comparison of utility or value. Once the desire is assumed to operate according to this utilitarian principle, the desire and its manifestation in labor or exchange can be sutured back into the logical structure of the pleasure/pain calculus. Many of the irrational impulses that Ruskin, Mill, and even Dickens saw as being at odds with and disruptive of the analyses offered by economic science are, in Jevons's text, effectively recontained within that analysis. Marginalist economic theory constructs a rationalist mathematical model that claims to account for the irrational, as well as rational, elements of human desire and motivation.

36. William Stanley Jevons, Preface to the 2nd Edition, 1879, in *Theory of Political Economy*, 4th ed. (London: MacMillan and Co., 1924), xvii.

37. Winch, "Marginalism and the Boundaries," 59–60. For other discussions of the relationship between Jevons's work and the professionalization of economics, see Black, "Jevons's Contribution," 162, 171, 175–76; Black, "W. S. Jevons and the Foundation,"

98–99, 107, 111–12; Schabas, *A World Ruled by Number,* 98–118, 138–39; and Sandra Peart, *The Economics of W. S. Jevons* (London: Routledge, 1996), 3–7, 75–84.

38. R. D. Collison Black discusses Jevons's influence on the teaching of economics in "Jevons's Contribution"; see esp.175. Margaret Schabas extensively discusses the critical response to *Theory of Political Economy* in *A World Ruled by Number,* 98–126.

39. Schabas, *A World Ruled by Number,* 139.

40. Ibid.

41. See Regenia Gagnier's extensive discussion of this feature of the marginal economic theory in *Insatiability of Human Wants.*

42. Deirdre McCloskey, *The Vices of Economists, the Virtues of the Bourgeoisie* (Amsterdam: Amsterdam University Press, 1996).

43. Perhaps the final irony of all these uneven discursive developments is that at the time of this writing, Ruskin's *Unto This Last* is in print, in paperback, with excellent notes, readily available for use in college classrooms. Jevons's *Theory,* in contrast, is long out of print because there is simply no market for it. It would not be read in economics classrooms; students of economics are too busy learning calculus and econometrics to study the history of their own discipline.

44. Wallerstein, "Should We Unthink the Nineteenth Century?" 191.

bibliography

Primary Sources

Aytoun, W. E. "Our Currency, Our Trade and Our Tariff." *Blackwoods* 62 (1847).
———. "Railways." *Blackwoods* 58 (November 1845): 633–48.
Bagehot, Walter. "The First Edinburgh Reviewers" (1855). *Collected Works of Walter Bagehot*, vol. 1. Ed. N. St. John–Stevas. Cambridge, Mass.: Harvard University Press, 1965.
[Banfield, Thomas Charles.] "The Bank Charter Act: Currency Principles." *Westminster Review* 47 (July 1847): 412–66.
———. "Coin and Currency: The Bank Charter Act." *British and Foreign Quarterly Review* 17, no. 33 (1844): 1–49.
"Currency and Banking." *Fraser's Magazine* 36 (December 1847): 728–32.
Dickens, Charles. *Dombey and Son* (1848). Ed. Alan Horsman. Oxford: Oxford University Press, 1982.
———. *Hard Times for These Times*. Ed. Paul S. Schlicke. Oxford: Oxford University Press, 1998.
———. *Oliver Twist*. Ed. Kathleen Tillotson. Oxford: Oxford University Press, 1999.
———. *Selected Letters of Charles Dickens*. Ed. F. W. Dupee. New York: Farrar, Straus and Cudahy, 1960.
[Empson, William.] "Mrs. Marcet—Miss Martineau." *Edinburgh Review* 57 (April 1833): 3–39.
Fisk, George. "The Moral Influence of the Commercial Spirit of the Day." In *Lectures Delivered before the Y.M.C.A.* or *The Exeter Hall Lecture Series* 3 (1848).
Francis, John. *History of the Bank of England, Its Times and Traditions*. London: Willoughby, 1847.
"The Grand General Junction and Indefinite Extension Railway Rhapsody." *Blackwoods* 58 (November 1845): 614–16.
Hall, John Parson. "Speculation: A Tale of a Bank." *Bentley's Miscellany* 21 (February 1847): 166–75.
[Hickson, W. E.] "History and Exposition of the Currency Question." *Westminster Review* 48 (January 1848): 448–82.
———. "Railway Investment." *Westminster Review* 44 (December 1845): 497–522.
"How We Got Up the Glenmutchkin Railway, and How We Got Out of It." *Blackwoods* 58 (October 1845): 453–67.

Jevons, William Stanley. *Theory of Political Economy*, 1st ed. London: Macmillan and Co., 1871.
———. *Theory of Political Economy*, 4th ed. London: Macmillan and Co., 1924.
Marcet, Mrs. [Jane]. *Conversations on Political Economy*. London: Longman, Hurst, Ress, Orme, and Brown, 1816.
Martineau, Harriet. *Berkeley the Banker*. London: Charles Fox, 1833.
———. *Cinnamon and Pearls*. London: Charles Fox, 1833.
———. *Demerara*. London: Charles Fox, 1832.
———. *Hill and Valley*. London: Charles Fox, 1832.
———. *A Manchester Strike*. London: Charles Fox, 1833.
———. *The Moral of Many Fables*. London: Charles Fox, 1834.
———. "Preface," in *Illustrations of Political Economy*, no. 1. London: Charles Fox, 1832.
———. *Weal and Woe in Garveloch*. London: Charles Fox, 1832.
Marx, Karl. *Capital*, vol. 1. Trans. Ben Fowkes. London: Penguin Books, 1976.
Mayhew, Henry. *The Unknown Mayhew: Selections from the* Morning Chronicle *1849–1850*. Ed. E. P. Thompson and Eileen Yeo. London: Merlin Press, 1971.
———. *London Labour and the London Poor*, 4 vols. (1861–62). Reprint ed. John Rosenberg. New York: Dover, 1968.
McCulloch, J. R. "The Abolition of the Corn Laws." *Edinburgh Review* 44 (September 1826): 319–59.
———. "Causes and Cure of Disturbances and Pauperism." *Edinburgh Review* 53 (March 1831): 43–63.
———. *A Discourse on the Rise, Progress, Peculiar Objects and Importance of Political Economy*. Edinburgh: Constable, 1825.
———. "Ireland." *Edinburgh Review* 37 (June 1822): 60–109.
———. "Note on Money, from Mr. M'Culloch's Edition of the Wealth of Nations." Edinburgh: A. Balfour, 1827.
———. *Outlines of Political Economy, with Some Inquiries Respecting Their Application*. Ed. John McVickar. New York: Augustus M. Kelley, 1966.
———. "Poor Laws." *Edinburgh Review* 57 (May 1828): 303–30.
———. *The Principles of Political Economy, with Some Inquiries Respecting their Application*, 5th ed. Edinburgh: Adam and Charles Black, 1864.
———. "Ricardo's *Political Economy*." *Edinburgh Review* 30 (June 1818): 59–87.
———. "The Rise and Fall of Profits." *Edinburgh Review* 40 (1824): 1–31.
———. "The Standard of National Prosperity." *Edinburgh Review* 40 (March 1824): 1–31.
———. "A Treatise on Metallic and Paper Money and Banks: Written for the Encyclopedia Britannica." London: Longman, Brown, Green, Longmans, and Roberts, 1858.
Mill, John Stuart. *Autobiography*. Ed. Jack Stillinger. Boston: Houghton Mifflin Co., 1969.
———. "Bentham." 1838. *Essays on Ethics, Religion and Society*. Ed. J. M. Robson. Toronto: University of Toronto Press, 1969.
———. "Coleridge." 1840. *Essays on Ethics, Religion and Society*. Ed. J. M. Robson. Toronto: University of Toronto Press, 1969.
———. "The Currency Question." *Westminster Review* 41 (June 1844): 579–98.
———. "On the Definition of Political Economy; and on the Method of Investigation Proper to It." *Collected Works IV: Essays on Economics and Society, 1824–1845*. Ed. J. M. Robson. London: University of Toronto Press; Routledge and Kegan Paul, 1967. 309–39.
———. *Principles of Political Economy, with Some of Their Applications to Social Philosophy*.

Ed. Sir William Ashley. London: Augustus M. Kelly Publishers, 1987.
"Miss Martineau's Little Novels." *The Spectator* (July 7, 1832): 639.
[Newmarch, William]. "The Financial Pressure." *Quarterly Review* 81 (June 1847): 230–73.
The Present State of the Currency Practically Considered: Proving the Justice and Necessity of Immediately and Effectually Revising the Currency Measures of 1819 and 1844. London: G. Briggs, 1847.
Ricardo, David. *The Principles of Political Economy and Taxation*. London: Dent and Sons, 1973.
Ruskin, John. *Munera Pulvis. The Works of John Ruskin*, vol. 17. Ed. E. T. Cook and Alexander Wedderburn. London: George Allen, 1905.
———. *Unto This Last and Other Writings*. Ed. Clive Wilmer. London: Penguin Books, 1985, 1997).
[Scope, George Poulett.] "Miss Martineau's Monthly Novels." *Quarterly Review* 49 (April 1833): 136–52.
Sheehan, John. "The Railway Queen." *Bentley's Miscellany* 18 (October 1845): 386–93.
Smith, Adam. *An Inquiry into the Nature and Causes of the Wealth of Nations*. Ed. Edwin Canaan. Chicago: Chicago University Press, 1976.
———. "The Principles Which Lead and Direct Philosophical Enquiries; Illustrated by the History of Astronomy." *Collected Works* III. Ed. R. H. Campbell and A. S. Skinner. Oxford and New York: Clarendon Press and Oxford University Press, 1976.
———. *The Theory of Moral Sentiments*. Ed. D. D. Raphael and A. L. Macfie. Indianapolis: Liberty Fund, 1984.
Steward, Dugald. "Account of the Life and Writings of Adam Smith, LL.D." In Adam Smith, *Collected Works*, vol. 3. Ed. R. H. Campbell and A. S. Skinner. Oxford and New York: Clarendon Press and Oxford University Press, 1976.

Secondary Sources

Althusser, Louis. "Ideology and the Ideological State Apparatus." In *Lenin and Philosophy and Other Essays*. Trans. Ben Brewster, 127–86. New York: Monthly Review Press, 1971.
Althusser, Louis, and Etienne Balibar. *Reading Capital*. Trans. Ben Brewster. London: New Left Books, 1970.
Altick, Richard. *The English Common Reader*. Chicago: University of Chicago Press, 1957.
Armstrong, Nancy. *Desire and Domestic Fiction: A Political History of the Novel*. Oxford: Oxford University Press, 1987.
Barker-Benfield, G. J. *The Culture of Sensibility*. Chicago: University of Chicago Press, 1992.
Beer, Max. *A History of British Socialism*. 2 vols. London, 1929.
Billet, Leonard. "The Just Economy: The Moral Basis of the *Wealth of Nations*." *Review of Social Economy* 34 (1976): 295–315.
Birch, Dinah. "Ruskin's Womanly Mind." *Essays in Criticism* 38 (1988): 308–24.
Black, R. D. Collison. "Jevons's Contribution to the Teaching of Political Economy in Manchester and London." In *The Market for Political Economy*. Ed. Alon Kadish and Keith Tribe, 162–83. London: Routledge, 1993.
———. "W. S. Jevons and the Foundation of Modern Economics." In *The Marginal Revolution in Economics*. Ed. R. D. Collison Black, A. W. Coats, and Craufurd D. W. Goodwin, 98–112. Durham, N.C.: Duke University Press, 1973.

Blaug, Mark. *Ricardian Economics*. New Haven, Conn.: Yale University Press, 1958.
Bowley, Marian. *Studies in the History of Economic Theory before 1870*. London: Macmillan, 1973.
Brown, Gillian. *Domestic Individualism: Imagining Self in Nineteenth-Century America*. Berkeley: University of California Press, 1990.
Brown, Vivian. *Adam Smith's Discourse: Canonicity, Commerce, and Conscience*. London and New York: Routledge, 1994.
Checkland, S. G. "The Advent of Academic Economics in England." *The Manchester School of Economic and Social Theory before 1870* 19 (1951): 43–70.
———. "The Propagation of Ricardian Economics in England." *Economica* (February 1949): 40–52.
———. *The Rise of Industrial Society in England, 1815–1885*. London: Longman, 1964.
Claeys, Gregory. *Machinery, Money, and the Millenium: From Moral Economy to Socialism, 1815–1860*. Princeton, N.J.: Princeton University Press, 1987.
Cole, G. D. H. *A History of Socialist Thought*. 5 vols. Vol. 1: *Socialist Thought: The Forerunners, 1789–1850*. London: MacMillan, 1977.
Collini, Stefan. "Political Theory and the 'Science of Society' in Victorian Britain." *Historical Journal* 23 (1980): 203–31.
Collini, Stefan, Donald Winch, and John Burrow, eds. *That Noble Science of Politics*. Cambridge: Cambridge University Press, 1983.
Daston, Lorraine, and Peter Galison. "The Image of Objectivity." *Representations* 40 (Fall 1992): 81–128.
Davidoff, Leonore, and Catherine Hall. *Family Fortunes: Men and Women of the English Middle Class, 1780–1850*. Chicago: University of Chicago Press, 1987.
de Marchi, N. B. "Mill and Cairns and the Emergence of Marginalism in England." In *The Marginal Revolution in Economics*. Ed. R. D. Collison Black, A. W. Coats, and Craufurd D. W. Goodwin, 78–97. Durham, N.C.: Duke University Press, 1973.
Dean, Mitchell. *The Constitution of Poverty: Toward a Genealogy of Liberal Governance*. London: Routledge, 1991.
Deane, Phyllis. *The Evolution of Economic Ideas*. Cambridge: Cambridge University Press, 1978.
Dreyfus, Herbert L., and Paul Rabinow. *Michel Foucault: Beyond Structuralism and Hermeneutics*. 2d ed. Chicago: University of Chicago Press, 1983.
Dumont, Louis. *From Mandeville to Marx*. Chicago: University of Chicago Press, 1977, 1983.
Fain, John. *Ruskin and the Economists*. Nashville, Tenn.: Vanderbilt University Press, 1956.
Fetter, Frank. "The Rise and Decline of Ricardian Economics." *History of Political Economy* 1 (1969): 67–84.
Fitzgibbons, Athol. *Adam Smith's System of Liberty, Wealth, and Virtue: The Moral and Political Foundations of The Wealth of Nations*. Oxford: Clarendon, 1995.
Fisch, Menachem. *William Whewell, Philosopher of Science*. Oxford: Clarendon Press, 1991.
Fontana, Biancamaria. *Rethinking the Politics of Commercial Society: The Edinburgh Review 1802–1832*. Cambridge: Cambridge University Press, 1985.
Forbes, Duncan. "'Scientific' Whiggism: Adam Smith and John Millar." *Cambridge Journal* 7 (1953–54): 645–70.
Foucault, Michel. *The Archaeology of Knowledge and the Discourse on Language*. Trans. A. M. Sheridan Smith. New York: Pantheon Books, 1972.

———. "Politics and the Study of Discourse." In *The Foucault Effect: Studies in Governmentality.* Ed. Graham Burchell, Colin Gordon, and Peter Miller. Chicago: Chicago University Press, 1991.

———. *The Use of Pleasure: The History of Sexuality,* vol. 2. Trans. Robert Hurley. New York: Vintage, 1990; Random House, 1985).

Gagnier, Regenia. *Subjectivities: A History of Self-Representation in Britain, 1832–1920.* New York and Oxford: Oxford University Press, 1991.

———. *The Insatiability of Human Wants.* Chicago: University of Chicago Press, 2000.

Gallagher, Catherine. "The Body versus the Social Body in the Works of Thomas Malthus and Henry Mayhew." In *The Making of a Modern Body: Sexuality and Society in the Nineteenth Century.* Ed. Catherine Gallagher and Thomas Laqueur. Berkeley: University of California Press, 1987.

———. *The Industrial Reformation of English Fiction, 1832–1867.* Chicago: University of Chicago Press, 1985.

Gordon, Scott. *History and Philosophy of Social Science.* New York: Routledge, 1991.

Grampp, William D. "Classical Economics and Its Moral Critics." *History of Political Economy* (1973): 359–74.

Gregory, T. E., ed. *Select Statutes, Documents, and Reports Relating to British Banking, 1832–1928,* vol. 1. London: Oxford University Press, 1929.

Gudeman, Steven. *Economics as Culture: Model and Metaphors of Livelihood.* London: Routledge and Kegan Paul, 1986.

Guillory, John. *Cultural Capital: The Problem of Literary Canon Formation.* Chicago: University of Chicago Press, 1993.

Harrington, Dana. "Gender, Commerce and the Transformation of Virtue in Eighteenth-Century Britain." *RSQ: Rhtoric Society Quarterly* 31, no. 3 (2001): 33–52.

Heavner, Eric. *Food, Sex and God: The Christian Social Theory of T. R. Malthus.* Ph.D. diss., Johns Hopkins University, Baltimore, Md., 1993.

Heilbroner, Robert. *Behind the Veil of Economics.* New York: W. W. Norton, 1988.

Henderson, Willie. *John Ruskin's Political Economy.* London and New York: Routledge, 2000.

Herbert, Christopher. *Culture and Anomie: Ethnographic Imagination in the Nineteenth Century.* Chicago: University of Chicago Press, 1991.

Hilton, Boyd. *The Age of Atonement: The Influence of Evangelicalism on Social and Economic Thought, 1795–1865.* Oxford: Clarendon, 1988.

———. "Chalmers as Political Economist." In *The Practical and the Pious: Essays on Thomas Chalmers (1780–1847).* Ed. A. C. Cheyne. Edinburgh: St. Andrews Press, 1985.

Himmelfarb, Gertrude. *The Idea of Poverty.* New York: Knopf, 1984.

Hirschman, Albert O. *The Passions and the Interests: Political Arguments for Capitalism before Its Prime.* Princeton, N.J.: Princeton University Press, 1977.

Hollander, Samuel. *The Economics of Adam Smith.* Toronto: University of Toronto Press, 1973.

———. *The Economics of David Ricardo.* Toronto: Heinemann, 1979.

———. *The Economics of John Stuart Mill,* vol. 2: *Political Economy.* Toronto: University of Toronto Press, 1985.

Hopfl, H. M. "From Savage to Scotsman: Conjectural History in the Scottish Enlightenment." *Journal of British Studies* 17 (1978): 24–40.

Houghton, Walter. E. "Periodical Literature and the Articulate Classes." In *The Victorian*

Periodical Press: Samplings and Soundings. Ed. Joanne Shattock and Michael Wolfe. Toronto: Leicester University Press; Toronto University Press, 1982.

Humphreys, Anne. *Henry Mayhew*. New York: Twayne Publishers, 1984.

———. *Travels into the Poor Man's Country: The Works of Henry Mayhew*. Firle, Sussex, and Athens: Caliban Books and University of Georgia Press, 1977.

Hutchinson, T. W. *On Revolutions and Progress in Economic Knowledge*. Cambridge: Cambridge University Press, 1978.

Jameson, Fredric. *The Political Unconscious*. Ithaca, N.Y.: Cornell University Press, 1981.

Johnson, Claudia L. *Equivocal Beings: Politics, Gender, and Sentimentality in the 1790s*. Chicago: University of Chicago Press, 1995.

Johnson, Edgar. *Charles Dickens: His Tragedy and Triumph*, vol. 2. New York: Simon and Schuster, 1952.

Jordanova, Ludmilla. "The Popularization of Medicine: Tissot on Onanism." *Textual Practice* 1 (1987): 68–79.

Kadish, Alon. *Historians, Economists, and Economic History*. London: Routledge, 1989.

———. "An Introduction to the Variety of Arguments for Free Trade." In *The Corn Laws: The Formation of Popular Economics in Britain*, vol. 1. Ed. Alon Kadish. London: William Pickering, 1996.

Kaplan, Fred. *Sacred Tears: Sentimentality in Victorian Literature*. Princeton, N.J.: Princeton University Press, 1987.

Kaufmann, David. *The Business of Common Life: Novels and Classical Economics between Revolution and Reform*. Baltimore, Md.: Johns Hopkins University Press, 1995.

Langer, Gary F. *The Coming of Age of Political Economy*. New York: Greenwood Press, 1987.

Lee, Alan. "Ruskin and Political Economy: *Unto This Last*." In *New Approaches to Ruskin*. Ed. Robert Hewison, 68–88. London: Routledge and Kegan Paul, 1981.

LeMahieu, D. L. *The Mind of William Paley*. Lincoln: University of Nebraska Press, 1976.

Lenoir, Timothy. "Discipline of Nature/Nature of Disciplines." In *Knowledges: Historical and Critical Studies in Disciplinarity*. Ed. Ellen Messer-Davidow, David R. Shumway, and David J. Sylvan. Charlottesville: University Press of Virginia, 1993.

Letwin, William. *Origin of Scientific Economics*. London: Methuen, 1963.

Meek, Ronald L. *Economics and Ideology and Other Essays: Studies in the Development of Economic Thought*. London: Chapman Hall, 1967.

Messer-Davidow, Ellen, David R. Shumway, and David J. Sylvan. *Knowledges: Historical and Critical Studies in Disciplinarity*. Charlottesville: University Press of Virginia, 1993.

Meyer, John W. "Society without Culture: A Nineteenth-Century Legacy." In *Re-Thinking the Nineteenth Century*. Ed. Francisco Ramirez. New York: Greenwood Press, 1988.

Miller, Thomas. *The Formation of College English*. Pittsburgh: University of Pittsburgh Press, 1997.

Mintowitz, Peter. *Profits, Priests, and Prices: Adam Smith's Emancipation of Economics from Politics and Religion*. Stanford, Calif.: Stanford University Press, 1993.

Mort, Frank. *Dangerous Sexualities: Medico-Moral Politics in England since 1830*. London: Routledge and Kegan Paul, 1987.

Moynihan, Julian. "Dealings with the Firm of Dombey and Son: Firmness versus Wetness." *Dickens and the Twentieth Century*. Ed. John Gross and Gabriel Pearson. Toronto: University of Toronto Press, 1962.

Nead, Lynda. *Myths of Sexuality: Representations of Women in Victorian Britain.* Oxford: Basil Blackwell, 1988.
Newton, Judith. "Engendering History for the Middle Class: Sex and Political Economy in the *Edinburgh Review.*" In *Rewriting the Victorians.* Ed. Linda Shires, 1–17. New York: Routledge and Kegan Paul, 1992.
———. "Making—and Remaking—History: Another Look at 'Patriarchy.'" In *Feminist Issues in Literary Scholarship.* Ed. Shari Benstock. Bloomington: Indiana University Press, 1987.
O'Brien, D. P. *J. R. McCulloch: A Study in Classical Economics.* New York: Barnes and Noble, 1970.
Olson, Richard. *The Emergence of the Social Sciences 1642–1792.* New York: Twayne Publishers, 1993.
———. *Science Deified, Science Defied.* Berkeley: University of California Press, 1990.
Oxford English Dictionary. 2d ed. New York: Oxford University Press, 1989.
Paul, Ellen Frankel. *Moral Revolution and Economic Science.* Westport, Conn.: Greenwood Press, 1979.
Peach, Terry. *Interpreting Ricardo.* Cambridge: Cambridge University Press, 1993.
Peart, Sandra. *The Economics of W. S. Jevons.* London: Routledge, 1996.
Peil, Jan. *Adam Smith and Economic Science: A Methodological Reinterpretation.* Cheltenham, U.K., and Northhampton, Mass.: Edward Elgar, 1999.
Perera, Suvendrini. "Wholesale, Retail and for Exportation: Empire and the Family Business in *Dombey and Son.*" *Victorian Studies* 33 (1990): 603–20.
Pichanick, Valerie Kossew. *Harriet Martineau: The Woman and Her Work, 1802–76.* Ann Arbor: University of Michigan Press, 1980.
Pocock, J. G. A. *The Machiavellian Moment: Florentine Political Thought and the Atlantic Republican Tradition.* Princeton, N.J.: Princeton University Press, 1975.
———. *Virtue, Commerce, History: Essays on Political Thought and History, Chiefly in the Eighteenth Century.* Cambridge: Cambridge University Press, 1985.
Polanyi, Karl. *The Great Transformation.* Boston: Beacon Press, 1944.
Poovey, Mary. "Aesthetics and Political Economy in the Eighteenth Century." In *Aesthetics and Ideology.* Ed. George Levine, 79–105. New Brunswick, N.J.: Rutgers University Press, 1994.
———. *A History of the Modern Fact: Problems of Knowledge in the Sciences of Wealth and Society.* Chicago: University of Chicago Press, 1998.
———. *Making a Social Body: British Cultural Formation 1830–1864.* Chicago: University of Chicago Press, 1995.
———. "Reading History in Literature: Speculation and Virtue in *Our Mutual Friend.*" In *Historical Criticism and the Challenge of Theory.* Ed. Janet Smarr. Urbana: University of Illinois Press, 1993.
———. *Uneven Developments: The Ideological Work of Gender in Mid-Victorian England.* Chicago: University of Chicago Press, 1988.
Rauch, Alan. *Useful Knowledge.* Durham, N.C.: Duke University Press, 2001.
Robbins, Lord. *The Evolution of Modern Economic Theory.* Chicago: Aldine Publishers, 1970.
Robson, John M. *The Improvement of Mankind: The Social and Political Philosophy of John Stuart Mill.* Toronto: University of Toronto Press, 1968.
Ryan, Alan. *J. S. Mill.* London: Routledge and Kegan Paul, 1974.
Sally, Razeen. *Classical Liberalism and the International Economic Order: Studies in Theory and Intellectual History.* London and New York: Routledge, 1998.

Samuels, Shirley. "Introduction." *The Culture of Sentiment: Race, Gender, and Sentimentality in Nineteenth-Century America.* Oxford: Oxford University Press, 1992.

Schabas, Margaret. *A World Ruled by Number: William Stanley Jevons and the Rise of Mathematical Economics.* Princeton, N.J.: Princeton University Press, 1990.

Schumpeter, Joseph. *History of Economic Analysis.* London: George Allen and Unwin, 1954.

Schwartz, Pedro. *The New Political Economy of J. S. Mill.* Durham, N.C.: Duke University Press, 1972.

Sedgwick, Eve Kosofsky. *Between Men: English Literature and Male Homosocial Desire.* New York: Columbia University Press, 1985.

Sen, Amartya. *On Ethics and Economics.* Oxford: Basil Blackwell, 1987.

Sherburne, James. *The Ambiguities of Abundance.* Cambridge, Mass.: Harvard University Press, 1972.

Shinn, Terry, and Richard Whitely, eds. *Expository Science: Forms and Functions of Popularisation.* Dordrecht: D. Reidel Publishing Co., 1985.

Simpson, David. "Introduction: The Moment of Materialism." In *Subject to History: Ideology, Class, Gender.* Ed. David Simpson. Ithaca, N.Y.: Cornell University Press, 1991.

———. *Romanticism, Nationalism, and the Revolution against Theory.* Chicago: University of Chicago Press, 1993.

Siskin, Clifford. *The Historicity of Romantic Discourse.* New York: Oxford University Press, 1988.

Spear, Jeffrey. *Dreams of English Eden: Ruskin and His Tradition in Social Criticism.* New York: Columbia University Press, 1984.

St. Clair, Oswald. *A Key to Ricardo.* London: Routledge and Kegan Paul, 1957.

Straffa, Peiro. *Production of Commodities by Means of Commodities: Prelude to a Critique of Economic Theory.* Cambridge: Cambridge University Press 1960.

Sutherland, Kathryn. "Adam Smith's Master Narrative: Women and the *Wealth of Nations*." In *Adam Smith's* Wealth of Nations: *New Interdisciplinary Essays.* Ed. Stephen Copley and Kathryn Sutherland. Manchester and New York: University of Manchester Press and St. Martin's Press, 1995.

Taylor, Barbara. *Eve and the New Jerusalem: Socialism and Feminism in the Nineteenth Century.* New York: Pantheon, 1983.

Teichegraeber, Richard F., III. *"Free Trade" and Moral Philosophy: Rethinking the Sources of Adam Smith's* Wealth of Nations. Durham, N.C.: Duke University Press, 1986.

Thomas, Gillian. *Harriet Martineau.* Boston: Twayne Publishers, 1985.

Thomas, William. *The Philosophical Radicals.* Oxford: Clarendon Press, 1979.

Thompson, E. P. "Mayhew and the *Morning Chronicle.*" *The Unknown Mayhew: Selections from the* Morning Chronicle, *1849–1850.* London: Merlin Press, 1971.

Thompson, James. *Models of Value: Eighteenth-Century Political Economy and the Novel.* Durham, N.C.: Duke University Press, 1996.

Thompson, Noel. *The People's Science.* Cambridge: Cambridge University Press, 1984.

Tompkins, Jane. "'Pray, therefore, without ceasing': From Tracts to Texts." *Genre* 16 (Winter 1983): 423–36.

Vance, Norman. *The Sinews of the Spirit: The Ideal of Christian Manliness in Victorian Literature and Social Thought.* Cambridge: Cambridge University Press, 1985.

Vargish, Thomas. *The Providential Aesthetic in Victorian Fiction.* Charlottesville: University Press of Virginia, 1985.

Walkowitz, Judith R. *Prostitution and Victorian Society: Women, Class, and the State.* Cambridge: Cambridge University Press, 1980.
Wallerstein, Immanuel. "The Development of the Concept of Development." *The Politics of the World Economy.* Cambridge: Cambridge University Press, 1984.
———. "Eurocentrism and Its Avatars: The Dilemmas of Social Science." *New Left Review* 226 (1997).
———. *Historical Capitalism, with Capitalist Civilization.* London: Verso, 1995.
———. "Should We Unthink the Nineteenth Century?" In *Rethinking the Nineteenth Century.* Ed. Francisco O. Ramirez. New York: Greenwood Press, 1988.
———. "A World-System Perspective on the Social Sciences." *The Capitalist World-Economy.* Cambridge: Cambridge University Press, 1979.
Waterman, A. C. *Revolution, Economics, and Religion: Christian Political Economy, 1798–1833.* Cambridge: Cambridge University Press, 1991.
Webb, R. K. *Harriet Martineau: A Radical Victorian.* London: Heinemann, 1960.
Wheatley, Vera. *The Life and Work of Harriet Martineau.* London: Secker and Warburg, 1957.
Williams, Raymond. *Culture and Society: 1780–1950.* New York: Columbia University Press, 1958, 1983.
———. *Marxism and Literature.* Oxford: Oxford University Press, 1977.
Winch, Donald. "Higher Maxims: Happiness versus Wealth in Malthus and Ricardo." In *That Noble Science of Politics.* Ed. Stephan Collini, Donald Winch, and John Burrow, 63–89. Cambridge: Cambridge University Press, 1983.
———. "Marginalism and the Boundaries of Economics Science." In *The Marginal Revolution in Economics.* Ed. R. D. Collison Black, A. W. Coats, and Craufurd D. W. Goodwin, 59–77. Durham, N.C.: Duke University Press, 1973.
———. *Riches and Poverty: An Intellectual History of Political Economy in Britain, 1750–1834.* Cambridge: Cambridge University Press, 1996.
Yeo, Eileen. "Mayhew as a Social Investigator." In *The Unknown Mayhew: Selections from the* Morning Chronicle *1849–1850.* Ed. E. P. Thompson and Eileen Yeo, 56–109. London: Merlin Press, 1971.
Yeo, Richard R. *Defining Science: William Whewell, Natural Knowledge, and Public Debate in Early Victorian Britain.* Cambridge: Cambridge University Press, 1993.
———. "Science and Intellectual Authority in Mid-Nineteenth-Century Britain: Robert Chambers and *Vestiges of the Natural History of Creation.*" *Victorian Studies* 28 (Autumn 1984): 1–31.
———. "Scientific Method and the Rhetoric of Science in Britain, 1830–1917." In *The Politics and Rhetoric of Scientific Method.* Ed. John Schuster and Richard R. Yeo. Dordrecht and Boston: D. Reidel, 1986.
Young, Jeffrey T. *Economics as Moral Science: The Political Economy of Adam Smith.* Cheltenham, U.K., and Lyme, N.Y.: Edward Elgar, 1997.

index

abstraction, 15, 18–20, 21, 27, 37, 39, 40, 45, 56, 58, 59, 77, 138–39, 140, 168, 169, 182
Althusser, Louis, xxi
Altick, Richard, 32, 33–34

Bagehot, Walter, 1, 2, 3
Banfield, Charles, 85–86, 88
Bank Charter Act, 79, 82–87, 107–8, 199n. 5, 199n. 7, 199nn. 10–11
banking, 15, 54, 70, 72, 73, 76, 82–87, 199n. 6. *See also* currency; money
Beer, Max, 15
Bentham, Jeremy, 37, 136, 175, 176
Berkeley the Banker (Martineau), 68–73
Blaug, Marc, 2, 34

capitalism: and civilization, 43–44, commercial, 59; competitive, 93–94, 96, 101, 133, 171; as dependent upon system of credit, currency, and banking, 72; and Dickens, 79, 81, 88, 93, 107; historical, xvii; industrial(-imperialist), xvii, xx, xxi, 22, 60; laissez-faire, 43, 45; and J. S. Mill, 183–84; as mode of production, xvii; model of, 76
Carlyle, Thomas, xv, xxv, 36, 136, 143, 164, 206n. 10, 207n. 14
censorship, 111
Chalmers, Thomas, 28
Checkland, S. G., 2, 20, 28, 34, 82
child labor, 61, 120, 124, 126–27
citizenship, 41
civilization, 42–43, 44, 187
Claeys, Gregory, 15
classical economic theory, 113; critics of, xxvi, 109, 110, 161, 173, 175, 178, 180 (*see also* Dickens, Charles; Jevons, W. Stanley; Mayhew, Henry); development of, 23; legacy of,

14–15; of Martineau, xxv, 30, 53, 56, 71, 73, 77; of McCulloch, 30, 49; revisions of, 180; of Ricardo, 14, 27
Cole, G. D. H., 15
Coleridge, Samuel, 136, 143, 145, 195n. 47, 207n. 14
communism, 147–49, 157
competition, xvi, 91–96; among family members, 120; anxieties about, 120; commercial, 106; constructing social dynamics as, xvi; free, 48–49; male, 100–103; Mill's discussion of, 139–40, 148–50, 154, 158; as a result of trade degradation, 128–30; trade societies as a solution to, 133; violence as a result of, 93, 99–104, 108; and working classes, 112–14, 124, 128–30, 202n. 12, 202n. 20
conjectural history, 28, 42–43, 44, 45, 196n. 23
Conversations on Political Economy (Marcet), 53, 54–55
Corn Laws, 45, 46–47, 50–51, 54
currency, 15, 69; bill, 199n. 11; crisis, 70, 71; depreciation of, 78; gold-based, 108; paper, 199n. 6; policy, 73; reform, 85; regulation, 82; stability of, 84; value of, 72. *See also* banking; money

Demerara (Martineau), 65–67
Descartes, Rene, xxiii, 4, 5
Dickens, Charles, xvii, xxiv, xxv; attacks on utilitarianism and materialist rationalism, 80–81; criticism of capitalist commercial and social systems, 96; criticism of discourse of political economy, xv–xvi, 184, 185; criticism of the Poor Laws, 80; and imperialism, 104; and J. S. Mill, 136; and

moral value, 100; and Ruskin, 164, 171; use of feminine influence, 198n. 2. *See also Dombey and Son; Hard Times; Oliver Twist*

Discourse on Political Economy (McCulloch), 19, 40–42, 43, 44

divine law, 3, 38

Dombay and Son (Dickens), 78–81, 87–108, 114, 132, 199n. 15

domesticity: anxieties about, 111; female, 13, 88, 92, 93, 112, 115, 116–17, 132, 172, 187, 199n. 15; male, 118; and virtue, 171, 193n. 30; working-class, 202nn. 10–11

economic law, xii, xiii, xiv, xv, xxv, 3, 12, 25, 27, 29, 30, 37, 38, 44, 45, 48, 49, 50, 51, 56, 66, 68, 70, 72, 82, 83, 84, 85, 87, 130, 158, 160, 165, 169, 179

economy, domestic, xii, 63, 64, 200n. 15

education, 26, 32, 33, 34, 41, 42, 56, 126, 135, 142, 143, 152, 155–56, 167, 176, 196n. 11

Essay on the Principle of Population (Malthus), xii, 15, 26, 195n. 47

ethics, xii, xiv, 5, 143, 158, 159, 164, 167, 173, 183, 189n. 3, 206n. 7

family wage, 112, 116, 119, 120, 123, 132, 133, 202n. 10, 203n. 24

Foucault, Michel, xvii–xx, xxi, xxii, 31, 189n. 5, 190n. 7, 190n. 11, 190n. 15

Fourierism, 149

Foxwell, H., 181, 182

France, boundary between England and, 96–97

free trade, 7, 8, 37, 44, 111

Gudeman, Stephen, 5, 28–29

Hard Times (Dickens), 80–81, 164

Hill and the Valley, The (Martineau), 73–76

Himmelfarb, Gertrude, 2, 202n. 17

Hobbes, Thomas, xxiii

Hume, David, xxiii, 5, 7

Illustrations of Political Economy (Martineau), xiv, 33, 53–59, 64, 68, 70, 71, 77

immigration, Irish, 47, 48–50

imperialism, 88, 104, 105, 107, 108

Jameson, Fredric, xxi

Jevons, W. Stanley, xi, xvii, xxiv, xxvi, 37, 159, 160; on consumption, 173–74; criticism of classical theory, 161, 164, 173, 185; educational background of, 181; on human psychology, 176–79, 180, 209nn. 34–35; on marginal utility theory, 182–84, 208–9n. 32; on mathematical science, 174–76, 178–79, 180, 182, 185, 208–9n. 32; and J. S. Mill, 161–62, 184; and Ricardo, 181; and Ruskin, 173–74, 178; on value, 175, 180, 182. *See also Theory of Political Economy*

Jones, Richard, 28

Keynes, Neville, 181, 182

Knight, Charles, 32, 33

knowledge, scientific, xxiv, 2, 6, 31, 32, 34, 41, 171, 186

labor: female, 109–11, 116, 124, 132–33, 202n. 10. *See also* domesticity; prostitution

laboring class, 25–26, 27, 58, 109–10, 111, 113, 121, 129, 145, 146, 151, 152, 204n. 42. *See also* working class

Leslie, T. E. Cliffe, 181

London Labour and the London Poor (Mayhew), 110, 111

Mackintosh, James, 23

Malthus, Thomas, xii, xiv, xv, xxiii, 1, 18, 20, 21, 26–27, 36, 37–38, 138, 191n. 2, 194n. 31, 195n. 47; population principle of, 15, 37, 67, 80, 113, 134, 157–58. *See also Essay on the Principle of Population*

Manchester Strike, A (Martineau), 59–65, 68, 77

Marcet, Jane, 36, 53–55. *See also Conversations on Political Economy*

Marshall, Alfred, xi, 162, 181, 182

Martineau, Harriet, xvii, xxi, xxiv, xxv, 21, 29, 30, 32, 36, 40, 184; compared and contrasted with Marcet, 53–55; and dramatic cycles of economic theory, 73; and economic theory in narrative forms, 35, 56–59, 66–67, 198n. 11; on morality, 55, 197n. 4; and popularization of scientific economic discourse, xiii; on science, 55–57; seeking to bridge distance between knowledge producer and consumer, 34. *See also Berkeley the Banker; Demerara; Hill and the Valley, The; Illustrations of Political Economy; Manchester Strike, A; Weal and Woe in Garveloch*

Marx, Karl, xvii, 14, 159, 161, 162

Marxist theory, xx–xxi, xxiii, 14–15

masculine subjectivity, 95, 97, 99, 107, 120, 132

masculinity: loss of, 125–28, 130; Ruskin on, 172; Victorian middle-class, 112, 114, 115–16, 202n. 22, 204n. 38; working-class, 112, 120, 132, 133, 201–2n. 10, 203n. 23

Mayhew, Henry, xvii, xxiv, xxv; as critic of discourse of political economy, xv–xvi, 184, 185; and J. S. Mill, 135, 201n. 4; on London's working poor, 109–133, 200n. 2, 200–201n. 4, 201n. 9, 202n. 20, 204n. 36, 204n. 37; publication of *Low Wages, Their Causes, Consequences and Remedies,* 111; and Ruskin, 171, 202n. 12. *See also London Labour and the London Poor*

McCulloch, John Ramsey, xvii, xxi, xxiv–xxv, 5, 21, 29, 30, 32, 53, 137, 184: as ally of James Mill, 37; on connection between civilization and capitalism, 43–45; on Corn Laws, 46–47, 50–51; critique of good intentions, 41; and definition of political economy, 18; and economic theory in narrative forms, 35; as first "professional" economist, 36; on ignorance, 41–42; on Irish immigration, 48–50; and Malthus, 37, 38; on mercantilist and French economical theories, 39; and natural truth, 39; political stance of, 37; on Poor Laws, 47–49, 50–51; popularity of, 36; and popularization of scientific economic discourse xiii; and Ricardian theory, xiii–xiv, 19, 34–35, 36, 40, 51–52; scientific and professional aspirations of, 33; seeking to bridge distance between knowledge producer and consumer, 34; and Smith, 39. *See also Discourse on Political Economy*

middle class: anxieties of, 110, 112; and domestic ideology, 116; fears of, 46, 50, 51; interests of, 58; in Martineau's works, 70–71, 72; masculinity of, 112, 114, 115–16, 202n. 22, 204n. 38; and Mayhew, 201n. 9; opposition to working class, 123; and Poor Laws, 50, 51; and prostitution, 124; as readers, xiii, 27, 32, 33, 34, 45, 46, 50, 123, 173; and Ricardian theory, 27, 28; and scientific economic theory, 136; women in, 133; as writers, xxv, 114, 116, 120

Mill, James, xii, xiii, xv, 1, 36, 37, 53, 59, 134, 137, 143, 156, 192n. 9; publication of *Elements of Political Economy,* xiii, xxvi

Mill, John Stuart, xvii, xxiii, xxiv, 5, 6, 19, 37, 53, 74, 164, 171; attempt to rewrite scientific political economy, 134–35; on competition, 139–40, 148, 154, 158; criticism from Ruskin and Jevons, 161–62, 184; and Dickens, 136; on distribution of property, 144; on education, 155–56, 158; on equality of women, 155; focus on individual, 156–59; on government intervention, 154–55; on laboring classes, 145–46; on laws of production and distribution, 140–41, 157, 160; and Mayhew, 135, 201n. 4; on narrative of economic growth, 183; on "peasant proprietorship," 151–52; on population control, 157–59; on private property, 148, 149, 150, 151, 153; on profit-sharing, 153, 205n. 18; on public money on nonproductive philanthropic projects, 143; publication of *Autobiography,* 135, 136; relationship with Harriet Taylor, 135, 146; and Ricardo, 138, 142, 143, 156, 157, 204–5n. 7; and socialism, 138, 142, 146–50, 151, 152, 158; and Smith, 137–38, 159; on solitude, 144–45

money: artificial counters of, 96; circulation of, 85; control of, 82; credit, 84, 85, 87, 199n. 10; definition of, 78–79, 85–86; desire for, 63, 76, 93, 100, 102, 103; earning, 33, 64, 75, 76, 114, 117, 167, 175; investment of, 143; principles of, 72, 73; Ricardo on, 135, 199n. 7; scarcity of, 199n. 11; value of, 78–79, 91, 98, 104, 107. *See also* Bank Charter Act; banking; currency; family wage

morality, 195n. 52; bourgeois, 30, 132; Christian, xii, 206n. 7; Dickens and, 79, 80, 103; discourse of, xi, xii, 189n. 3; domains of, xvii; and ethics, 5, 183, 206n. 7; individual, 13, 44, 58, 84, 205n. 13; issues of, xvi; Martineau on, 55, 76, 197n. 4; J. S. Mill and, 159; national, 44, 54–55; and prostitution, 124, 128; religion and, xiv; Ruskin and, 164, 167, 172; system of, 54; and virtue, 6, 9, 12, 75; working-class, 110, 116, 123, 124, 153

Morning Chronicle, 109–133, 135, 200n. 2, 201n. 4, 201n. 9, 202n. 12

narrative, fictional, xiv, 55–65, 77
nationalism, xi, 4
neoclassical economics, 164, 173. *See also* Jevons, W. Stanley
Newton, Sir Isaac, 4, 5

oeconomy, 17
Oliver Twist (Dickens), 80, 81
Overstone, Lord, 36

pauperism, 47–49, 50, 114, 115, 116, 119, 120, 124, 128. *See also* Poor Laws
peasant proprietorship, 151–52
Poor Laws, 4, 45, 46, 47–49, 50–51, 54, 80, 114–15
Poovey, Mary, xxi–xxiii, 163, 186, 202n. 11
popularization, 31–32, 34, 56
poverty, 24, 41, 46, 47, 48, 109–11, 113–15, 121, 157, 167, 183, 202n. 11, 207n. 17. *See also* pauperism; Poor Laws
Principles of Political Economy (McCulloch), 32, 36
Principles of Political Economy (J. S. Mill), 58, 134, 135, 136–60, 161–62, 180, 205n. 16
Principles of Political Economy and Taxation, The (Ricardo), xii, xiii, xiv, 3, 4, 5, 6, 13, 15, 17–18, 19, 20–23, 51, 53, 137, 176, 183, 194n. 43
prostitution, 110, 112, 121–25, 127–28, 130, 132, 133, 203–4n. 34
providentialism, xi, 28, 44–45
publishing industry, 32–33

Rauch, Alan, 32, 33
religion, xiv, xvi, xvii, 4, 18, 27, 28, 29, 38, 45, 168, 182, 195n. 48, 206n. 7
Ricardian economics, xiii, xiv, xv, xvi, xix, xxiv, xxvi, 1–30, 33, 34, 36–37, 40, 48, 50–52, 54, 59, 72–74, 77, 82, 113, 136–38, 142–43, 157, 195n. 48, 195n. 50, 204–5n. 7
Ricardo, David, xi, xvii, xxiii, 1, 5, 53, 137, 164, 169; and abstraction, 18–19, 21; establishment of universal theory, 20; and Jevons, 181; and labor theory of value, 14–15, 25–26; and "laws of nature," 4; and Malthus, 26, 37–38, 194n. 31; and McCulloch, xiii–xiv, 34; and J. S. Mill, 138, 142, 143, 156, 157, 204–5n. 7; and natural laws, 8; "neoclassical" liberalism of, 193n. 26; and "principal problem in Political Economy," 13–14; Quantity Theory of Money, 199n. 7; scientific approach to political economy, xii–xv; secularism of, 29–30; and Smith, 2–3, 5, 6, 7, 14, 15–16, 26, 39–40, 134; and sympathy, 12; theory of wages, 113; writing style of, 21–24, 27–29
Ruskin, John, xxiv, xxvi, 159, 160; audience of, 173; cannonization of, 186; on consumption, 169–70; criticism of economic science, 184–85; criticism of J. S. Mill, 161–62, 163–65, 168; and Dickens, 164, 171; on domesticity, 171–72; and Jevons, 173–74, 178; on masculinity, 172; and Mayhew, 171, 202n. 12; recontextualizing terms of economic science, 168–71; rejection of scientific economic theory, 161–67, 171–72; on term "merchant," 207n. 17; on value, 167–68; on wealth, 167–68, 169. *See also Unto This Last*

Say, Jean-Baptiste, 14, 169
scientific economic theory, xvi; xix; critics of, xv, xxiv, 136, 164, 165, 167, 169, 184 (*see also* Dickens, Charles; Mayhew, Henry); development of, xxiv; of Martineau, 53; of McCulloch, 36, 38, 51; of J. S. Mill, xxiv, 136, 160; popularization of, xiii; revisions of, 161–87; of Ricardo, xiii, 2, 3, 7, 8, 12, 28, 30, 38; Ruskin's rejection of, 164, 165, 167, 169, 184; of Smith, 2, 8, 9
Senior, Naussau, 6, 36, 37, 53, 137, 156
sentimentalism, 59–77, 80, 81, 170, 172, 197–98n. 9
slavery, 48, 54, 65–67, 75, 104, 119, 126–28, 128, 151
Smith, Adam, xi, xvii, xxiii, 5, 42, 80, 171; and civic virtue, 7, 9, 30; and division of labor, 16–17; as founder of scientific economics, 2; and industrialism, 26; and labor theory of value, 14; liberalism of, 193n. 26; and Malthus, 27; and McCulloch, 39; and J. S. Mill, 137–38, 159; notion of sympathy, 10–12; psychological model of, 9, 10, 11, 12, 193n. 27, 209n. 34; publication of *Inquiry into the Nature and Causes of the Wealth of Nations*, 17; and Ricardo, 2–3, 5, 6, 9, 14, 15–16, 26 39–40; three theoretical movements of, 9–13; theory of jurisprudence, 7–8; writing of "History of Astronomy," 38. *See also Theory of Moral Sentiments, The; Wealth of Nations, The*
socialism, 136, 142, 146–50, 151, 152, 158, 159
Society for the Diffusion of Useful Knowledge (SDUK), 32, 33, 34
Stewart, Dugald, 5, 42

taxation, 15, 41, 49–50, 55, 156, 157
Taylor, Harriet, 136, 146
Theory of Moral Sentiments, The (Smith), 2, 3, 6, 7, 9, 10, 81, 159, 192n. 13, 193n. 30, 209n. 34
Theory of Political Economy (Jevons), 162, 173–81, 183, 185, 209nn. 35–36, 210n. 43
Thompson, Noel, 15

Torrens, Robert, 36
trade societies, 118–19, 133, 203n. 25
Turgot, Anne-Robert-Jacques, 14

Unto This Last (Ruskin), 162, 163, 164–69, 171, 172, 173, 178, 184, 208nn. 18–23, 210n. 43
utilitarianism, 37, 80–81, 136, 150, 159, 175, 176, 209n. 35

virtue: bourgeois, 3, 7, 8, 30, 144, 151, 184, 192–93n. 15; civic, xiv, 7, 9, 30, 41; discourse of, xii; feminine moral, 81, 108, 122, 171; gendering of, 193n. 30; and morality, 6, 9, 12, 74, 75, 171, 189n. 3; of prudence and justice, 8, 152; Ricardo and, 30; Smith and, 9–13; social, xiv, 10, 42; wealth and, 47

Wallerstein, Immanuel, xxiii, 163, 186, 206n. 6
Weal and Woe in Garveloch (Martineau), 67–68, 70
wealth: Banfield on, 85; desire for, 19, 74, 76, 100, 145; in *Dombey,* 89, 91, 93, 94, 95, 96; material, xi, 2; Martineau on, 73–75; McCulloch on, 18, 41, 43–44; J. S. Mill on, 19, 140–41; and power, 4; Ricardo on, 27; Ruskin on, 167–68, 169; and virtue, 9, 47

Wealth of Nations, The (Smith), xii, 2, 5, 6, 7, 8, 9, 13, 14, 15, 16–17, 27, 39, 135, 137, 138, 159, 192n. 13
Whately, Richard, 28
Whewell, William, xxiii, 4, 28
Whitley, Richard, 31–32, 34, 35
women: as authors, 54; domestic, 112, 193n. 30, 199n. 15; empowerment of, 157; equality of, 155; and separate-spheres ideology, 172; as workers, 60, 112, 116, 120–21, 123–24, 132, 133, 155 (*see also* family wage; prostitution)
working class: education of, 26; as fictional characters, 45, 58, 70; gendered ideology of, 112, 116; males, 114, 116, 117, 119, 120, 127, 132, 204n. 35; Malthus and, 26–27; masculinity of, 112, 120, 132, 133, 201–2n. 10, 203n. 23; Mayhew on, 109–32, 200n. 2; 201n. 9; J. S. Mill on, 145–46; morality of, 110, 116, 123–24; as organizers, 173, 203n. 25; poverty among, 113–15; and prostitution, 110, 112, 121–25, 127–28, 130, 132, 133, 203–4n. 34; radicalism of, xxv; as readers, 33, 111; and separate-spheres ideology, 115, 116; urban, 112; women, 112, 120, 121; as writers, 116. *See also* laboring class

www.ingramcontent.com/pod-product-compliance
Lightning Source LLC
Chambersburg PA
CBHW030134240426
43672CB00005B/127